The William Freeman Murder Trial

The
WILLIAM FREEMAN
Murder Trial

INSANITY, POLITICS, AND RACE

ANDREW W. ARPEY

Syracuse University Press

Library of Congress Cataloging-in-Publication Data

Arpey, Andrew W.
The William Freeman murder trial : insanity, politics, and race /
Andrew W. Arpey.— 1st ed.
p. cm.
Includes bibliographical references and index.
ISBN 0–8156–0791–1 (alk. paper)
1. Freeman, William, 1824–1847—Trials, litigation, etc. 2. Trials (Murder)—New York
(State)—Auburn. 3. Insanity—Jurisprudence—New York (State)—Auburn—History—
19th century. I. Title.
KF223.F74 A77 2003
345.73'02523'0974768—dc22   2003021451

Manufactured in the United States of America

Contents

Illustrations

Andrew W. Arpey lives in Saratoga Springs, New York, where he was born. After receiving a B.A. from the State University of New York College at Cortland, he went on to earn his M.A. and Ph.D. from the State University of New York at Albany. Mr. Arpey is employed at the New York State Archives in Albany, New York. This is his first book.

Introduction

IN THE MID-1840s, George J. Mastin commissioned one or more artists to paint fourteen "bold, strong primitive pictures." Mastin, a "phrenologist, tailor, storekeeper, and farmer of Genoa, New York," displayed the paintings as part of a traveling show in central New York. The majority of the paintings were eight feet by ten, with two measuring ten feet by fourteen. They were done in oil on canvas, rolled on long wooden rollers, and stored in boxes specifically crafted to ease their transportation from town to town.[1]

In a broadside, Mastin noted that the featured paintings embraced "Landscapes, Historical, Scriptural and Tragical Scenes." The centerpiece of Mastin's exhibit, however, was a set of four paintings depicting the brutal assault of a white family by an African American man. In Mastin's words, these paintings represented "the Murder of the Van Ness Family by the Negro Freeman, which took place in Cayuga County, NY."[2]

Oil paintings were a novelty to many of the upstate New Yorkers that Mastin encountered in his travels. Besides original artwork, patrons enjoyed a variety of entertainment, including "sentimental and comic singing, a double clog dance and a lecture by Mr. Mastin on phrenology."[3] On some occasions, Mastin even took out his violin and beckoned his guests to dance to some fine fiddle music.[4] Mastin's broadside assured patrons that the paintings depicting the Van Nest killings "may be relied upon as being true likenesses of the family and also of the Negro." During the course of the show, Mastin spoke at length regarding the events and circumstances that had inspired these four particular works of art. The original manuscript copy of his lecture, roughly one thousand words in length, survives along with the original paintings.[5]

On March 12, 1846, William Freeman, a young man of mixed African and Native American descent, stabbed to death four members of the Van Nest family at their home in Fleming, New York. That summer in Auburn, Freeman was convicted and sentenced to hang for the murder of John G. Van Nest. At some point shortly following the conviction, George J. Mastin commissioned the four paintings depicting the tragedy.[6] The works were left unsigned, and were most likely produced by primitive or folk artists.[7] Decorators, carriage painters, sign painters, or tool manufacturers by trade, such craftsmen earned money by painting portraits and by depicting religious and historical scenes, landscapes, and scenes from everyday life. They were generally self-trained and unfamiliar with academic painting.[8] As a result, their levels of skill varied considerably. Unaffected by the main art currents of their time, folk artists painted "directly and spontaneously to express [their] own vision of life" to the best of their ability.[9] Most primitive artists remained unknown because, unlike professional artists, they did not "consider themselves as artists leaving identifiable works for posterity." They merely cultivated an adjunct craft that supplied a public demand and added income to their households.[10]

Most primitive or folk artists shared "a style of basically two-dimensional abstraction, in which flat patterns, expressive silhouettes, local areas of color, or contrasting areas of texture, were the primary means of defining and distinguishing forms." Most were "unconcerned with rendering things in perspective, fully modeled, or illuminated with single or consistent sources of light." Unencumbered by the techniques and perspectives of the formal schools, their works often reflected their own "intuitive and conceptual view of the world."[11] What they lacked in professional technique, however, these primitive artists compensated for in their attention to detail. Some recreated scenes from the world around them with such painstaking care that only photographs could have preserved a more detailed record.[12] The artists that Mastin commissioned to depict the Van Nest killings certainly conformed to this tradition.

The work of Mastin's artists betrays their lack of professional artistic training. However, the paintings succeed in capturing in vivid detail the brutality of the killings and the sheer terror that Freeman's victims endured. It is likely that Mastin's audience, viewing these paintings by candlelight

Freeman stabbing a sleeping child, with the child's father, John G. Van Nest, lying dead in the doorway. Unknown artist, *Freeman Stabbing Child,* ca. 1846. Oil on bed ticking; 7 ft. x 8 ft. 11 in. By permission of the Fenimore Art Museum, Cooperstown, N.Y.

while he recounted the bloody scene, were chilled to the bone by the thought of such a crime taking place in their midst. The painting that depicts the first moments of the affray is particularly disturbing. The scene is a bedroom, painted in the characteristically flat, two-dimensional style attributed to primitive artists. The painting indeed lacks careful attention to perspective and the interplay of light and shadow, but clearly captures Freeman in the process of committing his most unspeakable act. A black man, wearing a blue cap and blue coat extending to mid-thigh, is standing over a four-poster bed in which a young child is soundly sleeping. Mastin's artist plainly depicts the man as being of African descent. His complexion is painted in shades of dark brown that contrast sharply with the fair countenance of his victim. The attacker has pulled back the covers and raised a butcher-length knife up to shoulder level. The knife is already covered in red, as are both of the intruder's hands. Large red streaks can also be seen on the leg of his trousers. The image is so alarming that at first glance, the viewer may fail to notice another figure lying face down in the doorway adjacent to the bed. This figure is visible only from the waist upward, his white shirt stained crimson beneath his coat. The figure is Freeman's first victim, John G. Van Nest, the owner of the house and father of the sleeping child.[13]

One can almost envision the grimaces and hear the sighs of the patrons as Mastin described this first painting. He informed his listeners that Freeman stabbed John G. Van Nest with "such deadly Effect that he fell immediately Prostrate on his face." According to Mastin, Van Nest was found dead in this position with "his left hand in his Pocket, thereby showing Conclusively that he died literally without a struggle." Mastin told his audiences that Freeman stabbed the child, George Van Nest, "with such unabated ferocity that the knife Passed Entirely through his body." Through his paintings and passionate narration, the traveling showman invoked within the minds of his patrons images of a demon possessed and thirsting for blood.[14]

A second painting depicts the violent scene that took place outside the Van Nest residence. Again, the primitive style is clearly demonstrated in the artist's rendering of the structure. The house appears two-dimensional, and yet many fine details are captured. Each block of the foundation appears in perfect proportion and all window and door ornamentation is rendered with precision. A meticulously reproduced white picket fence extends the entire way from the foreground to the background of the painting. Although the attack took place after dark, the artist struggles to convey that effect. The scene is illuminated to a greater degree than one would expect even on the brightest of moonlit nights.

In the foreground, immediately beyond the picket fence, a woman wearing a long, white gown and bonnet struggles with a small, dark-skinned figure. Her gown is splattered almost its entire length with patches of red. In her right hand, she holds a small, thin object with which she is striking the wrist of the attacker. The assailant also appears to have a small object in his hand. In the background, a second woman clad in a long, dark dress appears to be running toward the house. A thick, crimson stain runs from her ab-

Mrs. Wyckoff struggling with William Freeman outside the Van Nest residence. Unknown artist, *Van Nest House*, ca. 1846. Oil on bed ticking; 6 ft. 11 in. x 8 ft. 9 in. By permission of the Fenimore Art Museum, Cooperstown, N.Y.

domen down to the hem of her dress. Mastin explained that John Van Nest's mother-in-law, Phoebe Wyckoff, encountered Freeman at the front of the house and managed to wound his wrist in the scuffle, "so far paralizing [*sic*] him for the time." Unfortunately, he told his audience, the elderly woman died two days later from the wounds she received in the scuffle. The woman in the background is John Van Nest's wife, Sarah, who was also mortally wounded by Freeman and yet tried to warn other members of the household that they were in grave danger.[15]

A third painting captures the scene inside the Van Nest house just after the attack ended. Three figures are gathered together in a room that is largely unfurnished. At the center, a young girl sits in a wooden chair with a small child upon her lap. The child slumps with eyes closed in the young girl's arms, his nightshirt stained pink beneath the waist. He closely resembles the child seen sleeping in the first painting. A woman in a floor-length blue gown stands just to one side, reaching as if to attend to the children. At the opposite side, a man is seated upon the floor with his eyes shut. He is dressed in a striped shirt and dark pants with blue suspenders. His light-colored shirt is completely stained beneath his right arm, the patch of scarlet extending from his breast to the waistline of his trousers. A black man can be seen peering in the window from outside the house. His eyes are focused intently upon the group inside, the whites contrasting sharply with the dark brown hue of his skin. The front of his coat is stained with rose-colored streaks. In his hands he is clutching an object that most closely resembles a spear. The object is long, thin, light in color, and pointed at the visible end.

Mastin identified the woman in the painting merely as Miss Holmes, who resided with the Van Nests. He recounted how she helped the wounded Mrs. Van Nest in her dying moments. After the attacker exited the house, Mastin noted, Miss Holmes found the family's hired man crouched on the floor of the sitting room. Mr. Van Arsdale, as Mastin referred to him, told Holmes that he had been stabbed in a scuffle with the attacker and was "going to faint." Mastin informed his audiences that Van Arsdale had "laid hold of a broom With which he struck at the negro several times" and eventually "succeeded in driving him from the house." Mastin's lecture notes make no reference to the young girl seated with the child on her lap.[16] Press reports, however, revealed that the Van Nests' nine-year-old daughter Julia comforted her infant brother in the moments prior to his death.[17] Mastin ended his description of the crime by noting that Freeman did not leave the property immediately following the assault. Miss Holmes, the lecturer noted, first "discovered the negro standing on the stoop with What she supposed to be a gun in his hand." This was not a gun at all, Mastin explained, but rather a club, as captured in the painting. Freeman "made a show at least of defiance if nothing more before quitting the scene of his Brutal butchery looking first in at one window and then at the other," Mastin exclaimed. Freeman finally kicked open the door with such force that his heel left behind a deep indentation. He did not reenter the house, however, choosing instead to hasten to the stable, where he stole a horse upon which to make his getaway.[18]

The fourth and final painting exhibited by Mastin depicts a gallows

Survivors comforting the dying child as Freeman watches through the window. Unknown artist, *Van Nest Family after Attack,* ca. 1846. Oil on bed ticking; 8 ft. 9 in. x 7 ft. By permission of the Fenimore Art Museum, Cooperstown, N.Y.

scene. A crowd of men, women, and children stand tightly packed around the scaffold. A dark-skinned figure in a white robe hangs upon the gallows, his eyes blindfolded with white cloth. A well-dressed gentleman looks with satisfaction upon the scene of the execution, his hands placed firmly upon his hips. Behind him, a woman stares with interest and gives a more subtle appearance of approval. A second male spectator glares upward at the scaffold, his lower lip curled in anger and disgust. One onlooker, however, appears frightened, if not shocked by the scene. Another man averts his eyes completely from the spectacle. By his side, a woman looks sadly toward the ground. There is just one black observer visible in the crowd. He stares intently at the figure upon the gallows but gives no appearance of emotion.

The gallows scene is the only one of the four paintings that does not de-

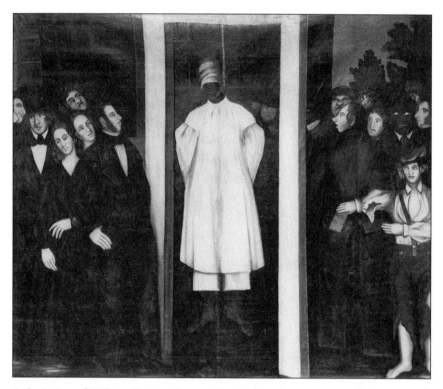

A depiction of William Freeman's execution by hanging—an event that never took place. Unknown artist, *Hanging Freeman,* ca. 1846. Oil on bed ticking; 7 ft. 6 in. x 8 ft. 6 in. By permission of the Fenimore Art Museum, Cooperstown, N.Y.

pict an actual event. Mastin's lecture notes, in fact, offer few details regarding Freeman's ultimate fate. Mastin did indicate, however, that Freeman's state of mind was a major issue in the criminal proceedings that took place in the summer of 1846. Patrons learned that Freeman was tried before two juries, one being required "to test Whether he was sane or insane." Mastin noted that "the Jury found him a Sane Man and He was Centenced [*sic*] to B hung on the 18th day of Sept 1846." Mastin closed with the observation that Freeman had "had a new trial Granted and Was not hung." Other sources examined in this study, though, reveal that Freeman was never retried, let alone executed, for the murders at Fleming. In fact, he became severely ill and died in his jail cell in the summer of 1847. Given the actual course of events following Freeman's conviction, Mastin's decision to complete the exhibit with a depiction of Freeman's execution seems mysterious. However, a closer examination of the events in Cayuga County during the first half of 1846 indicates that Mastin was no fool for anticipating such an end to this dramatic story.[19]

As Mastin's exhibition demonstrates, the Van Nest killings and William Freeman's trial became part of the cultural lore of antebellum New York. Artistic images and vivid descriptions of these events captivated antebellum audiences in much the same manner that dramatic television and movies do the present-day public. For a brief period of time, these events reverberated far beyond the Finger Lakes community in which they occurred. A host of issues that remain controversial even to this day came to the fore in a single, disturbing criminal case.

The Freeman case is clearly what K. N. Llewellyn and E. Adamson Hoebel refer to as a "case of hitch or trouble," or one in which ancient institutions are "tried against emergent forces." In such cases, long-standing traditions and deeply established patterns of behavior are questioned and challenged. These cases merit close attention because they reveal societal tensions with remarkable clarity. As Llewellyn and Hoebel note, it is cases of trouble "in which the play of variant urges can be felt and seen, in which emergent power-patterns, ancient security drives, religion, politics, personality, and cross-purposed views of justice tangle in the open." Traditions need not necessarily be discarded or overcome in favor of the establishment of some new precedent. The value of such cases for the study of cultures, past and present, lies in conflict, controversy, and the struggle with issues that defy permanent resolution.[20]

In the Freeman case, no precedent was established that shattered tradition, either in the legal or social world. Those that supported Freeman struggled against established social patterns and legal tradition; by and large, their efforts resulted in failure. However, history of prevailing forces, or of the victorious, is incomplete history. It is not enough simply to know that certain values held sway in antebellum New York, and indeed in America. The Freeman case reveals the interplay of opposing value systems and allows us to learn about ideas that were not only less popular, but were seen as threatening the American social structure. Certain values and traditions endured because the majority of nineteenth-century Americans believed that these established social and legal rules preserved the peace and security of society.

William Freeman, a free black in antebellum New York, committed an atrocious act that contributed to and was perceived in the context of an ongoing debate concerning the nature of crime and the purpose of punishment. The majority of antebellum Americans viewed crime as the product of human depravity and believed that vindictive punishment both deterred crime and coincided with human instinct. Freeman's defenders challenged this view, albeit unsuccessfully, incorporating recent advances in the study of mental illness. Antigallows reformers jumped into the fray, arguing that vindictive punishment only conditioned criminals to be violent and unforgiving. Prosecutors successfully portrayed these attitudes as constituting a legitimate threat to the safety and security of Americans. Without examining the challenges posed by Freeman's defenders, we could never hope to truly understand why Freeman was convicted. More than just a reflection of the social and legal attitudes of antebellum America, the Freeman case illustrates the intensity with which antebellum Americans defended attitudes and doctrines that they felt were closely linked to their own security.

Racial attitudes clearly influenced the manner in which the lawyers, physicians, politicians, newspaper editors, and townspeople that participated in the case, or monitored it from afar, perceived the man and the act. Freeman's defenders pleaded passionately for jurors and the public to treat Freeman as a human being, deserving all protection guaranteed under the law to whites. Prosecutors and numerous commentators argued that Freeman's evil was directly linked to his racial background. Furthermore, they drew the community's attention to the possibility that misguided reformers were using Freeman's race as an excuse for his behavior. Environmental excuses for crime, if granted credence by the legal system, could pose a grave threat to the security of the community. The Freeman case allows us to view the active defense of traditional social viewpoints, a defense made necessary by the commitment and courage of Freeman's defenders.

The gravity of the Freeman case drew the attention of some of the most influential political figures in antebellum New York. Although a few partisan barbs were exchanged in the press and there were limited efforts to fash-

CORRECT LIKENESS OF WM. FREEMAN. THE MURDERER.
As sketched in his cell, by our young Artist, George L. Clough.

Sketch of William Freeman in his jail cell by George L. Clough.
Auburn Journal and Advertiser, March 25, 1846.

ion the case into partisan capital, the issues essentially cut across party lines. New York State's Democratic attorney general was asked to prosecute the case because of the challenges it presented for the administration of justice and the threat many perceived that it posed to the security of the community. A former governor and leading New York Whig defended Freeman for personal rather than partisan reasons. Among these was concern over the treatment of the mentally ill and of nonwhites by the criminal justice system. Precisely because of the nonpartisan nature of the issues involved and their relevance to society at large, the Freeman case discloses much about the political climate of Jacksonian New York.

———◊◊◊———

Despite all that it has to offer, the Freeman case has never been the subject of a full-length scholarly study. The only detailed treatment is Earl Conrad's *Mr. Seward for the Defense,* a sympathetic, romanticized account completely void of historical documentation.[21] Most of the scholarly attention given the Freeman case stems, without a doubt, from William Henry Seward's involvement as defense counsel. Still, Seward's modern biographers have tended to examine the trial only briefly, in an effort to illustrate Seward's development personally and as a politician. The legal complexity of the case and its place in the political debate concerning the punishment of criminals are given scant attention. Focusing on partisan politics in New York and Seward's political and personal attitudes toward blacks, the biographers also fail to fully illuminate the dialogue that Freeman's race inspired following the killings and during the trial.[22] This study goes much deeper, exploring antebellum attitudes regarding crime, capital punishment, mental illness, race, and manhood as these attitudes were reflected in and shaped by one highly charged case.

The William Freeman Murder Trial

1

The Van Nest Killings

AUBURN, NEW YORK, is situated in the center of Cayuga County, twenty-five miles to the southwest of Syracuse. Nestled in the Finger Lakes region of the state, Auburn rests only a few miles northwest of Owasco Lake's northern shore. In 1846, the village of Auburn was a growing community, twice as populated as Rochester and roughly equal in population to Syracuse.[1] Observers noted how the "business streets" of the village were "crowded with people engaged on their everlasting 'trading.' " The beauty of Auburn's public buildings was compared to those of America's larger cities.[2] The New York State Prison at Auburn had opened in 1817 and provided a major source of jobs and income for local residents. In the antebellum era, the village participated actively in the antislavery movement. In the years following the Freeman trial, Auburn became the home of Harriet Tubman, as well as a station on the Underground Railroad, in which she played a leading role. Auburn residents in general, however, were far from willing to accept former slaves and the descendants of slaves as social equals.[3]

Auburn was residentially segregated, with blacks isolated in a settlement called New Guinea in the southernmost portion of the village.[4] The formal education of the black community was thoroughly neglected until Auburn's Presbyterian Society established a Sunday school for the benefit of blacks in 1818. That decision brought such public ridicule and opposition that for a period of time, no volunteers could be found who were willing to brave the onslaught and teach at the school. Public education was not made available to black children until September 1846, when an all-black public school district was formed. Prior to that date, public opposition and the threat of violence barred blacks from attending the village's public schools with white children.[5] The first black church was not established in Auburn until 1840. Blacks were admitted to white churches before and after that date, but they were hardly welcomed as equals.[6] Concerned white citizens cited neglect of religious training as well as of formal education when explaining immoral behavior and crime among Auburn blacks.[7]

The village of Auburn and its surrounding communities became fixated with issues involving the administration of justice beginning in early 1846, with the trial of Henry Wyatt. Wyatt, a convict in the state prison, was tried in the Court of Oyer and Terminer in Cayuga County in February for the murder of James Gordon, a fellow inmate. William Henry Seward, former governor of New York, and his colleagues Christopher Morgan and Samuel Blatchford defended Wyatt. Cayuga County district attorney Luman Sherwood prosecuted with Bowen Whiting, judge of the Seventh Circuit, presiding. Seward and his colleagues argued that Wyatt suffered from moral insanity, a form of mental illness that affected the emotions while leaving the intellect in many cases undisturbed. The murder of Gordon, Wyatt's counsel and expert medical witnesses argued, was not precipitated by motive but by an irresistible impulse. The jury was ultimately unable to agree on a verdict, with up to seven of its members at times favoring acquittal on the ground of insanity. A new trial was ordered, which took place the following June.[8]

The significance of Wyatt's first trial, independent of the violent events that took place subsequently, is a matter of conjecture. Innovations in the common law seemed to be affecting the manner in which insanity, as a legal excuse for criminal acts, was defined in the United States. Trials in Boston, New York City, and now Auburn proved that at least some members of the community who served on juries were willing to consider a definition of insanity that encompassed recent advances in the study of mental illness. However, Wyatt's first trial was never to be assessed independently of the horrific events that took place within three weeks of the trial's close. The second hearing of Wyatt's case, which occurred after the fatal night of March 12, also cannot be viewed outside of the context of the intervening events. The year 1846, in Auburn, was characterized by what came to be viewed as a series of interrelated occurrences.[9]

On Friday, March 13, 1846, the editor of the *Albany Evening Journal* received details, via telegraph from Utica, of a "Most Horrible Murder" that had taken place the previous evening. The earliest details of the bloody scene were shocking, and were made all the more terrifying by the fact that the perpetrator was still at large. "We hear this morning by Mr. Frink, Conductor from Auburn, that the house of Mr. Van Ness, a farmer and supervisor of the town of Fleming, on Owasco Lake, four miles from Auburn, was entered last night about 9$^1/_2$ o'clock by some one in the disguise of a negro," the report stated, "and Mr. Van Ness, his wife and child, were stabbed by the villain, and are dead.—His mother-in-law and hired man were also stabbed but are still living." Sarah Van Nest was reported to have "ran about sixty rods when her bowels gushed out, and she fell dead." John Van Nest apparently attempted to go upstairs to retrieve his gun, but he fell dead upon the steps. Their two-year-old child was "torn open from its shoulder entirely across its abdomen." The hired man was reported to have sustained serious injuries fighting the killer off with a broomstick, saving the lives of the remaining occupants of the house. The killer made his escape by stealing one of the family's horses, which he rode to Auburn where the horse "fell down." No further traces had been discovered.[10]

The local newspapers featured further details of the scene when they went to print on the thirteenth of March. The *Auburn Daily Advertiser* identified Mrs. Wykoff (Wyckoff), the mother of Sarah Van Nest, and Cornelius Van Arsdale, the hired man, as the two "dangerously, if not mortally wounded" survivors of the brutal attack. The killer was believed to have entered the front door of the residence, where he met and "butchered" John Van Nest before Van Nest could alert his family. Van Nest was found lying "with his face in the back kitchen, with his feet on the step," fatally stabbed in the breast. The young child, who was not immediately identified by name or gender, was found dead in the bed where it had been sleeping. Sarah Van Nest was also apparently stabbed inside the house, but she was able to escape through a back door. Once outside, she alerted a young houseguest, later identified as Helen Holmes, through a bedroom window. Holmes unlocked a third door, allowing Mrs. Van Nest to reenter the house after which she collapsed on Holmes's bed. It was there that Sarah Van Nest, pregnant and "soon expected to be confined," was found dead when rescuers arrived at the scene.[11]

After the affray on the ground floor, the killer procured a candle and proceeded upstairs. He inquired if there was a man there, to which Van Arsdale, who had been roused from bed by the commotion, answered affirmatively. Immediately thereafter, the intruder stabbed Van Arsdale and a scuffle ensued. Van Arsdale apparently seized the candlestick from the attacker and threw it at him, forcing him to either fall or jump down the stairs. Van Arsdale then pursued the intruder with a broomstick and forced him out of the house. Upon exiting, the killer encountered Phoebe Wyckoff at the front gate. Having just fled the house in search of help, Mrs. Wyckoff was attacked and mortally wounded, but not thwarted in her effort to run "over 100 rods" to a neighbor's house. The morning after the brutal attack, she was described as "senseless," and "not likely to recover." Van Arsdale was reported to be "perfectly sensible," but still in a "very precarious state." [12]

After the intruder left the house, Helen Holmes saw him standing nearby with what appeared to her to be a gun. Finally, he went to the barn and took the horse upon which he fled the scene. Van Arsdale described the attacker as approximately five feet six inches tall, "thick set," and either a negro, or someone disguised as a negro. The knife used in the attack split into two pieces at some point, one of which was found in the house and the other outside in the yard. Peter Williamson, a neighbor who had been a guest at the Van Nest home until approximately half past nine on the night of the killings, reported hearing suspicious noises on his way home. He stated that he had not managed to walk far toward home when he heard a dog bark followed by the sound of a shriek. Not long after, a man aboard Mrs. Wyckoff's horse rode past "urging him on as fast as he could." This was the horse that was later found abandoned near Auburn. The *Advertiser* assumed that the killer fled eastward, given that a second horse had been stolen from a residence approximately two and one-half miles east of Auburn. [13]

It took relatively little time for word to spread that authorities were in pursuit of a suspect. The *Daily Cayuga Tocsin,* another Auburn-based journal, reported on the day following the crime that the "murderer" was believed to be "a negro man by the name of William Freeman." Freeman was identified as having been previously sentenced to five years in the state prison for stealing a horse. The *Tocsin* reported that upon Freeman's trial, "Van Nest, or some one of his family is said to have been a witness against him." The killings were acts of "premeditated revenge," the *Tocsin* surmised, adding that "the devil incarnate" was being closely pursued and would soon be taken.[14] The *Advertiser* also indicated in its March 13 reports that Freeman was suspected of the crime. The *Advertiser* reported that Freeman had been seen in Auburn the previous evening, and that the murder weapon had been identified as "having been recently made for him." Freeman was described as being twenty-one years old, five feet five or six inches high, and "square built—rather thick set." He was reported to have been wearing a blue roundabout coat and cloth cap, with "pantaloons of a different color" on the evening of the killings. In contrast to the *Tocsin,* however, the *Advertiser* maintained that the motive for the bloody deed was a mystery. The *Advertiser* dismissed as thoroughly unfounded the rumor that Freeman's motive was revenge upon Van Nest for testifying against him.[15]

On Saturday, March 14, newspaper editors in Albany learned via telegraph that the "murderer of the Van Ness family" had been taken at Fulton, Oswego County, the previous day. These first reports did not name Freeman but stated that the man in custody had acknowledged the killings at Fleming. The killer had been seen at Syracuse on Friday morning and later went to Fulton where he "offered to sell his horse to the tavern keeper, Mr. V. Low." This "caused suspicion that the horse was stolen," and soon after the suspect departed he was "pursued on this suspicion and taken." The suspect bore the marks of a blow that was reported to be the result of the scuffle with Cornelius Van Arsdale.[16]

The *Auburn Daily Advertiser* printed further details on Saturday, including the identity of the suspect. William Freeman, the *Advertiser* reported, was apprehended Friday afternoon at Phoenix, Oswego County. This location was actually ten miles closer to Syracuse than Fulton, the location given in the first telegraph accounts. Besides confessing the deed, Freeman confessed his intention to kill the entire family, "which he was only prevented from doing by breaking his knife, and cutting his wrist severely." Among the people who pursued and apprehended Freeman was a man by the name of George Burrington. It was Burrington's horse that had been stolen Thursday evening from his residence along the Skaneateles Road, several miles east of Auburn. Freeman was first transported to the Van Nest home in Fleming, where Van Arsdale and Helen Holmes readily identified him as the "murderer." While at the Van Nest residence, Freeman "appeared to be exceedingly agitated," which the *Advertiser* deemed understandable since "a state of excitement was every where presented never before equaled in this vicinity."[17]

In fact, the *Advertiser* exclaimed, there was cause for concern that Freeman would never make it safely to the Cayuga County jail. Due to the "unparalleled excitement in the community, apprehensions were entertained, that a more speedy and summary mode of punishment than that provided by the laws, would have been attempted."[18] As constables escorted Freeman through Auburn on the way to Fleming, a group of townspeople "made a rush for him," and were only prevented from "tearing him to pieces" by the constables "putting spurs to their horses." The *Daily Cayuga Tocsin* reported that in Fleming, an angry crowd gathered outside the Van Nest house and demanded that Freeman be "taken from the hands of the officers and strung up on the first tree." One of the local justices calmed the crowd, however, by claiming that others had probably instigated Freeman to commit the crimes.[19]

Fearing that the worst was yet to come, the authorities sent riders from Fleming ahead to the courthouse in Auburn, in order to serve as a decoy while Freeman was quickly slipped into the nearby Cayuga County jail through the side door. Distracted but not deterred by the deception, the crowd charged the jail with such force as to destroy the surrounding fence.[20] There would be no lynching, however. The *Advertiser* concluded that "great credit" was due to the officers and citizens of Cayuga County "for thus speedily apprehending and securing the murderer."[21]

Just as William Freeman was being escorted back to the crime scene on Saturday, March 14, Mrs. Wyckoff died of the injuries received in the attack.[22] Four members of a prominent and highly regarded Cayuga County family had now perished at his hands. The editors of the *Daily Cayuga Tocsin* mourned the loss of the family patriarch, calling John G. Van Nest "one of the most estimable and respected citizens in the community." Just thirty-eight years of age, he had been a supervisor of his town, and was "held in deservedly high estimation by all who knew him." The *Tocsin* noted that as soon as word of the "dreadful calamity" reached the community, an "immense concourse of his neighbors and friends thronged to his residence."[23]

The funeral for the four slain victims took place on Sunday and was attended by a crowd estimated to have numbered three thousand persons.[24] On Monday, March 16, a rumor circulated throughout the state that Cornelius Van Arsdale had also died of his wounds. The rumor turned out to be unfounded, however, and newspapers quickly printed retractions. On March 19, the *Albany Evening Journal* reported that Van Arsdale was "recovering and will probably be able to testify on the trial." The *Rochester Daily Advertiser* printed news that Van Arsdale "was considerable [*sic*] better, and would immediately get well."[25]

Of the eight people present when William Freeman entered the Van Nest residence on the night of March 12, three remarkably escaped injury. Helen Holmes, the young houseguest who hurried to assist the fatally wounded Sarah Van Nest, remained unharmed.[26] The Van Nest's elder son, Peter, who slept in the front parlor with his grandmother, also escaped confrontation with the killer.[27] The Van Nest's nine-year-old daughter, Julia, was physically unscathed although she observed firsthand the results of Freeman's fury. Young Julia "displayed the fortitude of riper years," going to the bedside of her mother to receive "the dying blessing and advice of an expiring parent." While Freeman was still on the property, the now orphaned child proceeded to where her infant brother George was "crying in its last agonies, and sought to soothe its anguish."[28] Had the seriously injured Van Arsdale failed to resist Freeman, these young survivors might not have been so fortunate.

Freeman's arrest did not result in an immediately satisfactory answer to the question being asked across the state: why did this man violently kill this particular family? That the victims included a pregnant woman, a two-year-old child, and an elderly woman made the crime seem incomprehensibly brutal and bizarre. Reports continued to circulate that Freeman claimed a Mr. Van Ness had been a witness against him in the grand larceny trial that resulted in Freeman's imprisonment.[29] According to one report, Freeman discovered afterward that he had mistakenly killed the wrong Van Nest.[30] Other reports quoted Freeman as saying that he was "imprisoned wrongfully" and that he "ought to have pay" for his time. Freeman, according to this hypothesis, found that there was no redress for his grievance and "was determined to have vengeance."[31] One report stated that Freeman's response to all inquiries regarding motive was that he "was five years in State Prison wrongfully, and that he had made up his mind that somebody must pay for it!"[32] These contradictory reports foreshadowed the opposing arguments that would be heard during Freeman's trial. Were the killings premeditated acts of vengeance directed at specifically targeted enemies? Or were the Van Nests, on the other hand, merely the unfortunate victims in Freeman's confused effort to seek compensation for incarceration that he believed he had not deserved? The question of motive remained highly relevant and yet agonizingly elusive.

By the early part of the week following the killings, the local authorities had questioned William Freeman at length regarding the violent night of March 12, 1846. Freeman gushed with details about the affray and his flight, but his motive still remained a mystery. Freeman told authorities that he did not carry a gun to the Van Nests', but rather a club with a five or six inch blade affixed at one end. Helen Holmes more than likely mistook this club for a gun as she watched Freeman prepare to flee the crime scene. Freeman hid the club at the gate before proceeding to the front door of the house. He believed that the knife he had carried with him into the house broke during the scuffle with Van Arsdale. Although somewhat confused regarding his confrontation with Phoebe Wyckoff, Freeman believed that he stabbed her at the gate using the blade in the end of the club. He also contended that Mrs. Wyckoff cut his wrist with a butcher knife during the confrontation.[33]

Freeman stated that he proceeded on foot for several miles after the horse stolen from the Van Nests fell near New Guinea. He admitted stealing Burrington's horse, which he mounted bareback and rode in the direction of Syracuse. He passed through Syracuse shortly after daylight on March 13 and proceeded through Salina, Liverpool, and Clay Corners to Phoenix.[34] To inquiries regarding why he killed the Van Nests, Freeman in one instance appeared indifferent, and finally answered that he "had no reason at all."[35] At other times he spoke of his wrongful imprisonment, for which he insisted the state owed him compensation. Since he could not "get pay" in any other manner, he took his revenge by killing the Van Nests. To one of the local judges, Freeman specifically denied ever having been told that John Van Nest sent him to state prison. Freeman named several other individuals as having sworn him into prison, including two people that had indeed testified against him five years earlier.[36] While the legal system moved quickly forward in the process of determining his fate, the struggle to ascertain what motivated Freeman to commit such acts of savagery was just beginning.

Shortly after the killings, a coroner's inquest was commenced and testimony taken from the survivors of the attack. The confusion and sheer panic that Freeman's victims felt the night of March 12 is glaringly apparent in the testimony of Phoebe Wyckoff, Sarah Van Nest's elderly mother. Mrs. Wyckoff awoke to the frantic cries of her daughter shouting, "John is dead; and I am dead—they have killed me and they will kill you." Mrs. Wyckoff then heard the sound of someone in the front hallway, just outside of her bedroom. She also thought she heard another intruder toward the back of the house. For whatever reason, she entered the hallway herself and thought she heard a voice from the back of the house shout "John stab her!" Just then, she was stabbed with what she described as "a kind of long thing." Her version conflicted with that of Freeman, who believed he stabbed her outside at the front gate. Her description of the weapon, however, coincided with Freeman's belief that he used the long-handled instrument to deliver the blow that eventually claimed her life.[37]

The physicians who attended both the slain victims and the survivors presented details of the wounds inflicted by the killer. Dr. Joseph T. Pitney determined that John G. Van Nest suffered a wound to the right cavity of the heart, "which must inevitably have caused instant death." Dr. Pitney determined that Sarah Van Nest received a wound "penetrating through the lower edge of the left lobe of the liver, down towards the left side of the spine." The official cause of death was "a fatal hemorrhage," resulting from a severed vein or blood vessels in the abdomen. The Van Nest's two-year-old son, George, also died from a fatal hemorrhage caused by a wound "extending entirely through the left side of the abdomen." The doctor found several feet of the young boy's intestines protruding, portions of which were completely severed. Mrs. Wyckoff was wounded in the lower abdomen, a portion of her intestines also having protruded through the laceration. Dr. Pitney replaced the intestines and stitched the wound, but to no avail. Cornelius Van Arsdale received a wound two or three inches long to the left side of his breastbone. The wound penetrated the chest cavity, seriously injuring Van Arsdale's lung. The doctor testified that all of the wounds, with the exception of Mrs.

Wyckoff's, were "inflicted by the blade of a knife, and one very similar to the one a piece of which is now before the jury."[38]

The coroner's inquest also brought to light details regarding William Freeman's movements during the days leading up to the assault. Helen Holmes testified that Freeman had visited the Van Nest residence ten days prior to the killings. Upon his arrival that day, Freeman told John Van Nest that he lived in Auburn and could not find work. Holmes quickly perceived that Freeman was "hard of hearing," observing the manner in which he placed his ear close to Van Nest. Freeman, on that occasion, both approached and left the property by means of the barnyard, using only the back door of the house. George W. Hyatt, an Auburn blacksmith and toolmaker, recognized the remains of the knife found at the Van Nest residence. The Monday prior to the killings, Hyatt had affixed a handle to the same knife and sold it to "a colored man." Upon hearing Hyatt's description of the purchaser, Nathaniel Lynch, one of Freeman's former employers, informed Hyatt that Freeman was most likely the man. Hyatt also testified that the "colored man" assisted him in sharpening the blade, and called upon him to put a rivet in a jackknife that same day.[39]

Nathaniel Lynch stated that he learned through mutual acquaintances that Freeman had recently had a knife made and also had bored a hole in a walnut club. William B. Patten, a resident of Auburn, testified that he encountered Freeman in the vicinity of the Van Nest residence on the night of the killings. Patten was traveling home on horseback at approximately nine o'clock, when he passed Freeman walking southward toward Fleming. Freeman, Patten testified, "had a gun concealed, partly by the barrel being under his coat, with the breech hanging below the skirt of his coat." Patten mistook, as did Helen Holmes, the club-and-blade instrument that Freeman carried for a gun.[40]

As the perpetrator of a brutal attack the likes of which had never been seen in Cayuga County, Freeman became the subject of tremendous curiosity across the state. The *Auburn Journal and Advertiser* attempted to extinguish rumors by providing what it deemed a "correct" biographical sketch of "William Freeman, The Murderer." Freeman's exact date of birth was not known, but he was believed to have been born around 1823 or 1824 in the village of Auburn. He was the son of the late James Freeman, who died of poisoning when William was just three years old. Freeman's mother was "of Indian origin," having come to Auburn from Pittsfield, Massachusetts. William had no brothers; hence rumors circulating across the state that his sibling was recently executed were completely unfounded. Freeman had lived in or near Auburn his entire life. In the fall of 1840, he was convicted of stealing a horse and sentenced to five years in the state prison at Auburn. Since his release in the fall of 1845, he had found no particular employment, "except occasionally sawing wood about town." [41]

Physically, Freeman was described as "about 5 feet 5 inches high, thick set, short legged." His weight was estimated at just 110 pounds and he was not known to have any "prominent traits." The *Auburn Journal* noted, however, that he had "a downcast bearing of his head and eyes," and was "seldom or never known to smile." This contrasted with the "happy disposition and appearance" Freeman was said to have had as a young boy. He was "remarkably deaf," a condition that "constantly increased upon him since his incarceration in the State Prison." The *Auburn Journal* also observed that violence was not something new to William Freeman. While in prison, some three and one-half years before the Van Nest killings, Freeman purportedly "attempted on one occasion to dirk with a knife, Mr. James E. Tyler, one of the then assistant keepers." [42]

The brutality of the killings and Freeman's bizarre behavior following his capture thrust his mental health into question. Many men volunteered to interview Freeman in his cell, and later offered information to Freeman's counsel or the district attorney, depending upon their impressions of Freeman's mental condition. [43] According to one local newspaper, local residents "of every class and sex" flocked to the county jail to cast their eyes upon Freeman. At one point, a jailor became so annoyed by the number of people that he was "obliged to give admittance" to Freeman's cell, that he joked about hiring another "negro" to stand chained outside the jail. "But," the jailor quipped in regard to the would-be impersonator, "I am afraid they would Lynch the nigger!" [44] This process, referred to by Earl Conrad as the "manufacture of witnesses," continued throughout the spring, picking up in intensity as Freeman's trial approached. Freeman's counsel and the public prosecutor also dispatched physicians to ascertain Freeman's mental condition. [45] It is important to note, however, that not all of the testimony later presented at Freeman's trial was produced by interviews subsequent to his arrest. Townspeople, family members, and former employers testified as to Freeman's appearance, demeanor, and actions prior to the Van Nest killings.

Anger and suspicion regarding the man in custody for the atrocities committed at Fleming only increased with time. "Since his confinement he has endeavored to convince him [*sic*] that he is insane, by talking to himself, saying that they were asleep that he killed, and using all sorts of incoherent expressions," the *Rochester Daily Advertiser* reported several days after Freeman's arrest. The journal also noted that local residents were "still so much excited upon the subject that each is suggesting some mode of punishment in comparison with which hanging would be a mere pastime!" Viewed in the context of the recent unwillingness of a Cayuga County jury to convict Henry Wyatt, the *Rochester Daily Advertiser*'s suspicion that Freeman feigned insanity was not surprising. To many observers, insanity seemed but a clever and yet dangerous conspiracy concocted by crafty lawyers to spare their depraved clients deserved and necessary punishment.[46]

2

Human Depravity vs. Environmentalism

THE PUBLIC RESPONSE TO A TRAGEDY

FROM THE VERY MOMENT that word of the Van Nest killings began to spread across New York by means of the telegraph, the partisan press debated the relevance of William Freeman and his violent acts. The killings and Freeman's trial were covered with interest by journals from as far away as New York City. The courtroom contest between John Van Buren, son of the former president, and former Whig governor William H. Seward gave the case the appearance of a partisan showdown. One might expect to find that largely partisan political considerations inspired both the major legal participants and the coverage given the case by the press. Although the subsequent involvement of leading New York politicians eventually resulted in limited efforts to make partisan political capital from the case, the most widely discussed and most heated political issues to arise in the wake of the Van Nest killings were not strictly partisan in nature. Sympathy for Freeman emanated from limited circles; a hostile public rendered it highly unlikely that William H. Seward or any other politically connected defense attorney would attempt to use the Freeman case for partisan purposes. Despite Seward's personal connection with the Wyatt case, fellow New York Whigs did not hesitate to link the Van Nest killings to the Wyatt trial.

Public response to Freeman's brutal acts was extremely emotional, as evidenced in the harsh rhetoric and vitriolic prose found in the partisan press. This response was not, however, divided along partisan lines. Political debate focused primarily on the functioning of the criminal justice system, namely the appropriate punishment of criminals. As Louis P. Masur notes, in the mid-1840s, "public conflict over capital punishment was on the rise." He adds, "Throughout the Northeast, legislatures considered bills and petitions for the elimination of the gallows, newspapers and periodicals featured numerous essays for and against the death penalty, and some professionals formed local and national societies for the abolition of capital punishment."[1] Yet, as Masur and Philip English Mackey both note, abolition of capital punishment was not a partisan reform movement in the antebellum era.[2] Officers in the New York State Society for the Abolition of Capital Punishment were fairly evenly distributed between the Democratic and Whig parties.[3] Public sentiment in favor of retention of the gallows also crossed party lines in New York, its strength resulting in the ultimate failure of the reform effort to achieve its goal of either statutory or constitutional change. Freeman's acts were seized upon by both supporters and opponents of capital punishment as evidence in support of their given stance. These responses illustrate basic antebellum perceptions of the link between punishment, crime, religion, and manhood.

The earliest responses to the Van Nest killings were rife with signs that the Freeman case would indeed be a case of trouble. Both Democratic and Whig journals called for retribution and blamed the Van Nest killings on the failure of the criminal justice system in the case of Henry Wyatt. Opponents of the gallows, also representing both parties, most strongly advocated calmness and warned that retributive punishment nurtured a vindictive spirit in the community. The killings also fueled an ongoing biblical debate on the appropriate Christian response to murder. Gallows supporters referred to the Old Testament in support of retribution, whereas reformers cited the forgiveness and humanity exemplified by Jesus Christ. In this process, reformers also challenged the popular rejection of compassion and forgiveness as masculine virtues.

The Van Nest killings intensified the antebellum debate concerning the nature of crime. Was William Freeman a depraved human being who deserved appropriately vindictive punishment, or was he the product of his social environment and therefore entitled to a measure of human sympathy? Certain reformers argued that perhaps society bore a share of the responsibility for the killings. Freeman's racial background added an additional element of controversy to this debate. Many of the voices that screamed for retribution did not hesitate to cite the killer's race as a source of his depravity. These commentators claimed that Freeman's violent behavior was consistent with that of the races to which he traced his lineage. Freeman's defenders in the public at large, most of which opposed capital punishment in general, tended to view social conditions as contributing to crime. William Freeman descended from both black slaves and Native Americans; his defenders drew attention to the cruelty with which Freeman's ancestors were treated by whites. In these commentators' view, nonwhite peoples were denied the advantages that uplift human beings from social conditions most often characterized by poverty, vice, and crime.

In examining the responses to the Van Nest killings, it is important to bear in mind the narrow time frame between the conclusion of Henry Wyatt's first trial and the "horrid massacre" at Fleming. Wyatt was convicted on charges of burglary and larceny in June 1844 and sentenced to a term of ten years in Auburn State Prison.[4] On March 16, 1845, he stabbed fellow convict James Gordon to death with half of a pair of shears. Wyatt believed that Gordon had been heard talking about Wyatt's involvement in a murder in Ohio. The principal keeper at Auburn Prison had, in fact, been informed by an attorney in Ohio that Wyatt was implicated in a murder in that state. Whether Gordon had any role in implicating Wyatt remains unclear. The crucial point was the manner in which William H. Seward and his legal partners defended Wyatt, arguing that he had been "flogged and tortured with an inhuman instrument of torture" while in prison. Wyatt was thereby "driven to desperation," with homicide being the end result of his inability to resist his passions. Wyatt's trial commenced at Auburn on February 11, 1846, one month and a day prior to the Van Nest killings. A portion of the jury found the defense of moral insanity interposed by Seward convincing, and an agreement on a verdict could not be reached.[5]

Once word spread that four members of the Van Nest family had been brutally killed just several miles from the site of Wyatt's trial, connections began to be made. Prosecutors later maintained that William Freeman himself had attended the Wyatt trial, a claim contested by the defense. Regardless of whether Freeman actually attended, the journals that favored a strict imposition of retributive criminal sanctions, including the death penalty, blamed the death of the Van Nests on the outcome of the first Wyatt trial. Just two days after the crime, the *Daily Cayuga Tocsin,* a Democratic organ with free-soil leanings, proclaimed that this "most revolting butchery of five persons" had "no parallel in the annals of crime in this community." The Auburn-based *Tocsin* then asked a penetrating question: "How far the late trial of Wyatt, and the doubts cast by its proceedings and results upon the power of the criminal tribunals of the land to protect the lives of our citizens, may have sharpened the assassin's knife, and steeled his heart, the public, who are conversant with it, must determine."[6] The editors of the *Tocsin* claimed with confidence that "not one man in this county can be found now, who does not see how naturally such horrible scenes flow from the events of the past two months."[7] Justice delayed, by virtue of Wyatt's first trial, was seen as justice denied with all the accompanying threats to the security of society.

New York's Democratic Party was deeply divided along ideological lines in 1846. A minority faction resisted the majority's "hard-money, antibanking, anticorporation policies." In 1844, this "probusiness, procanal expansion" minority, known as the Hunkers, aligned with Governor William C. Bouck and established the *Albany Argus.* The main target of the *Argus* was the *Albany Evening Atlas,* which "represented the party's antibanking, anticanal wing" and claimed John Van Buren among its associates. The split between the Hunkers and the opposing faction, known as the radicals, worsened over the issue of slavery's extension into the territories. Many radicals, including Martin and John Van Buren, eventually departed Democratic ranks and joined the Free Soil Party.[8]

Nevertheless, the *Cayuga Patriot,* an Auburn-based Hunker organ that was highly critical of John Van Buren and the radical faction of the party, agreed with the *Tocsin*'s interpretation of the events of early 1846. "Freeman has been proved to have attended the [Wyatt] trial, and the result might well have emboldened desperate men to gratify their malicious propensities," the *Patriot* exclaimed. The editors went on to express a deeper dismay at the threat being posed to society at large. The *Patriot* disavowed all sympathy with "that *good Samaritan's humanity,* which would *clear the guilty,* regardless of his slaughtered victims, and the public safety." The allusion, of course, was to the influence of the movement opposing capital punishment upon the willingness of juries to convict accused murderers.[9]

In the wake of the killings, the *Albany Argus,* edited by Edwin Croswell, reported that everyone in Auburn spoke of the "acquittal" of Wyatt with "indignation and shame." The *Argus* claimed that the desire to convict Wyatt upon his retrial was so strong that the venue would probably be changed from Auburn. The journal candidly expressed its conclusions as to the source of the problem with Wyatt's first trial: "It is to be hoped that those who are scrupulous with regard to capital punishment, will hereafter be excluded from acting on a jury, unless they have sufficient *mind* to know that [it] is not within *their* PROVINCE to acquit a prisoner *because* they are not in favor of hanging." The *Argus* exclaimed that jurors must "act conformably with their oath and acquit or convict according to evidence, and leave the Executive and the laws of the land to decide the rest." [10] This commentary appeared in an article entitled "The Horrible Murders in Cayuga," directly following details of the Van Nest slayings. The charge was a serious one, which the *Report of the Trial of Henry Wyatt* does not support. Only one juror sworn in Wyatt's first trial admitted supporting the abolition of capital punishment, and he swore to obey the law "as it is." The other eleven jurors admitted no conscientious scruples that might deter them from finding the defendant guilty based on the evidence.[11]

The *Argus's* accusations might not have been well founded, but they demonstrated very clearly that organ's position with regard to the administration of justice. Capital punishment was law in New York, and the campaign for its abolition was undermining the administration of justice by rendering juries sympathetic to cold-blooded killers. If murderers such as Wyatt were allowed to commit their crimes with impunity, the *Argus* reasoned that the lesson would not be lost on the likes of depraved individuals such as Freeman. These killings were rooted in the community's temptation to view violent criminals as sick rather than depraved. The *Argus* urged the community to open its eyes and see what the future held if necessary punishments were withheld.

The *Morning Courier and New York Enquirer,* a conservative Whig journal, joined in the protest regarding the interference of conscientious scruples in the jury's hearing of Wyatt's case.[12] The *Courier and Enquirer* doubted the veracity of the *New York Daily Tribune's* contention that "four-fifths of the Jurors on the recent trial of Wyatt who were not objected to on other grounds were set aside on the ground of their admitted hostility to Capital Punishment." The *Courier and Enquirer* implied that objections to the death penalty had rendered certain jurors unwilling to convict Wyatt, since otherwise the case against him was so strong. The *Tribune,* edited by Whig Horace Greeley who supported a variety of reform movements including the abolition of capital punishment, retorted that "the material facts, that many were so set aside and that those who tried and did not convict Wyatt were all of the other sort, remain unmoved." [13] Again, the *Report of the Trial of Henry Wyatt* supports the *Tribune's* contention, but we learn from the attitude expressed in the *Courier and Enquirer* that disgust with the administration of justice was bipartisan. [14] Both Whig and Democratic journals expressed suspicion regarding the effect that the antigallows reform movement was having on the administration of justice.

The far-reaching impact of the events in Auburn during the early months of 1846 is demonstrated by the editorial comments of *New York Herald.* The *Herald,* a Democratic journal edited by James Gordon Bennett, enjoyed a cordial relationship with Democratic state legislator John L. O'Sullivan and tended to support causes with which O'Sullivan was involved. O'Sullivan, however, was one of antebellum America's most dedicated supporters of the campaign to abolish capital punishment. His *Report in Favor of the Abolition of the Punishment of Death,* presented to the New York State Legislature in 1841, was widely cited by supporters and opponents of the death penalty. The *Herald* drew the line with O'Sullivan when it came to this particular cause. [15]

In the context of the events of the first half of 1846, the *Herald* could scarcely restrain itself:

> The fact is that many desperate characters in these days of "reform," plan and commit murder, with the explicit belief that the Fourier and universal abolition philosophers of the present time, will exert themselves in their behalf, and obtain for them full pardon, or a commutation of punishment to imprisonment for life. The new theories which have been lately broached

upon the subject of capital punishment, have spread themselves among all classes of society, so that even judges and jurors are tinctured with them. Understanding this feeling, and knowing that so soon as arrested as a murderer, he will excite the sympathies of a class of sickly sentimentalists, a man who is so hardened as to commit a murder, is willing to risk his chance of hanging, fully believing that the various causes we have mentioned will prevent it.

The *Herald* published details of the Van Nest killings in March and continued to monitor the trials of Wyatt and Freeman that summer. Although not specifically cited, it is very likely that the Wyatt trial and the Van Nest killings helped to inspire this particular editorial.[16]

A desperate desire to reinvigorate the criminal justice system in the days immediately following the Van Nest killings clearly crossed party lines. The *New York Morning Express,* edited by conservative Whigs James Brooks and William B. Townsend, focused on themes essentially similar to those of the Democratic organs. In the administration of justice, the editors complained, the cards were stacked in favor of the criminal. "These wretches estimate the chances of escape as nicely as the experienced gamester the delicate points in his game," the *Express* noted. Among the factors working in the criminal's favor were "the probabilities and possibilities of disagreement among the jurymen, either on the ground of stupidity, obstinacy, prejudice, or corrupt motive." Finally, the Whig journal lamented criminals' "reliance upon the effects that so many anti-death-penalty movements must, by this time, in this enlightened age of the world, have had upon the minds of the community."[17] The editors traced a direct line from the movement opposing capital punishment to the jury's failure to convict the "murderer" Wyatt, ultimately to Freeman's deduction that he could exact violent revenge with excellent chances of impunity.

In the wake of the unsuccessful effort to lynch William Freeman, press commentators explained the spirit of the Auburn mob in language that closely resembles the southern defense of lynching in the late nineteenth and early twentieth centuries. Slow and irregular justice was blamed in each instance for failing to effectively deter crime and uphold the social order. "Faced with what many whites perceived as increasing black-on-white crime," Stewart E. Tolnay and E. M. Beck note, "some thought that the formal system of criminal justice was too weak, slow, and uncertain to mete out fitting punishment." The "law's delay," corrupt lawyers, and "legal dodges" such as the insanity defense all became "stock defenses of mob violence" in general. This "popular justice apology" was the standard response to northern critics of southern mob violence in the late nineteenth century.[18]

The *Morning Courier and New York Enquirer* commented extensively on what it perceived to be the sources of the spirit of mob justice in Auburn. The desire to lynch Freeman "furnishes pretty pregnant evidence of the state of things in store for us in this country, and which is soon to come upon us, unless the mawkish and maudlin movements of a false philanthropy are speedily checked by a more rational and healthful public sentiment." The *Courier and Enquirer* congratulated the local community for thwarting the efforts of the mob but claimed that "it is impossible for a calm observer of events not to see in the circumstances, one of the legitimate consequences of the pestilent cant of the day." Freeman had confessed and his guilt was unquestionable. Therefore it was necessary, "not only for the vindication of public justice but for the safety of society, that he should be put to death." The desire for summary justice was based on "the utter uncertainty of his punishment if he should be left in the custody of the law." This uncertainty, according to the *Courier and Enquirer,* was an evil by-product of the antigallows movement.[19]

The *Courier and Enquirer* lamented the corruption of juries caused by the reform movement, claiming "there were besides, plenty of chances that at least one knave or fool might be empannelled [*sic*], and that would be sufficient" to save Freeman from his rightful end. The Auburn mob likely felt as well that, "if such a miracle should occur as an actual sentence, there would be objections enough ready to carry the case to two or three superior tribunals till it would be 'legal murder' to hang the criminal." If the above impediments to justice were overcome, the editors were certain that opponents of the gallows would flood the executive office with petitions asking that the "murderer" Freeman's sentence be commuted to life in prison. The mob were justified in believing that the "philanthropists" would not cease at commutation of punishment, but rather would push for full executive pardon. The *Courier and Enquirer* concluded by calling the assemblage at Auburn "the natural and necessary result of the present deplorable laxity in the administration of criminal law, and of the constant warfare which a sickly sentimentalism is making upon the enforcement of penalty against transgressors." [20]

These sentiments were fervently echoed in the columns of the *Albany Argus*. After reviewing the report of the attempt to lynch Freeman, the *Argus* claimed, "We do not regret that in this instance the wretch [escaped] the just retribution of an excited popular feeling; but we applaud this honest and indignant feeling, show itself as it may." The *Argus* agreed that the source of this "honest and indignant feeling" was lack of confidence in the administration of justice. "The law's delays and quibbles are such, and such the mistaken and false humanity of the anti–capital punishment advocates, who sometimes creep upon juries," the *Argus* explained, "that even in the most undoubted cases of murder" the perpetrator was as likely to escape as to suffer just punishment.[21] In the wake of the first Wyatt trial, the Van Nest killings were seen as a frightening example of where misguided reform movements could lead. The public understandably took upon itself a duty that the justice system was failing to fulfill.

The *Daily Cayuga Tocsin* printed a reaction to the near lynching of William Freeman that was perhaps the most sympathetic to the impulses that drove the mob. "Responsibility can never be imposed without its appropriate privilege," the *Tocsin* argued, "and the moment the privilege of protection is withheld by the government, the people will understand, practically, that all obligation to the laws of that government is determined and ended." In this scenario, the editors asserted, "Society immediately reverts to the primal condition of things; and that necessity which is the law of the case, is at once, and energetically applied." The contributor, who selected the pseudonym "Fleming" in direct reference to the Van Nest killings, viewed the outcome of the first Wyatt trial in the severest terms. The State of New York had violated its obligations under the social contract, which freed its citizens to abandon their obligation to obey the law. "Fleming" portrayed the Wyatt trial as a case of "sickly sentimental sympathy, puerile imbecility, and atrocious humbug." Just punishment had been denied out of sympathy for a killer, rendering it perfectly natural for the community to protect itself by whatever means necessary.[22]

Public responses to the Van Nest killings also clearly illustrate the tendency of gallows supporters to cite the Old Testament in support of capital punishment. As Masur notes, in antebellum America, arguments regarding morality "flowed directly from those who sought to re-establish the connection between the moral government of God and the secular polity of man." We find in the attacks, tendered from press and pulpit, at Freeman and his defenders, support for Masur's contention that "the defense of capital punishment centered on the belief that divine authority should govern human affairs, that religion should provide the principles of morality by which civil government operated." Capital punishment represented one means of maintaining moral and religious order in a time of great social change. Even though the reformers actually shared this desire for an ordered society, defenders of the gallows viewed them as anarchists, and their methods as radical. Ministers of the Calvinist denominations preached to their congregations that "the bible authorized death and that civil government, as a representative of divine government, had an obligation to execute murderers."[23] The Calvinist clergy themselves were leaders in the effort to defend the gallows from the reformers' assault.[24]

The Van Nests were communicants of the Sand Beach Church, which was denominationally Dutch Reformed Calvinist. At the funeral service held for John G. Van Nest, his wife, son, and mother-in-law, the Reverend A. B. Winfield lashed out in acerbic tones that illustrate the theological defense of the gallows. "If ever there was a just rebuke upon the falsely so-called sympathy of the day, here it is," Winfield began. Unless one loved the murderer more than his victims, the minister continued, the sight of the killings would force the admission that "the law of God which requires that 'he that sheddeth man's blood, by man shall his blood be shed,' is just, is reasonable." The reformers charged that capital punishment was "barbarous, cruel, savage," he added. To Winfield this amounted to charging God with commanding that which was barbarous, cruel, and savage. "Most daring blasphemy!" he concluded.[25]

The *Courier and Enquirer* responded with religious themes in answering the critics of capital punishment in the context of the events of early 1846. "We are on the rock of divine ordinance, as the highest *proof* (if you object to its being regarded as a present binding statute), that punishment, in its very nature, is meant to be retributive," the editors exclaimed. Divine law prescribed the taking of life for life, this being "God's method of restraining men from the commission of crime." The increase or diminution of offenses, however, did not at all effect this "immutable and unassailable position." The editors reasoned that a multitude of factors must be considered in any effort to explain the crime rate. Yet diminution of crime, the editors observed, "will generally be found to be in correspondence with the faithful preaching of the divine law, and the divine gospel, together with a rigidly enforced system of criminal jurisprudence based on the Scriptures." Crimes like Freeman's were linked to what the *Courier and Enquirer* called "infidel theology, or *atheology*," which regarded punishment as merely the "curative process of an hospital." Greeley's *Tribune* was lambasted for spreading such blasphemy and equating sin with disease. Under the "pretence of social reform," all crime was erroneously being attributed to some mode in which society had failed the criminal, instead of to the "hard to be checked depravity of men." [26]

The *New York Express* joined in the attack on Freeman's apologists, namely the *Tribune,* employing religious themes in the process. The *Express* admitted understanding human aversion to the shedding of blood but declared that a "wise Providence" had also implanted a natural desire for retribution in man's character "for wise purposes." In addition to human sympathy, "as deep an instinct is implanted by the hand of God, to sanction His primal eldest decree to the children of noah [*sic*], that, at the hand of man He would, (in all time) *require* the blood of the shedder of blood." The editors claimed that "the great poet of human nature" made "Blood will have blood" the instinctive exclamation of "one whom he represents as exhibiting the true workings of the human conscience." [27]

In the columns of the *Herald,* religious themes were mingled with the exigencies of public security. Citizens would face having to band together in armed groups and the organization of society would be threatened all because "one of its organic laws will be futile, and wretches who break all human and Divine laws are converted into demigods, instead of expiating their villany [*sic*] on the gallows." The paper expressed a longing for bygone days when "The murderer—he who had shed his brother's blood deliberately and inexcusably" was considered a "wretch who should be disposed of as quickly as possible, and snatched out of the midst of the society whose fundamental laws he had broken." These "fundamental laws" were the laws that most closely reflected the will of the Almighty, as expressed in the Old Testament.[28]

A corollary to the demand for obedience to scriptural commands in the administration of justice was repugnance to the idea that criminals could be reformed. This reformist idea contradicted Calvinist theology concerning the depravity of man. Gallows supporters regarded Freeman, and Wyatt for that matter, as excellent examples of depraved human beings upon which the reforming mission of the penitentiary had no positive effect. The *New York Morning Telegraph,* an independent and intensely pro-capital-punishment journal, pondered whether Freeman's life should be spared in favor of life imprisonment. "Shall he again be trusted to the reforming process of State Prison confinement, which in his case has proved to be worse than vain?" the *Telegraph* demanded.[29] The *Courier and Enquirer* included in its columns an editorial from another conservative Whig journal that expressed indignation at the idea of returning Freeman to the penitentiary. "Would this tiger nature have quailed at a thought of a return to those prison walls whence he was recently liberated?" the *Rochester Daily American* asked. Freeman was depraved by nature, the *American* contended, and he had exited prison unaltered in temperament. Society's depraved could not be reformed, and therefore the aim of criminal punishment should be to demonstrate that the price for taking human life was life itself.[30]

If the penitentiary failed to reform criminals, progallows commentators pointed out that it likewise failed to deter them from committing further crime. The *Rochester Daily American* did not believe that Freeman feared incarceration enough to refrain from killing the Van Nests. "Why did the bloody fiend of that atrocious butchery tremble when proofs of his guilt accumulate to the exclusion of all doubt?" the *American* demanded. The answer, in the editors' opinion, was because Freeman knew that murder carried the penalty of death. The *Courier and Enquirer* agreed wholeheartedly with the sentiments expressed in the *American,* indicating its own support of punishment based on instinctively and divinely supported retribution, as well as deterrence of crime.[31] The *Morning Telegraph* also criticized the failure of the penitentiary to deter convicts from committing further crime. "Will the long cherished grudges, which are known to lurk in

the hearts of convicted offenders, be softened down by the proposed abolition of the death punishment?" the editors asked. Vindictive punishment,
these commentators concluded, was supported by human instinct, divine
law, and the plain and simple fact that fear of death was all that deterred offenders like Freeman.[32]

The sheer brutality of William Freeman's crimes, especially that he had
stabbed both a pregnant woman and her two-year-old child to death, made
it extremely difficult to publicly express sympathy for him. This did not
mean, however, that sympathy was not forthcoming. The voices that
pleaded most loudly for calmness, for fairness, and for allowing Freeman his
full legal rights were those of activists opposing capital punishment. In the
wake of the Van Nest killings and the failed effort to lynch William Freeman, the Whig-affiliated *Auburn Journal and Advertiser* devoted considerable
space in its columns to the words of John Austin. Austin was a clergyman of
the Universalist church in Auburn, who wrote under the pseudonym "Justice."[33] Universalist associations were, in fact, very actively campaigning for
the abolition of capital punishment in Cayuga County in 1846.[34] Capital
punishment violated Universalist teachings that stressed "the salvation of
mankind, a benevolent, noncoercive God, and the rejection of eternal, everlasting punishment." Man was essentially "moral, reasonable, educable, and
savable," but capital punishment often meant that human beings were sent to
their death, unreformed and unrepentant. Universalists believed that punishment should be calculated to reform criminals, not to exact a retribution
that went against the true will of God.[35]

John Austin in no way tried to downplay the cruelty of the Van Nest
slayings. Freeman was "a brutal wretch, who violated every principle of
manhood and compassion," Austin agreed. "A just feeling of indignation at a
crime so awful as this, and a loathing abhorrence of the spirit by which its
perpetrator was actuated, is both proper and commendable," he added. This,
however, did not justify the spirit of *"revenge and blood-thirstiness,"* including
pleas for summary justice, that the crimes awakened in the community.
Freeman was still a human being who was entitled to some consideration
from a Christian community. "One evil can never justify another," Austin
wrote. Because Freeman "thirsted for the blood of his victims," did it justify
the community in "thirsting for his blood"? Because Freeman took the lives

of others in a "violent and lawless manner," was the community justified in taking his life in a violent and lawless manner? "Because he showed no feeling, no pity, no commiseration for others, does it justify us in showing no feeling, no pity for him?—Can two wrongs ever make a right?" Austin demanded. Ultimately, "Justice" concluded that any man that was disposed to answer these inquiries in the affirmative had "evidently lost his place in mingling in a civilized and Christian community." Such persons, Austin reasoned, had "adopted principles of action which alone belong to barbarians and brutes." A Christian community stood little to gain by taking Freeman's life either legally or illegally.[36]

Austin, like those who spoke out in favor of capital punishment, drew the community's attention to the authority of the Bible. "I think it would be well not to cast the book entirely aside, amid circumstances so trying as these," he warned. Austin however, schooled in the liberal theology of Universalism, focused on the lessons of the New Testament regarding the guilty. "Does it teach us to indulge in feelings of revenge and retaliation?—does it direct us to demand 'an eye for an eye, and a tooth for a tooth'?" he asked his readers. "No," Austin replied, "it peremptorily forbids it." The voice of God instructed his children to " 'avenge not yourselves; but rather give place unto wrath,' "the clergyman argued.[37] Austin also called upon his faith in answering those who criticized him personally for cautioning the community against the desire for vengeance. "I am firm in my consciousness that my motives will be appreciated and approved by the enlightened and candid portion of the community, and by One above, who scrutinizes all the thoughts of our hearts," he wrote. Reiterating his indignation at Freeman's cruelty, Austin emphasized that he "still strove to school [his] feelings toward the brutalized murderer into a frame that should receive the sanction of the Master of christians [sic], and accord with the spirit he manifested towards the blinded, the guilty, the depraved."[38]

In this commentary, Austin revealed his own conception of manhood. Freeman's behavior "violated every principle of manhood," Austin maintained, because it was violent, insensitive, vindictive, and completely lacking in emotional control or restraint. If the men of the community responded with equal violence, vindictiveness, and absence of compassion or restraint, then they had no greater claim to true manhood than did Freeman. Austin's conception challenged the more widely held antebellum image of ruthless, aggressive, self-interested, ambitious, and power-hungry American manhood.[39] Self-sacrifice and compassion, truly "anathema to this crude masculine stereotype," were commonly deemed feminine virtues. However, reformers, evangelical Christians, and transcendentalists criticized "belligerent, combative masculinity" as one source of America's moral and political problems. These predominantly northern cultural groups concluded that the Mexican War and immoral forms of oppression that centered on women, blacks, and Native Americans resulted in part from American conceptions of manhood. Universalist and reformer himself, it is likely that Austin shared this belief that true manhood involved a different set of virtues.[40]

A student of the New Testament, it is also likely that John Austin shared with other reformers, particularly abolitionists, an admiration for the image of manhood embodied in Jesus Christ. Among those who wanted to revise the notion of masculinity in America, "Christ-like values" were idealized rather than "aggressive and competitive ones." Cynthia Griffin Wolff observes that the image of Jesus as "at one and the same time 'heroic,' 'loving,' and 'manly'—permeated abolitionist thought and literature." Jesus united what reformers viewed as the best virtues of women and men within one perfect, harmonious being. He was nonviolent, compassionate, forgiving, self-sacrificing, and yet strong. Jesus rejected vengeance but possessed the courage to oppose injustice even in the "highest places."[41] Exponents of the doctrine of separate social spheres claimed that men's aggressive and self-interested nature was not socially destructive if tempered by the positive moral influence of women in the home.[42] Abolitionists, suffragists, and evangelical Christians observed evidence to the contrary in the society around them. Along with John Austin, they believed that Americans should look to Jesus as the ultimate model of a Christian man.[43] Thus we see that at least among certain segments of northern society, the notion of aggressive and self-interested masculinity did not go unchallenged. Even when contemplating the fate of William Freeman, Austin and other reformers including Horace Greeley urged the community to act in accordance with the spirit manifested by Christ.

As previously noted, Greeley's *New York Tribune* was castigated in the spring of 1846 for its opposition to capital punishment. Opposition to the gallows was not a strictly sectarian movement, but reformers did tend in any case to be dissenters from the Calvinist denominations.[44] Greeley's reaction to the thirst for vengeance brought on by the first Wyatt trial and the Van Nest killings illustrates this clearly. "God is perfectly able to execute His own judgements, and when He says 'He that taketh the sword shall perish by the sword,' we do not understand Him as requiring any of us to take swords and kill all swordsmen," Greeley wrote. No case was strengthened, he maintained, "except with the very weak or very ignorant by such assertions as that 'the law of death for Murder was *beyond all denial* established by God as *perpetual.*'" That was the very point most earnestly denied by the reformers, Greeley contended, "and *our* side undoubtingly believe that *all* such retributive penalties, so far as ever sanctioned, were expressly abrogated by Christ."[45] The *Tribune*'s attack on retribution and the gallows, similar to that of John Austin, drew its inspiration from the New Testament. The reformers stressed that the Calvinist justification for punishment, cited by the pro-capital-punishment forces, clearly ignored the changes brought about by the life and death of Christ.

In the weeks following the Van Nest killings, Greeley's editorials became increasingly explicit. He directed his readers to the Gospel according to Matthew, claiming that Christ's words repealed the law given by God to Moses. The Mosaic Law of "eye for eye, tooth for tooth," that appeared in Exodus and Leviticus was "plainly repealed by Christ in Matt. v. 38, 39," the editor argued. Greeley's reference was to the New Testament passage in which Christ teaches, "When a person strikes you on the right cheek, turn and offer him the other." Greeley concluded, "the *spirit* of Christ's precept applies as fully to the requirement of 'Life for life' in Exod. xxi. 23, as to that of 'eye for eye' immediately following it." Whatever had been God's purpose in commanding the "law of Retaliatory Infliction" in the time of Moses, Greeley advanced that Christ had abolished it "as calculated to do harm rather than good."[46] Even in Mosaic times, Greeley added, criminals were punished primarily to deter them from further crime rather than to uphold God's law.[47] Supporters of the gallows, even in the case of William Freeman, would have to find a better argument than the scriptural one to convince the Whig editor.

Opponents of capital punishment were disturbed by the tendency of gallows supporters to blame Freeman's crimes on laxity in the administration of justice. John Austin asked, "Is it well for men who address the public amid this excitement, to speak lightly of our Courts of Justice—to pour contempt upon the proceedings of Judges, Counsellors and Juries, for a conscientious discharge of their duty, under the solemn responsibilities which they felt resting upon them?" Such criticism, according to Austin, diminished the community's confidence in the "efficacious operation of our laws." The ultimate effect, he reasoned, was to "countenance and encourage the multitude to take the power into their own hands, and administer justice according to the Lynch code, rather than submit to the operations of laws originating in wise legislation, and sanctioned by long experience!" Those that were quick to blame the reformers seemed, to Austin, to be the true cultivators of anarchy.[48]

Austin took issue particularly with a contributor to the *Daily Cayuga Tocsin* who wrote under the pseudonym "Vindex." "What security have we as a community, if the cause of public justice is to be perverted by the ingenious presentation of fallacious and pernicious dogmas?" the *Tocsin* writer asked. Austin responded with a firm defense of the proceedings in the first Wyatt trial, insisting that public justice had been guided by "the most enlightened minds that have appeared upon the stage of human life." In Austin's opinion, judges "justly famed for intelligence, great legal knowledge and experience, and strict impartiality" had presided over the case. In addition, "Learned and able advocates were engaged, both in behalf of the people and the prisoner, who displayed a legal acumen and ability, seldom if ever before exhibited in this community." The trial had been conducted in accordance with the "most enlightened and well established principles of legal jurisprudence." Furthermore, Austin retorted, Henry Wyatt had not been *acquitted*. Ever cognizant of the connections being drawn between Wyatt's first trial and the Van Nest slayings, Austin feared that the events of early 1846 were being used as an excuse to disregard the law and contemplate summary justice. In his view, abandonment of the legal system threatened the security of the community far more than the law's imperfections.[49]

William Freeman's acts were unspeakable, Austin admitted. Yet Freeman's death, whether by legal means or not, would not eliminate crime.

Furthermore, Austin feared that the community's thirst for vengeance would lead to anarchy. There would be others after Freeman who would come along and commit deeds that would outrage the community. The danger in lynching Freeman was that once the community got "a taste of lawless power," it would require "less provocation to call it into existence" in each ensuing instance.[50] If Freeman's legal rights were trampled, in time it would require little more than the expression of a dissenting or unpopular opinion to put a citizen's legal rights in jeopardy.

As a final note, antigallows reformers faced the difficult situation of having to advocate some form of punishment that deterred crime, while facing the harsh reality that the disciplinary regime of the penitentiary failed to reform many criminals. As we have seen, gallows supporters used the failure of the penitentiary to reform Freeman during his five-year sentence for grand larceny as evidence in support of the death penalty. Freeman, progallows commentators asserted, possessed a permanently depraved heart and no amount of incarceration would effect a beneficent change. The *New York Morning Telegraph* feared that a sentence of life imprisonment for Freeman would merely signal to other "convicted offenders" that they could settle "long-cherished grudges" against the state without fear for their own persons. Nothing short of Freeman's execution would send a message to other convicts, and society at large, that death was the price for murder.[51]

In Freeman's case, it was simpler for reformers to emphasize that the thorough vindictiveness of the criminal justice system drove this man to desperation. The *Tribune* took great interest in Freeman's past, noting that he had "felt the full weight of vindictive (perhaps mistaken) justice, in years of joyless, cramped, lashed, ill-fed, unrewarded toil." Freeman had exited prison, "resolved to have revenge in turn," and resolved that such vengeance would far outweigh the precipitating offense. According to Greeley, the "State" had punished a sixteen-year-old boy, who had been duped by a crafty horse thief, with five years of harsh punishment. Freeman decided to retaliate for the "State's" offense by brutally killing a family that had done him no harm. He had learned the lesson of vindictive and disproportionate punishment at the hands of his teacher, the "State."[52] John Austin likewise observed that Freeman had been "beaten with bludgeons into deafness and comparative idiocy—at length released, with faculties shattered or benumbed, every evil passion magnified and burning with revenge against those whom he believed had injured him."[53] The death penalty, reformers maintained, was but vindictive, retributive justice taken to its ultimate conclusion.

William Lloyd Garrison, although not as active a participant in the effort to abolish the death penalty, shared Greeley and Austin's beliefs regarding the evils of vindictive punishment. Furthermore, his remarks illustrate the non-partisan nature of the antebellum death penalty debate, which was both reflected in and influenced by public response to the Van Nest killings. Because of Garrison's disavowal of all affiliation with political parties, Michael F. Holt describes him as an "apolitical abolitionist."[54] Garrison wondered "what provocation to commit some terrible outrage after his release, may not have been given to William Freeman, during his five years' incarceration in that dreadful prison?" Shortly after the killings, Garrison fumed, "Of course, it is to be expected that the friends of the gallows will seize on this occurrence to help prop it up." Garrison hoped that "Humanity and Common Sense, instead of finding in this tragedy any reason for perpetuating that barbarous instrument of retaliation, will only be stimulated to make fresh efforts for its overthrow." As the ultimate expression of human vengefulness, the gallows, in Garrison's opinion, depraved rather than saved society and tended to the "cheapening of human life."[55]

William Freeman's racial background also became the subject of pointed commentary in the days and weeks immediately following the killings. Both Democratic and Whig journals raised the issue of Freeman's race in attempting to explain the brutal attack at Fleming. It is important to note, however, that race was an element of the larger debate concerning the nature of crime and the purpose of punishment. Freeman's father was a black slave who had obtained his own freedom by purchase just nine years prior to his son's birth. Freeman's mother was of mixed ancestry, being part black and part Native American.[56] This intensified the controversy surrounding Freeman, but his acts of butchery would have inspired indignation and vengefulness from a majority of the public regardless of his race. Likewise, Freeman's race generated added interest and sympathy among the small but vocal group of reformers that opposed capital punishment.

Following the slayings, the Whig-affiliated *Syracuse Journal* claimed that "Wm. Freeman, the murderer of the Van Nest family, is a cousin of the Freeman who was executed in this county some five or six years since, for murder." The editors concluded that there "must be some bad blood running in the veins of the Freeman tribe," since they had "heard it stated, that Wm. Freeman is one-quarter Indian, his mother having been one-half Indian."[57] The implication was that Freeman's violent nature was traceable to his Native American ancestry. That a blood relative was executed for murder provided evidence that this conclusion was perfectly logical. It made no difference to the editors that a cousin on Freeman's father's side would not necessarily share his Native American ancestry. The *Syracuse Star* likewise attempted to establish that a Dan Freeman, who was executed in Syracuse and was more than likely the same person referred to in the *Syracuse Journal,* was William Freeman's brother.[58] The implication, again, was that there was a pattern of savagery and depravity in the Freeman family, resulting from the mixture of two inferior races.

The Auburn area papers responded with assertions that reports linking other members of William Freeman's family to violent crime were untrue. The *Auburn Daily Advertiser* refuted the *Syracuse Star* by asserting, accurately, that William Freeman had no brothers.[59] The *Cayuga Patriot* stated that the Freeman executed in Onondaga County was not William Freeman's cousin, as the *Syracuse Journal* claimed. The editors also noted that the *Patriot* had been credited incorrectly by the *Albany Argus* as the source of this claim. Merely unsubstantiated rumors, these claims nevertheless demonstrated the willingness of the press to entertain racial explanations for the Van Nest killings. Such explanations, as can be seen, circulated widely around the state.[60]

The *Albany Argus,* besides reprinting the comments regarding "bad blood running through the veins of the Freeman tribe," made its own connection between Freeman's depravity and his race. Lamenting that antigallows reformers took great pains to save murderers from just punishment, the *Argus* complained that "the wretch, however *black* in heart and in skin" was still likely to be spared. William Freeman was not simply a murderer; he was a *black* murderer. It was shameful enough that misguided philanthropists interceded between evil doers and the punishment they deserved. Interceding for those who were also black was intolerable.[61] It was no coincidence that the *Argus* spoke for the conservative faction of the New York Democratic Party, a party for which hostility to free blacks was "part of the political stock in trade." [62] It is also important to note that "black" was not the preferred term used to refer to people of African descent in the antebellum era. Freeman was regularly referred to as "the negro," but the expression "black" was chosen specifically in this case to conger the images of evil, depravity, and sin. His heart *and* his skin were black indicating that Freeman was the embodiment of everything that whites should fear. If the ordinary white man was inherently depraved and required the restraint of divine and civil laws, it was even more necessary that the newly freed black be so restrained. [63] Calvinism melded together with racism resulted in dehumanizing images of black men who ran afoul of the law. [64]

The *Rochester Daily Advertiser,* an organ of the radical faction of the New York Democratic Party, created an image very similar to that of its conservative counterpart. The *Advertiser* referred to Freeman in one instance as "This black wretch." [65] On a separate occasion, while spewing venom over the insanity plea serving as the saving grace of murderers, the *Advertiser* called Freeman "the black demon." [66] "Wretch" was used as a general term of condemnation for criminals at this time. That Freeman was a "black wretch" amplified his depravity. His "blackness" was referred to, rather than his being a "negro," in order to conjure the worst images and fears that readers possessed of people of African descent. The phrase "black demon" simply took this process a step further. Direct connection was made between Freeman's race and his evil ways. The use of the term "black" served both to denote Freeman's race and to intensify the image of evil embodied in the word "demon." In this view, the community had abundant reason to fear for its safety since Freeman was both a free black, with all of the concomitant images of insurrection and depravity, *and* the perpetrator of an atrocious crime. [67]

The conservative Whig journal the *New York Express* lashed out at Greeley's *New York Daily Tribune* for taking pity upon Freeman because of his race. As noted earlier, the *Express* supported the gallows and was highly critical of progressive Whigs who supported greater political participation for blacks. The editors complained that Freeman was an ideal candidate for the sympathies of the *Tribune,* which opposed capital punishment. After all, he was not merely an accused murderer but "a black man,—some say, a half-blood Indian," as well. The *Express* chastised the *Tribune* for possessing "such a romantic regard for the colored race, that it seems to have a greater attachment for it than for its own." The *Express* suspected that the "murders" presented the *Tribune* with an "opening for the play of a double sympathy," an opportunity that was eagerly exploited. The editors could stomach no such sympathy for the individual that they deemed "the *last and worst of the murderers.*" According to the *Express,* the *Tribune* apologized for Freeman, claiming that he had been " 'trained for the gallows,' by the injustice and prejudice of the community, who have actually 'educated him for a murderer.' " The *Express* took issue with this reasoning, asserting that "every man in the same original position, in society, with this malefactor, would be justified in being a criminal, by throwing the blame thereof upon 'The State,' or 'the age.' " The *Express* accepted no responsibility for William Freeman's actions, believing that crime resulted from human depravity. No degree of environmental influence exculpated Freeman from his guilt; he was a murderer who deserved to be punished as a murderer.[68]

Another organ of the radical Democrats, the *Albany Evening Atlas,* categorized Freeman as "of the lowest and most unprotected class of society."[69] It is important not to read sympathy for blacks into the words chosen by the *Atlas.* Although the radical Democrats, or Barnburners, opposed the extension of slavery beyond the states where it already existed, they were by no means friendly to the interests of free blacks in New York. As Phyllis F. Field notes, the New York Democratic Party was unified in its hostility to blacks. The Democrats appealed to whites' most basic fears of blacks when issues involving black participation in the community came to the political fore. The Democrats went so far as to portray the Whig Party as "dangerous, fanatical 'nigger lovers' " in order to quell the efforts of some Whigs to increase black political rights.[70] The *Atlas* merely noted the low social station from which William Freeman came, neither offering him sympathy because of it nor holding society in any way responsible. The *Atlas* perceived Freeman as a depraved, violent, repeat offender who also happened to be black. The editors protested that Freeman's fate only became a matter of controversy because he committed a capital crime and attracted the attention of antigallows reformers. Otherwise, the editors concluded that, black or white, Freeman would have been convicted and sentenced with little fanfare or community concern.

Freeman's defenders in the public at large expressed very different conclusions regarding the link between race and crime. Most opponents of the death penalty in antebellum America, including John Austin, believed that social conditions contributed to crime. They found environmental explanations for crime especially convincing in reference to blacks. When blacks such as Freeman were put on trial for capital crimes, the opponents of the death penalty seized the opportunity to express both their disdain for capital punishment and their sympathy for an oppressed race.[71]

In addition to his general criticism of retributive justice, Austin discussed in detail the role of society in making Freeman a killer. He closed one lengthy article in the *Auburn Journal and Advertiser* with an extended admonishment of the community that began with the observation that blacks belonged "to a degraded *caste.*" In the community, a "most heartless, cruel prejudice rests against them, for the reason that God has given them complexions a few shades darker than some of the rest of our citizens." For this reason only, Austin observed, "they are set aside and denied the privileges of the meanest and most unworthy of white men." Denied admission to white churches, "with none to instruct them intelligently in their religious and moral duties," Austin concluded that blacks existed "almost wholly without the benefits of moral, religious or intellectual culture." Unable to sustain their own schools, and "shut out from both public and private schools among the whites," blacks grew up "almost literally heathen, in the midst of an enlightened and christian [*sic*] community." Ultimately, the black community fell victim to "unworthy prejudices which compel them to exist under circumstances where they are exposed to imbibe all the vices, without being able to become imbued with the virtues, of those around them." Given the social circumstances, Austin asked readers, "Who can wonder that they fall into crime?"[72]

Austin then turned his attention directly to Freeman, demanding, "To these causes must we not trace the guilt of the miserable wretch whose hands are now reeking with the blood of murdered worth and innocence?" According to Austin, Freeman was "Born in ignominy—with a mental organ-

ization but little superior to the brute creation—raised in total ignorance—
what little mind he naturally possessed unimproved, unenlightened by religion or education." Freeman consequently fell "early and easily into crime,"
which led to his subjection to the harsh discipline of the state prison. He
emerged from a long sentence, with little left of his faculties and a burning
passion to seek revenge against those that he believed were guilty of causing
him harm. Austin asked, "is not society in some degree, accountable for this
sad catastrophe?" Could the killings not be "traced as one of the legitimate
effects of the utter indifference and neglect manifested towards the colored
population of this place?" The words " 'fiend'—'brute'—'wretch' " were on
every tongue in the village, Austin observed. Yet, he demanded, had any
member of "our enlightened and wealthy population interposed to prevent
[Freeman] from becoming the wretch that he is?" Austin pleaded for the
erection of a "convenient church" and the provision of a "faithful ministry"
for the benefit of the black community. He ended by asking, "Should there
not be immediately, one or two good schools opened and sustained at the
public expense, expressly for the instruction of colored children?" [73]

The editors of the *Auburn Journal and Advertiser* defended John Austin
when the *Daily Cayuga Tocsin* printed an article criticizing "Justice" for stating that blacks were "every way excusable for falling early and easily into
crime." The editors of the *Auburn Journal and Advertiser* focused on the *Tocsin*
article's use of the phrase "every way excusable." The *Journal* editors accurately noted that these words did not appear in Austin's article and further
denied that they were his intended meaning. "Justice" had merely alluded to
the "miserable, neglected condition of the African race—their ignorance,
poverty, wretchedness," and asked "is not society *in some degree,* accountable
for this sad catastrophe?" The *Journal* did not wish to be construed as excusing Freeman's brutality in any way, which would have been a dangerous position to assume given popular outrage. The editors took great pains to
clarify their support of law, of right, and of justice. They went on record,
however, as supporting the "love of truth and fairness" manifested by "Justice." The editors agreed that white prejudice and neglect of the black race
were partially to blame for making Freeman a criminal. They did not want
to express overt sympathy for Freeman but rather an enlightened understanding of the circumstances from which he came. The editors' remarks

notwithstanding, it seems as though John Austin was significantly more critical of society and more willing to hold the community responsible than was the journal in which his writings appeared.[74]

Like John Austin, Horace Greeley responded passionately to those voices that attempted to link Freeman's criminality to his race. As noted, the *Tribune* portrayed Freeman as living proof that vindictive punishment only taught criminals that vengeance was the proper way to answer any offense. Furthermore, the *Tribune* denied that Freeman's depravity was the natural product of his racial background. Freeman had never been given opportunity for improvement in life, the editor asserted, and therefore society was implicated in the brutal crimes committed at Fleming. "Born of an outcast and trampled race, daily exposed from his cradle to unmerited insults and indignities, growing up to vice a poor, friendless orphan," Freeman was arrested "in boyhood on a charge of horse-stealing." Not surprisingly, Freeman was convicted and sent to state prison, Greeley observed, since "a poor negro boy caught on a stolen horse has a poor chance of acquittal." Greeley believed that Freeman had been tricked into possessing stolen property and was subsequently convicted because he was black. The harsh discipline of the state prison then nurtured in him a desire for revenge that resulted in the deaths of four innocent people. Despite the indignation that his columns inspired, most notably at the editorial offices of the *New York Express,* Greeley remained steadfast in his faith that William Freeman had been the victim of injustice long before he spilled the blood of the Van Nests.[75]

The *Albany Argus,* as noted, complained that even black criminals garnered the sympathies and protection of misguided philanthropists who sought to abolish the death penalty. The *Argus* feared that William Freeman, who was not just a mass murderer but a black as well, would likely be spared the punishment he deserved. Greeley refused to accept the *Argus's* implication that, because the *Tribune* spoke out against the death penalty, it was in some way responsible for the Van Nest murders. "The *Argus* is wrong—we fear wilfully [*sic*] so," Greeley averred, being that facts "abundantly prove that men with black *skins* can be hung easily enough, however it may be with those of black *hearts.*" Freeman "obviously had no ground of hope to escape hanging if caught," the *Tribune* editor argued, recalling "several instances in which black men have been hung for murdering white ones." Greeley challenged his critics to produce one case in which "the palpable author of such a murder has escaped the gallows." He remained steadfast in his own conviction that blacks suffered the punishment of death at higher rates than whites convicted of capital crimes. According to Greeley, race was indeed a factor that influenced the administration of justice, but not in the manner suggested by the *Argus*. William Freeman deserved the sympathy of society, but society had given him no reason prior to the Van Nest killings to assume that such sympathy would be forthcoming.[76]

Lastly, William Lloyd Garrison's *Liberator* expressed grave concern that segments of the white community would seize upon the Van Nest killings as evidence that the entire black race was violent and depraved. The *Liberator*, the major organ of the Boston clique of immediatist abolitionists, was outraged by what it called Freeman's "most dreadful deed." Since Freeman "happened to have a colored skin," however, Garrison's paper was certain that "the wicked persecutors of the colored people will hold them all responsible for it, and thus try to inflame and immortalize that fierce yet vulgar prejudice, which has so long prevailed against them." The deed was Freeman's own, the editor concluded, and "the consequences should be confined to him alone." After all, the *Liberator* continued, "the colored population of this country have given the strongest evidence of possessing incomparably more humane feelings, of having a much stronger aversion to the shedding of blood, than their white enslavers." Blacks had been "robbed, scourged, bought and sold like cattle, subjected to every outrage that cruelty could invent or tyranny inflict," Garrison reminded readers. Thousands had been "flogged to death, stabbed, mutilated, and shot down, by those monsters who have possessed unlimited and irresponsible control over them." Incredible in Garrison's mind was that hundreds of blacks had not been "driven by desperation to commit the most shocking atrocities, by way of retaliation." By Garrison's estimation, the Van Nest killings were an atypical and yet understandable product of centuries of enslavement and oppression.[77]

Antebellum perceptions of the link between punishment, crime, religion, and manhood were revealed in public responses to the brutal slaughter of John G. Van Nest and his family. The Van Nest killings occurred at a time when Americans were involved in an emotionally charged debate over the punishment of criminals. When word spread of the atrocities at Fleming, voices from both major political parties placed blame on laxity in the administration of justice owing to the efforts of antigallows reformers. The brutal nature of the killings, coming as they did on the heels of the failure to convict Henry Wyatt, underscored the danger inherent in misdirected benevolence. Commentators who disagreed on a variety of other sensitive political issues had little difficulty seeing eye to eye on this one. Freeman was a depraved human being, these critics shouted, his life a violent example of the failure of the penitentiary to reform criminals or deter crime. The good of the community demanded that he be treated as God and human instinct directed.

Opponents of the gallows challenged the Old Testament justification of capital punishment, bringing to the fore a liberal creed that emphasized God's benevolence and universal salvation. Criminal punishment, they argued, was best used to initiate a reformative process, rather than as retribution. Taking Freeman's life, legally or illegally, was both unmanly and unchristian. Retribution would do nothing to change the fact that his victims were dead. It would merely nurture a spirit of vindictiveness and immorality among the community. Unfortunately for William Freeman, opponents of the death penalty were in the minority. Their presence in the community was a mixed blessing. Their support of Freeman ensured that he would receive qualified legal representation. On the other hand, their activities exacerbated public feelings of insecurity and intensified the popular desire for a traditional form of punishment.

Public responses to the Van Nest killings also illuminate antebellum conceptions of the link between race, crime, and the administration of justice. The killings were brutal beyond anything that the residents of central New York could have imagined happening in their own backyard. Observers across the state shared their outrage. The victims were respectable and *white*. Among them were a mother, her unborn child, and two-year-old son. At a time when blacks were spurned from participation in white society, and Native Americans were portrayed in stereotypically derogatory terms, sympathy for a killer who traced his lineage to both groups was not likely to be great. To numerous observers, Freeman's actions reinforced the worst images of violence and depravity associated with African Americans and Native Americans. Participation of these groups in society engendered feelings of insecurity among antebellum whites. Failure to punish criminal elements within these groups was looked upon as foolhardy.

Sympathy for Freeman was forthcoming, but only from opponents of capital punishment, abolitionists, and as we shall soon see, those who felt genuine sympathy for the mentally ill. These commentators placed a portion of the blame for the Van Nest killings on society. They believed that environmental factors destroyed the life of a young man who had been born with spirit and intelligence. Vengeance consumed Freeman's thoughts while he was imprisoned and during his brief period of freedom prior to the killings.

While responses to the killings give us a glimpse of racial attitudes in the antebellum North, they were a small part of the larger debate concerning the nature of crime and purpose of punishment. Freeman was certainly more evil and his punishment more essential, in many observers' minds, because he was black and Native American. He also drew greater sympathy and stiffer resolve from his defenders because of his race. The Van Nest killings would have fueled the debate over the punishment of criminals regardless of Freeman's race, however. Such brutal acts, coming as they did on the heels of the controversial Wyatt trial, would have inspired outrage from gallows supporters even had Freeman been white. These attacks would in turn have provoked responses from antigallows reformers. Had Freeman been a white ex-convict, the public still would have speculated on the causes and implications of such a horrific event. Freeman's race did, however, help onlookers explain events that truly defied explanation. If the killings were the product of depravity, it soothed the emotions of white observers to believe that nonwhites were more likely to sink to such depths. Environmental explanations offered other observers hope that such brutality could be prevented in the future.

3

Mental Illness in Antebellum America

SCIENCE, THE PUBLIC, AND THE COURTS

SHORTLY AFTER THE VAN NEST KILLINGS, Governor Silas Wright responded to the popular demand for a special term of the circuit court for Cayuga County. The governor ordered that a special term be scheduled to commence on June 1, 1846, for the purpose of both retrying Henry Wyatt and trying William Freeman.[1] During the May term of the Cayuga County Court of General Sessions, a grand jury was convened to hear the evidence against William Freeman.[2] On May 18, the Grand Jury of the County of Cayuga returned a single indictment against Freeman, charging him with the murder of John G. Van Nest. Freeman was arraigned at the outset of the special term of the Cayuga County Court of Oyer and Terminer on June 1, 1846.[3] William Henry Seward, along with Seneca Wood, Christopher Morgan, and Samuel Blatchford, appeared voluntarily on behalf of Freeman. Seward informed the court that he and his colleagues had found Freeman "as the Court see him, deaf, and unable even to hear the indictments found against him." They requested that a plea of insanity be entered in Freeman's behalf. Statutory law in New York forbade the trial of insane persons for crimes or offenses, making necessary a preliminary consideration of Freeman's present state of mind. District Attorney Luman Sherwood moved to take up the retrial of Wyatt before considering the issue of whether William Freeman was sane for the purpose of standing trial.[4]

At the time of the trials of Wyatt and Freeman, jurists, legislators, physicians, and laymen were engaged in a struggle to define insanity in some manner that would be usable in courts of law. As far as criminal law was concerned, the debate focused on what degree or variety of mental impairment absolved an individual of responsibility for behavior that the law defined as criminal. Statutory law in New York was of little assistance to the courts dealing with accused criminals who employed insanity as an affirmative defense. The law merely stipulated, "No act done by a person in a state of insanity can be punished as an offence; and no insane person can be tried, sentenced to any punishment, or punished for any crime or offence, while he continues in that state." The legislature offered the courts no help in identifying just which individuals were to be considered "in a state of insanity." [5] Distinguishing between the depraved and the demented was a task that remained predominantly within the realm of the common law during the antebellum period.

European legal theorists had grappled with this dilemma for centuries. Prior to 1800, English legal authorities such as Lord Edward Coke and Sir Matthew Hale maintained that only idiocy nullified legal responsibility for criminal acts. To escape punishment, they reasoned, the accused "must be in such a state of prostrated intellect, as to not know his name, nor his condition, nor his relation toward others." Lord Erskine, who defended James Hadfield during his trial for attempting to assassinate King George III of England, moved English common law away from the "wild beast" interpretation associated with Coke and Hale. Erskine introduced the concept that delusion could precipitate behavior in individuals whose ability to reason remained intact. Delusion, "where there was no frenzy or raving madness, is the true character of insanity," he argued. In the 1812 Bellingham murder trial, Lord Chief Justice Mansfield ruled that the accused must be unable to distinguish right from wrong and unaware that murder was "a crime against the laws of God and nature." Reflecting Erskine's influence, Mansfield allowed that morbid delusion could excuse a criminal act in situations where the law would excuse a similar act that stemmed from real circumstances. Although Mansfield expanded the legal definition of insanity beyond the wild beast test, his formula still demanded that the accused be so bereft of moral judgment and conscience as not to comprehend the gravity of his offense.[6]

Finally in 1843, the Lords Justices of England formulated the McNaughtan rules in response to a number of legal questions posed by the House of Lords.[7] The rules stated first of all, that sanity was presumed to be man's natural state and must be disproved to the satisfaction of the jury. To establish a defense on the ground of insanity, it was necessary to prove that the accused "was labouring under such a defect of reason, from disease of the mind, as not to know the nature and quality of the act he was doing, or if he did know it, that he did not know he was doing what was wrong." If the defense claimed that the accused was laboring under an insane delusion when the act was committed, the accused "must be considered in the same situation as to responsibility as if the facts with respect to which the delusions exist were real." Leonard W. Levy notes that the rules, "although in some respects grievously erroneous and deficient from the standpoint of psychiatry, are the basis of the modern law of insanity in criminal cases and have been followed in thousands of English and American decisions."[8]

The McNaughtan rules quickly formed the core of the definition of legal insanity as it was applied in antebellum American courts. This does not mean, however, that American courts accepted the rules as completely satisfactory. Being that the theory of criminal law holds "that no act, however reprehensible or even fatal in its consequences, is punishable unless the doer, exercising his will and understanding, voluntarily and knowingly intends a criminal deed," some jurists believed that the McNaughtan rules were too narrow.[9] One group of antebellum psychiatric theories, known collectively as "moral insanity," postulated that some forms of mental illness could pervert the emotions or subvert the will of an individual without disturbing his intellect or understanding. Persons suffering from moral insanity, while intellectually aware that society considered certain behavior immoral, antisocial, or even criminal, sometimes failed to control their impulses and engaged in the behavior anyway.[10] In many cases, no logical motive for the behavior could be discovered. The McNaughtan rules, on the other hand, stemmed from "an immutable philosophical and moral concept which assumes an inherent capacity in man to distinguish right from wrong and to make necessary moral decisions." The rules focused only on whether the accused had the intellectual capacity to understand that his behavior was wrong.[11]

As Thomas Maeder observes, however, the majority of antebellum jurists rejected the theory that criminal acts could be irresistible impulses of people whose intellectual faculties were unimpaired.[12] Levy agrees, noting that over a century after the McNaughtan rules were formulated, "a large majority of the state courts" had not appended to the rules some manner of testing for the presence of uncontrollable impulses.[13] The difficulty of identifying those who committed crimes because they could not control their actions appeared insurmountable. Many violent crimes were committed in the absence of any motive that was considered adequate or logical, given the brutality of the offense. Conservative jurists feared that a majority of criminals might be included in a legal definition of insanity that was broad enough to encompass persons who intellectually understood that they acted wrongly, yet committed apparently motiveless crimes.[14] These jurists urged a strict adherence to McNaughtan rules and portrayed any attempt to expand the legal definition of insanity as dangerous to the safety of society.

Furthermore, as Norman Dain observes, in the antebellum period most people still expected an insane person to have "no more reason than a brute animal or to be totally wild and ungovernable." As far as the medical profession was concerned, "with the possible exception of a few psychiatrists, there was no movement among physicians to explain anti-social acts as the result of mental illness." Physicians who supported an accused murderer's claim of insanity "flouted public opinion," which tended to view crime as the result of human depravity.[15] David Brion Davis adds that one of the principal assumptions of early-nineteenth-century theology, moral philosophy, and law was the belief that man inherently possessed capacity to distinguish good from evil. The only exception was the human being whose mind had been alienated by physical disease, thereby separating his actions from this inherent moral capacity. In cases of total insanity or idiocy, the causal connection between an evil heart or moral sense and an unlawful act was obliterated. A person that clearly did not understand the nature of his actions could not be assumed to have chosen the path of criminality. Moral insanity, however, "seemed to imply that the understanding was only partially damaged, and that certain actions, at least, reflected the true nature and quality of the heart."[16]

The outcome of the first Wyatt trial merely exacerbated community suspicions regarding the insanity defense. Just days after the Van Nest killings, the *Albany Argus* stated, "After the expression we have recently had of public justice in Auburn, none scarcely doubt that some fallacious and newfangled plea will be interposed between the murderer and a just retribution." [17] The *Morning Courier and New York Enquirer* likewise anticipated a "convenient plea of insanity" in the Freeman case and worried that the "technical petti- foggery" of Freeman's counsel might "befog the court and jury." [18] After Freeman's arraignment, the *Rochester Daily Advertiser* seethed over the fact that a plea of insanity had been entered on his behalf and expressed concern that Seward would use "all his talents and influence to make it effectual." Disgusted by the "pretty state of things" exhibited in recent criminal trials, the *Advertiser* warned that a few more acquittals on insanity pleas "and Judge Lynch's court will be frequently summoned to execute summary justice, which our regular tribunals deny." [19] While the *Advertiser* certainly exagger- ated the general effectiveness of the insanity defense, the editors' disdain for insanity as a legal excuse for crime is unmistakable. Just as clear is their per- ception of imminent danger.

Community wishes were most influential in determining the course that criminal justice took in American courts through the middle of the nine- teenth century. As James C. Mohr has determined, "attitudes toward the culpability of the insane were neither systematic nor systematically applied" in the antebellum period. Juries tended to excuse on grounds of insanity irk- some but harmless village idiots who committed minor offenses. Most de- fendants that clearly committed the illegal acts for which they were prosecuted were punished, regardless of their mental capacities, psychologi- cal states, or ability to control their emotions. In general, the more heinous the crime, the less likely were antebellum juries to excuse the action on the basis of mental incapacity. In many jurisdictions, violent offenders found not guilty by reason of insanity were simply turned back out into society. This rendered juries even less likely to entertain insanity pleas on behalf of ac- cused murderers. [20]

Nevertheless, important innovations in the common law with regard to insanity were introduced just prior to the Freeman trial. These innovations reflected the influence of the testimony of Dr. Isaac Ray, given during the 1844 murder trial of Abner Rogers, regarding uncontrollable impulses brought on by mental disease. Strongly influenced by French medicine and

French law and "deeply committed to the scientific method," Ray published *A Treatise on the Medical Jurisprudence of Insanity* in 1838. Drawing upon the latest theories from both France and England, Ray categorized various types and degrees of mental illness and recommended ways in which enlightened courts should identify and respond to each variety. He was firmly convinced that certain varieties of mental illness, known collectively as moral insanity, "reduced the judgmental powers and emotional control of the people afflicted." Ray directed pointed criticism at American courts for upholding conceptions of insanity and legal precedents that were rigid and inappropriate. He looked forward to a day when medical experts would play critical roles in court proceedings as detectors of mental illness.[21]

Proponents of moral insanity, including Isaac Ray, were influenced by phrenology, a theory of "brain localization" developed in the early nineteenth century by Europeans Franz Gall and J. G. Spurzheim. Phrenological theory "divided the physical brain into many areas, each responsible for a different behavioral, cognitive, or emotional trait."[22] The theory postulated that virtues, vices, criminality, sexuality, deviancies, affection, social affiliation, and benevolence could all be traced to regulative centers in the brain which, when diseased, resulted in various forms of mental and moral degradation.[23] Environment and education were important in that areas of the brain, like muscles, were strengthened or atrophied depending upon level of use. Localization of brain function complimented the theory of moral insanity since both asserted that some faculties could be diseased or underdeveloped while others remained healthy.[24] Ray maintained the basic phrenological position that insanity was a physical disease that should be treated as such, and not as the "moral blight for which laymen in general, and judges and juries in particular, tended to punish its unfortunate victims."[25] Phrenology was viewed suspiciously by Calvinist Protestantism since the theory also included a congenital component. Moral insanity could result not only from disease but also from an "inherited, insufficiently developed moral faculty." The theory contradicted religious assertions that immoral behavior was a choice, resulting from a sinful nature.[26]

Since the technology that would allow medical professionals to examine the brains of living persons was far in the future, phrenologists focused on the external appearance of the human head. They believed that the relative state of development of the various faculty-controlling centers of the brain could be determined by examining the external contours of the skull. Many physicians and psychiatrists were impressed by the theory and attempted in good faith to link human behavior to the physical characteristics of the head. On the other hand, practical phrenologists took advantage of unsuspecting people by providing individual character readings for a price.[27] Practical phrenologists purported to reveal for each customer his virtues, his limitations, and the manner in which he could improve himself and achieve success in life. Commencing work in 1835, Orson S. Fowler, the most famous commercial exploiter of phrenology, claimed by 1842 to have earned nearly $75,000 from lectures, publications, and individual examinations. The popular appeal of practical phrenology was so broad that by 1847, Fowler's *American Phrenological Journal* had twenty thousand subscribers, among the largest monthly circulations in the nation.[28]

Reflecting the influence of Ray, Chief Justice Lemuel Shaw of the Supreme Judicial Court of Massachusetts individualized the knowledge test stipulated in the McNaughtan rules. During the trial of Abner Rogers, Shaw stipulated that beyond knowing the nature of his act or knowing that it was wrong under the law, the accused must "be able to apply 'to his own case' an otherwise abstract understanding of the nature of his act." Shaw hereby opened the door to moral insanity as an excuse for crime. He expressed a conviction that in certain cases of mental illness, an individual may not consider his own actions wrong, despite knowing that society judged them to be so.[29] Shaw also appended an irresistible impulse test to the McNaughtan rules in his charge to the jury. "If it is proved to the satisfaction of the jury, that the mind of the accused was in a diseased and unsound state," he directed, "the question will be, whether the disease existed to so high a degree, that for the time being, it overwhelmed the reason, conscience, and judgement, and whether the prisoner in committing the homicide, acted from an irresistible and uncontrollable impulse." If this was the case, Shaw added, then the act was "not the act of a voluntary agent, but the involuntary act of the body, without the concurrence of a mind directing it."[30] Ray's testimony had convinced Shaw that disease could overcome an individual's intellectual ability to resist engaging in certain behavior. It was Shaw himself, however, who was in the position to encourage the law to keep pace with advances in science.

Shaw used the term "partial insanity" to refer to the type of mental illness elucidated by Ray. "The conduct may be in many respects regular, the mind acute, and the conduct apparently governed by the rules of propriety, and at the same time there may be insane delusion by which the mind is perverted," he informed the jury. The most common form that the disease took was monomania, where "the mind broods over *one idea,* and can not be reasoned out of it." This form of insanity could operate as an excuse for a criminal act in two types of cases, according to Shaw. The first type were cases where the delusion was such that "the person under its influence has a real or firm belief of some fact, not true in itself, but which if it were true, would excuse his act." The second, and far more controversial type of cases, were those in which the state of delusion indicated to an "experienced person" that the mind of the accused was in a diseased state. Medical experts knew that the tendency of this diseased state of mind was "to break out into sudden paroxysms of violence, venting itself in acts of homicide, or other acts of violence toward friend or foe indiscriminately." Even in the absence of previous indications of violence, these acts taken in conjunction with previous symptoms and indications would "enable an experienced person to say, that the outbreak was of such a character, that, for the time being, it must have overborne memory and reason." Ultimately, such acts could be deemed the result of disease and not the products of a "mind capable of choosing." The accused was not "acted upon by motives" or "governed by the will," according to Shaw, and therefore lacked the "malice aforethought" which constituted murder.[31]

In May 1845, Judge John Worth Edmonds, presiding over the Court of Oyer and Terminer in New York City, brought Shaw's innovations to New York State. In his charge to the jury during the murder trial of Andrew Kleim, Edmonds stated that "the question whether the accused knew the difference between right and wrong is not to be put generally, but in reference to the very act with which he is charged." Edmonds's language indicated an appreciation of Shaw's concern that certain defendants might understand that murder was wrong in general, but not be able to apply that premise to their own actions. Furthermore, Edmonds incorporated Shaw's innovations regarding irresistible impulses, albeit with caution. "If some controlling disease was in truth the acting power within him, which he could not resist or if he had not a sufficient use of his reason to control the passions which prompted the act complained of, he is not responsible," Edmonds instructed. He cautioned, however, that the court "must be sure not to be misled by a mere impulse of passion, an idle frantic humor or unaccountable mode of action, but inquire whether it is an absolute dispossession of the free and natural agency of the mind." Quoting Lord Erskine, Edmonds added that reason need not be "hurled from her seat," it being "enough that Distraction sits down beside her, holds her trembling in her place, and frightens her from her propriety." Edmonds, again closely echoing Shaw's remarks during the Rogers trial, stressed that "the moral as well as the intellectual faculties may be so disordered by the disease as to deprive the mind of its controlling and directing power."[32]

Judge Bowen Whiting presided over Henry Wyatt's first trial and once again took the bench for Wyatt's retrial in June. His charges to the jury in both trials indicated the influence of Shaw with regard to the legal definition of insanity. In the first trial, Whiting stated, "I shall read to you the charge drawn up by Chief Justice Shaw, with great labor and research as being better than any thing I could say to you myself." He then added, "This court holds that case [the trial of Abner Rogers] to be authority, and declaratory of what is the law of the land upon this subject."[33] In the second trial, Whiting proclaimed that Shaw had provided the rule of law used in the Kleim case, "which I shall give in this case, and which is the law of the land, and by which you must decide this case." Like Edmonds had done in the Kleim trial, Whiting deferred to Shaw's definition of insanity, viewing it as the common law in criminal cases.[34]

Given the brutality of the Van Nest killings and William Freeman's racial background, Seward and his colleagues faced an uphill battle in convincing a jury to acquit by reason of insanity. Recent precedents indicated that American juries could be persuaded to accept moral insanity as a legal defense. It would be no easy task, however, to convince a Cayuga County jury that Freeman was anything but a vicious, depraved demon bent on revenge. Prosecutors faced the less daunting but critical task of convincing a jury to focus on the idea that Freeman was not insane by the McNaughtan definition. To facilitate this process, the prosecutors would certainly assure jurors that the McNaughtan rules were specifically formulated to protect society from killers like Freeman.

Under these circumstances, it is difficult to fathom why such a publicly visible figure as Seward would defend Freeman. Partisan politics and sympathy for the condition of blacks certainly influenced Seward's decision, although these factors have been overemphasized. They serve as a fine starting point, however, in our effort to fully comprehend the implications of the case as well as Seward's motives.

The year 1846 was very volatile, both in terms of national and state politics. The Mexican War began in May, bringing the question of the expansion of slavery to the fore of national politics. The Wilmot Proviso was introduced in Congress in August, exacerbating the split between the radical, or Barnburner, and conservative, or Hunker factions of New York's Democratic Party. In the summer of 1846, New York was in the process of revising its state constitution. One important issue being considered was African American suffrage. The 1821 constitution had placed a prohibitive $250 freehold property qualification on black voters.[35] To the self-described "progressive" wing of the New York Whig Party, led by Seward, Greeley, and *Albany Evening Journal* editor Thurlow Weed, unrestricted black suffrage meant tremendous political benefits. First of all, since New York blacks voted overwhelmingly Whig, ten thousand newly enfranchised voters would certainly aid the Whig cause. Secondly, suffrage reform was viewed as a way to attract political abolitionists away from the Liberty Party and into the Whig ranks.[36] The Liberty Party had polled 4.7 percent of the total vote cast in the state in 1845, enough to tip the balance given the close competition between the two major parties.[37] The "progressive" Whigs pointed to the cool, if not downright hostile, attitude of the Democrats toward black suffrage. If blacks, free or slave, were ever to benefit from true change, it would result from the efforts of one of the two major parties. Desertion of the Whig Party would only strengthen the Democrats, assuring that change would be long in coming.[38]

The Van Nest killings came at a very inauspicious time for the Weed-Seward-Greeley wing of the Whig Party. The conservative wing of the party was already opposed to any attempt to revise the constitution or "to portray the Whig Party as a friend of black suffrage."[39] If anything, the Van Nest killings provided opponents of black suffrage with evidence that blacks did not deserve greater participation in American society. The press reactions to

Freeman's crime did make reference to his racial background, as demonstrated in chapter 2. There was little connection made, however, to the suffrage question. The *Rochester Daily Advertiser* fumed over the fact that an Auburn publisher had gone to the trouble of having a lithograph of Freeman produced for sale. Still, the editors stated, "Lest we should shock the nervous system of some of our whig contemporaries, we state that this 'puff' has *positively* nothing to do with the suffrage question."[40] Nevertheless, Seward worried in the weeks following the crime that political damage had been done.

On March 22, he wrote to a contemporary, "The Loco Focos (Barnburners) have been focusing on the prejudices of the Whigs against Negro suffrage, now roused by the late tragedy in which a Negro immolated a white family as a sacrifice to hellish revenge."[41] Seward confided to Weed, "This prejudice against Negroes by reason of the Van Nest Murders is an auxiliary of Loco Focoism also."[42] It is likely, as Glyndon Van Deusen has noted, that part of the reason why Seward undertook Freeman's defense was to counteract what he saw as negative publicity for the Whig Party. Something had to be done to prevent the political abolitionists from getting the impression that the Whig Party had abandoned the cause of black rights because of William Freeman. Such an impression could spoil Whig efforts to court political abolitionists, thereby increasing the ranks of the Liberty Party and ultimately benefitting the Democrats. Standing up for the legal rights of a black man accused of multiple murder would demonstrate the Whig Party's commitment to black rights in general.[43]

Public opinion was overwhelmingly opposed to unrestricted black suffrage, however. The Democrats were certainly aware of this, and Thurlow Weed, who was one of the most astute political analysts of his time, undoubtedly was aware as well. When the Democratic-controlled convention voted, in the early summer of 1846, to submit the suffrage question directly to the voters in the form of a referendum instead of writing a provision into the new constitution, Weed backed away from the issue. Public campaigning for black suffrage at that point would only exacerbate the disagreements between the factions of the Whig Party and serve to annoy unsympathetic voters.[44] It is doubtful that, given his close scrutiny of statewide politics, Weed ever thought that Freeman's case could be forged directly into political capital. Defending a black man who brutally slaughtered four members of a prominent and respected white family could do little to further the Whig cause. The *Albany Evening Journal* made no effort to elicit sympathy for Freeman based on his race and did not link Seward's role in defending Freeman directly to any political issue involving blacks. It is likely that Seward, while personally sympathetic toward the extension of black rights and privately hopeful that defending Freeman would please political abolitionists, based his decision more on personal factors than partisan politics.[45]

The Seward-Weed correspondence and other sources support the contention that personal factors had the greatest influence on the former governor's decision to defend Freeman. In late May, just prior to the opening of the constitutional convention, Seward admitted to Weed, "It is unlikely that I shall be asked for advice about the Convention, at all, and I certainly shall not volunteer it." He reiterated his own support of universal suffrage, but he was "satisfied a large number of the Whig Delegates will not [support it]." Seward's personal support of black suffrage remained strong at this time, but he was aware that politically, it was a losing battle. It is unlikely that he based the very controversial decision of defending Freeman primarily on partisan calculations given this context. Evidence of a strain in the relationship between Seward and Weed further supports the contention that partisan motives were not paramount in Seward's decision to defend Freeman.[46]

In May 1846, Seward confided to Weed that defending Freeman "will rain a storm of prejudice and passion which will try the fortitude of my friends—But I shall do my duty, I care not whether I am to be ever forgiven for it, or not."[47] However, Seward's letters to Weed, throughout the summer of 1846, betrayed a strong sense of guilt on Seward's part for having placed Weed in a difficult spot. Weed's loyalty as a friend and political backer was strong, and it seems to have been put to the test.[48] Seward made offers to Weed to "retire you of myself," and asked Weed to "drop [him] and save yourself."[49] Seward admitted having impaired Weed's "fortunes of all sorts," implying both financial indebtedness to Weed and impairment of Weed's public reputation.[50] "I entered those trials," Seward claimed, ". . . ignorant that the telegraphic sympathy between myself and you my first last and very best of friends was disturbed and deranged." After the close of Freeman's trial, Seward acknowledged, "I rise from these fruitless labors exhausted in mind and body and covered with public reproach, stunned with duns and protests, and not yet quite forgiven by you for involuntary injuries."[51]

Writing in the fall to James Bowen, a prominent New York City Whig and Seward advisor, the former governor declared that "in that unavoidable and most righteous conflict, every friend I had here but my wife and sister, and *every* friend abroad abandoned me." The correspondence and the columns of the *Evening Journal* indicate that Weed did not "abandon" his friend. Seward, in defending Freeman, does seem to have ignored warnings from Weed that doing so would be politically damaging rather than productive. Public reproach spilled over from Seward to his closest political associate, hence putting a strain on their relationship. Being in constant communication with Weed, it is almost certain that Seward was aware of the bad publicity his own legal career was thrusting upon his political supporters. However, sincere aversion to the punishment of the insane and a perceived need to advertise his professional skills caused him to proceed.[52]

Van Deusen is led to overestimate the role of race in Seward's decision to defend Freeman by the mistaken belief that Henry Wyatt was also black. He is accurate in his conclusion that Freeman's story appealed to Seward's personal sympathy for the suffering of American blacks. However, he interprets the Wyatt and Freeman cases as politically useful because they involved "two Negroes," when in fact Wyatt was white.[53] The Auburn Prison Register of Male Inmates Discharged listed Wyatt's complexion as "dark," in contrast to Freeman whose complexion was recorded specifically as "negro." Other inmates, who were of mixed ancestry, were identified specifically as "mulatto."[54] During Wyatt's first trial, there was some controversy regarding whether Wyatt had made the following remark to an assistant keeper who was about to punish him: "It is hard for one white man to take off his shirt to be flogged by another." This issue would not have been disputed had Wyatt been black.[55] Likewise, Earl Conrad refers to Wyatt as "a white man with a dark stubble of beard."[56]

Freeman was constantly referred to in press reports as "the negro Freeman," and as we have seen, specific racial interpretations of the Van Nest killings appeared in the press.[57] Van Deusen may have been led astray by the sole instance in which it was implied that Wyatt was black. For reasons unknown, the *Albany Evening Atlas* claimed in one report that *both* Wyatt and

Freeman were "of the lowest and most unprotected class of society."[58] Nowhere else was Wyatt referred to in any manner that indicated he was nonwhite. That being the case, Seward's actions in the summer of 1846 take on greater clarity. Seward continued to defend Wyatt through his second trial, despite public outcry that the outcome of the first trial had inspired the Van Nest killings. Seward was both deeply opposed to slavery on humanitarian grounds and sympathetic to the circumstances under which free blacks in the United States were forced to live. He was also convinced that the Whig Party was the best vehicle for change.[59] Yet equal devotion to Wyatt and Freeman in this most intimidating environment supports the contention that factors other than partisan politics played the more crucial role in motivating Seward.

A correspondent of the *New York Daily Tribune* reported from Auburn, two days after the killings, that "A lawyer of standing in town ran down the street an hour or two since, crying out 'Would that Seward were here to see this deed!' " The correspondent commented on how "shamefully wrong and unjust" it was to link Seward's actions, as Wyatt's counsel, to the horrible crimes at Fleming.[60] As noted earlier, it was generally in the context of the debate over capital punishment that the outcome of Wyatt's first trial was criticized. Critics in the press did not generally trace the legal assistance of Wyatt or Freeman to the partisan machinations of the Whigs. Plenty of harsh words, as shown, were tendered by conservative Whig journals. Partisan or not, popular connections drawn between the first Wyatt trial and the Van Nest slayings temporarily stifled Seward's ability to reap political benefits from any public activity. In a letter to Weed, Seward admitted expecting his closest advisor to "tell me the plain truth that my political career could not be revived." When he received this sobering information from Weed, Seward claimed to have "accepted it gratefully and with certain resignation." His public career at a low point, Seward concentrated on his reputation as an attorney, while at the same time being driven by a firm conviction that William Freeman was unquestionably insane.[61]

While governor, Seward did not express any public support for the abolition of capital punishment. The leading historian of the anti-death-penalty movement in New York, Philip English Mackey, does not attribute to Seward any active role.[62] Seward did favor pardons, however, for offenders who were insane. "While governor," Van Deusen notes, "his sympathetic interest in insane prisoners had been so marked that in 1843 Dorothea Lynde Dix had come to Auburn for his advice on steps that might be taken to improve the lot of the demented." Van Deusen attributes Seward's role in the Wyatt and Freeman trials in part to this sympathy for the insane. The evidence supports this contention, and it deserves greater emphasis than that given by Van Deusen, Seward's most eminent modern biographer.[63]

On the day of William Freeman's arraignment, Seward informed the court that "humane persons, sanctioned by [Freeman's] request," had requested that Seward and his partners assist Freeman in his defense. The "humane persons" had suggested that Freeman "was and is insane." Although shocked at the "atrocity of the crimes charged against the prisoner," Seward indicated that he and his colleagues "feared the still greater atrocity that, through any fault of ours, an individual bereft of his reason should be cut off as a malefactor." On the advice of these "humane persons," Seward asked that a plea of not guilty by reason of insanity be entered on the record.[64] "Humane persons" was, in fact, a reference to opponents of capital punishment, particularly John Austin. In his testimony at Freeman's trial, Austin said, "Previously to this trial, I called on Governor Seward, and conversed with him about the prisoner and his deplorable condition."[65] Seward also mentioned Austin's interest in the case to Weed, writing that "No Priest, (except one Universalist)" had visited Freeman.[66] Austin, as shown, opposed capital punishment as a matter of principle and seized upon Seward's opposition to the criminal punishment of the insane. Seward became thoroughly convinced that Freeman was insane and considered it his duty as a lawyer, as a Christian, and as a man to prevent him from being punished as a murderer.

Seward's choice of the words "bereft of his reason" seems inappropriate, given that Freeman's chances for acquittal hinged upon the doctrine of moral insanity. Seward had employed moral insanity, with encouraging results, in defense of Wyatt in February. By June 1, when Freeman was arraigned, Seward was prepared to employ moral insanity in back-to-back murder trials. He was thoroughly familiar with the doctrine and undoubtedly certain that it would be Freeman's best mode of defense. However, medical experts believed that individuals suffering from moral insanity were still rational on many subjects. Experts used the term to refer to people who exhibited signs of mental illness while retaining some ability to reason correctly. It is likely that Seward chose his words for emphasis. After all, the defense would later insist that Freeman was unable to reason correctly on the subject of his wrongful imprisonment. Although he may not have been completely "bereft of his reason," the defense would claim that Freeman's failure to properly exercise that reason resulted in the Van Nest killings. In Seward's mind, the killings were unquestionably the product of insanity. The crucial point that he wanted to emphasize was that the insane must not be punished for criminal acts.

The Seward-Weed correspondence further supports the contention that sympathy for the insane was the predominant factor in Seward's decision to defend Freeman. Repeatedly, Seward confided his private thoughts regarding Freeman's case to Weed. Just three days prior to Freeman's arraignment, Seward wrote, "He is deaf, demented, ignorant; and his conduct is unexplainable on any premise of sanity."[67] As Freeman's preliminary trial approached, the former governor again stressed, "Freeman is a demented idiot made so by blows which extinguished every thing in his breast but a blind passion of revenge." With complete confidence in the righteousness of the cause, he assured Weed that Freeman would "be acquitted at once and with the public consent."[68] During the trial on the indictment, Seward told his friend, "I have been doing what has seemed to me a necessary and high duty."[69] Believing that he faced an unsympathetic, if not hostile, judge, and aware of public scrutiny, he lamented that he was "crushed between the nether mill-stones of judicial tyranny and popular anger." Affirming his commitment to the insane, Seward assured Weed that there would be "a consoling reflection by and by that I was not guilty of hanging the poor wretches whom the State Prison tormentors drive to madness."[70] Following the trial, Seward professed, "If I know the line of personal or that of professional duty, I have adhered to it faithfully and unflinchingly."[71]

Duty, in fact, meant more to Seward than adherence to Christian principles or professional integrity. He was incensed with the prosecutors because they catered to public sentiment, regardless in his opinion of the nature of that sentiment. The desire for retribution was so strong in Freeman's case that, in Seward's opinion, it was easy for the prosecutors to jump on the bandwagon and receive acclamation for attempting to give the people what they wanted. New York State attorney general John Van Buren, whose assistance at the special term of the Cayuga County Court of Oyer and Terminer was requested by the county and approved by Governor Wright, particularly annoyed Seward.[72] The son of Martin Van Buren won "golden praise from the vicious and vulgar," according to Seward, because he vigorously prosecuted Freeman despite what Seward regarded as clear evidence that Freeman was insane. Instead of doing what was right, even at risk of public reproach, Van Buren did what was politically expedient and safe. The attorney general, in Seward's words, lacked "principle, decency, or manliness" because he placed his own reputation ahead of truth and justice. It is likely, given early-nineteenth-century social attitudes, that Seward viewed his own role in Freeman's case as precisely what Van Buren's was not, an assertion of manliness.[73]

Douglas L. Wilson suggests that antebellum Americans carried the concept of manliness "into the political realm by labeling candor—the moral courage to speak one's opinions freely without fearing consequences—as manly." Political dissent, if managed effectively and done without perceivable evidence of fear, "could be acknowledged as a mark of manliness and honor." While the ultimate proof of manliness was "physical courage and the willingness to meet others in combat, to fight," the courage to take a stand in the face of popular indignation was also valued as an assertion of manhood. True respectability in the long run came from honorable action, even if that action brought temporary personal or even financial hardship.[74] For Seward, to adhere to the line of duty was to be a man. He believed unflinchingly that Freeman was insane, and he was willing to forever associate himself with the defense of a man who inspired rage in the community. Knowing that his defense of Freeman threatened to harm the reputations of his friends, political advisors, and family, Seward persevered because of his faith in the righteousness of the cause.[75] The insane must not be punished for their actions, however brutal, if those actions were beyond their capacity to control. To shrink from this challenge, simply because of "popular anger," was to be less than a man.

Furthermore, while partisan concerns did not play a pivotal role in his decision to defend Freeman, Seward still evaluated Van Buren's behavior according to Whig principles. As Michael F. Holt notes, "Whigs portrayed themselves as the party of probity, respectability, morality, and reason—as 'the party of law, of order, of enterprise, of improvement, of beneficence, of hope, and of humanity.' " Within their definition of improvement, Whigs clearly incorporated "self-improvement and self-discipline." Whigs believed "that men must be educated, that individuals must control carnal appetites and other dangerous passions with their reason, and that they must develop habits of sobriety, thrift, industry, and self-control." In contrast, Holt observes, Whigs portrayed the Democrats as "wild-eyed radicals, lawless and lazy drunkards, and a contemptible and dangerous rabble." Whigs such as Lyman Beecher and Horace Greeley associated the Democratic Party with intemperance, Sabbath breaking, debauchery, vice, and "ruff-scuff generally."[76] Daniel Walker Howe likewise notes the Whigs' identification "with the cause of 'reason' against the party of 'passion.' " Howe quotes one former Whig who recollected in 1859 that his party had "placed their whole hopes on the right and justice of their cause, while their antagonists sought theirs in the passions of the multitude."[77]

Whigs were highly wary of the tendency of the multitude to act first and deliberate later, "when inquiry and reasoning are perhaps of no effect but to induce an unavailing repentance." Ever skeptical of the people's capacity for self-government and convinced of their selfishness, Whigs warned that "the present desire will always outweigh the remote good in minds governed solely by the utilitarian principle." Whigs, John Ashworth adds, "believed it to be axiomatic that government required the services of an elite" consisting of the "wisest, best, and most experienced men." They feared that a "constant infusion of the popular will would threaten 'that lofty independence and integrity of mind which should characterize the representatives of the people' " in a republican government. The American republic was best served by the unbiased judgment of men of "special talent and wisdom" that acted according to the dictates of reason rather than the "caprice of popular favor."[78] Both Ashworth and Rush Welter observe that the Whigs held constitutions in such high esteem because the people were "liable individually and collectively" to be swayed by their passions and interests. The will of the majority was not necessarily right, and therefore must be subjected to necessary checks and restrictions.[79]

Seward suspected Van Buren of pandering, in the typical manner of a

Democratic politician, to the lower impulses in human nature in prosecuting Freeman. The Van Nest killings had ignited the passions of the "vicious and vulgar," the gratification of which Seward deemed politically opportunistic and shameful. The desire to convict and execute Freeman, Seward avouched, was prompted by emotion and a profound lack of understanding and sympathy. In Seward's mind, Van Buren was very much the demagogue, seeking influence among the populace by appealing to ignorance and prejudice. In defending Freeman, Seward believed that he exemplified the very principles that made his party superior to the Democrats. He exercised reason and judgment in resisting the will of the populace. He defended the legal rights of a man whose brutal acts had nearly resulted in the execution of summary justice.

The role of sympathy for the insane, although far more important than partisan political considerations, must be viewed in conjunction with the purely personal considerations that motivated Seward. After declining to seek a third term as governor of New York, Seward returned to Auburn in 1843 encumbered by debts that were large enough to prompt some friends to suggest that he file for bankruptcy.[80] Van Deusen notes that Seward hoped his efforts on behalf of Freeman and Wyatt would bolster his legal reputation, thereby attracting lucrative business.[81] The evidence, in fact, shows financial considerations to have been a powerful motivating force deserving relatively greater emphasis than the racial and partisan considerations upon which Van Deusen focuses.

In June 1846, Seward informed Weed, "My pecuniary fortunes depend on my professional ability—Duty obliges me to establish this—I am endeavoring to do so in this Court."[82] Looking back on the summer's work, Seward confided to Weed that he had approached the murder trials "sure of business enough afterwards."[83] Within weeks of the close of the Freeman trial, Seward wrote, "I find a world of work here and hereafter hope to profit professionally by the enormous outlay of time in my late murder trials, they have given me very effective advertisement." He had "never had better business prospects," he rejoiced.[84] "While you and so many generous friends have been studying plans for my political advancement," Seward informed Bowen, "I have during the last four years been chiefly bent upon effecting an honorable re-entrance at the crowded Bar of the State, a measure absolutely essential in regard to all my prospects."[85] The Wyatt and Freeman trials formed the core of Seward's effort to enhance his legal reputation during the year 1846.

Committed to protecting the mentally ill from criminal punishment and hopeful that his efforts would bolster his personal and professional fortunes, Seward harbored no illusions about the tasks ahead. He feared that lingering anger and suspicion would prohibit both Wyatt and Freeman from receiving fair trials. As the district attorney moved on the trial of Wyatt, Seward indicated his intention to ask that the trial of Freeman be put over to the next Oyer and Terminer, in the hope that public emotions would calm enough for an impartial hearing.[86]

On June 2, as Wyatt's retrial was set to commence, Seward formally petitioned the court to have it "put over, to the end that it may be brought on hereafter in this county, when popular prejudice and passion shall have subsided, or may be transferred to some other county." In the petition, written in the first person on behalf of Wyatt, Seward discussed the impact of the events of the previous winter. The public mind viewed moral insanity, the mode of defense used in Wyatt's first trial, as a new theory that threatened the administration of justice despite that "it was well established in medical science and in the law." In the wake of the Van Nest killings, the petition alleged, "the Press, and the Pulpit, and the political assemblage, and every social circle, eagerly believed and thoughtlessly published, that my partial escape from justice had excited Freeman to commit his crimes, by diminishing the salutary effect of the fear of capital punishment upon his mind." Seward was convinced that Wyatt's fate was inseparable from the desire for vengeance inspired by the Van Nest killings. He was mystified, however, by the logic that assumed Freeman capable of learning anything from Wyatt's first trial.[87]

Seward argued that Freeman "did not even know that such a trial had been held" or that such a man as Henry Wyatt existed. Being deaf, Seward added, Freeman could not have understood the trial proceedings even if he had, as some alleged, been present in the courtroom. Being "unable to deduce the simplest conclusion from the plainest premises," Freeman lacked the intellectual capacity to process the legal and scientific principles used to defend Wyatt, the former governor asserted. Yet it was "regarded throughout the country as an offence against the safety and welfare of the State, for counsel to appear for either me or the other accused person," the petition alleged. "The Clergy and the Press, disdaining scientific examination, have combined with advocates of vindictive retaliation as a sound principle of justice, and have rendered the very name and nature of my defence, a *mockery* and a *by-word,*" the petition concluded. Seward offered a copy of the sermon given at the Van Nest's funeral, as well as copies of newspaper articles as evidence of the climate of public opinion. The court ruled out this evidence, and Wyatt's petition was denied. The court informed Wyatt's counsel that it did not presume the power to postpone the trial unless an attempt to impanel a jury in Auburn failed. The course of justice moved slowly but resolutely forward.[88]

Wyatt's chances of acquittal were remote given the publicity generated by the events that followed his first trial and popular convictions regarding crime and punishment. However, the combined influence of the antigallows movement and psychiatry still caused considerable uneasiness. Any unnecessary delay or a change of venue would have undoubtedly exacerbated this feeling. Furthermore, Wyatt was still represented by an attorney who, however berated for his choice of clients, was greatly revered for his talent in the courtroom. The state's top prosecutor would not have been summoned to Auburn if the people of Cayuga County or Governor Wright had viewed Wyatt's conviction as a foregone conclusion. Judge Whiting more than likely feared that public faith in the criminal justice system would be seriously compromised if the court did not make a concerted effort to move the process forward.

4

Controversial Verdict, Controversial Defense

IN THE SUMMER OF 1846, the village of Auburn was preparing to host the New York State Agricultural Fair, scheduled for September. Observers in town to witness or participate in the trials of Wyatt and Freeman marveled at the splendor of Auburn in summer. One newspaper correspondent was particularly taken with the surroundings. "This village certainly deserves the title of 'Sweet Auburn,' " he began. "Now that the beautiful gardens which surround almost every dwelling are clothed in the brightest foliage, and scattered round and sprinkled over with a vast profusion of every colored flower, and the distant hills and valleys seem to rejoice in their rich variety of living green," he added, "the most fastidious foreign tourist could find nothing here to deprecate."[1] Explicit details of the Wyatt and Freeman trial proceedings were not immediately available to nonparticipants. Out-of-town correspondents informed their editors, and the local papers explained to their readers that the Cayuga County Oyer and Terminer had ordered an injunction on the press, barring the publication of testimony until after the cases were decided.[2]

The retrial of Henry Wyatt took over three weeks to complete. Sixteen days were spent in the process of impanelling a jury.[3] Seward objected to the first panel of potential jurors, claiming that District Attorney Luman Sherwood had improperly interfered in the selection of the panel and had arranged the selection of biased candidates.[4] Ultimately over 160 potential jurors were summoned, with the exhaustion of the initial panel forcing the court to summon an additional 100 men.[5] Seward objected to the district attorney's request for the second panel, arguing that the circumstances proved that an impartial jury could not be obtained in Cayuga County.[6] The court disagreed and the proceedings continued; the trial itself took six days after the jury was selected.[7] The facts of the case were unchanged from the first trial, and moral insanity was once again presented as a legal excuse for the murder of James Gordon. Seward called upon the services of additional medical experts, who testified that Wyatt was insane when he killed Gordon. Amariah Brigham, superintendent of the New York State Lunatic Asylum at Utica, and John McCall, president of the New York State Medical Society, made their first of several appearances in Auburn as expert medical witnesses for Seward's clients.[8]

"Seldom has there been a trial in which greater wisdom, more enlightened experience, or more profound learning, on these nice and difficult subjects, as well as on the philosophy of the human mind generally, has been exhibited by both witnesses and counsel than in this," the *Auburn Journal and Advertiser* reported. The editors of that journal believed that the Wyatt trial clearly demonstrated how "mental as well as physical science is stamped with that proud and peculiar boast of our age and country, *progress.*"[9] Other observers reacted far differently, condemning the protracted nature of the proceedings and the expense to the taxpayers of the county.[10] The insanity defense was once again criticized as a creative device used to delay and impede the administration of justice.[11] On June 23, the jury returned a verdict of guilty after deliberating for one and one-half hours. The following day Wyatt was sentenced to hang on August 17, 1846.[12] Judge Bowen Whiting expressed his satisfaction that Wyatt's rights had been faithfully protected. Wyatt's counsel, the judge informed the convicted murderer, had devoted "the best efforts which learning and eloquence, animated by zeal and fidelity, enabled them to put forth in your behalf." The law and "the good of that society of which [he] might have been an honest and useful member" now demanded that Wyatt's life be taken.[13] Seward believed that the court conducted Wyatt's trial unfairly, and he predicted that the conviction would "ultimately be reversed."[14]

The Wyatt case having been settled, the court immediately proceeded to take up the issue of Freeman's sanity for the purpose of standing trial. At Seward's urging, the preliminary issue was argued before a jury, as opposed to the alternative method of a private court examination of Freeman. The jury was impanelled on Wednesday, June 24, with the preliminary trial commencing the following day.[15] At Seward's request, the court assigned as Freeman's official counsel the distinguished David Wright. Wright had been a member of the bar in New York for twelve years and had developed a legal practice having "a wide and extended range." He lent his talents as a courtroom orator, concisely delivering the opening argument for the defense in both of Freeman's trials.[16] Seward, however, still took upon himself the brunt of the burden of defending Freeman. He examined and cross-examined the witnesses and delivered exhaustingly lengthy summations at the close of each trial.[17]

David Wright presented the jury with the basic facts supporting the conclusion that Freeman was not presently sane for the purpose of standing trial. Freeman was hereditarily predisposed to insanity, his ancestors having become insane "for causes apparently trivial." Wright claimed Freeman had been wrongfully imprisoned for stealing a horse, a fact the prosecution contested. Freeman had been disciplined severely while in the state prison at Auburn, and a blow to his head had caused partial deafness. He was now indifferent to his fate, his vacant stare and idiotic smile evidence of a diseased mind. Laying the groundwork for the argument that Freeman was morally insane, Wright juxtaposed the sheer brutality of the killings with the apparent absence of motive. Freeman had no grudge against the Van Nests that could possibly have compelled a sane mind to take their lives in such brutal fashion. Wright concluded by remarking that Freeman neither understood the plea interposed in his behalf nor the nature of the current investigation to determine his state of mind. In short, he was completely unable to participate in his own defense.[18]

The district attorney informed the jury that "if they found that the prisoner was competent to distinguish between right and wrong, the prosecution would insist that he was legally sane, and answerable to the law for his crime."[19] This was a markedly different approach from that of the defense, which focused on Freeman's capacity to appreciate the specific situation in which he now found himself. This disagreement regarding the proper legal definition of sanity for the purpose of standing trial foreshadowed the conflicting approaches to insanity that would characterize the trial on the indictment. Both sides called a multitude of laymen witnesses "to testify as to the prisoner's *former* character, habits and conduct from his childhood." In addition, medical witnesses of various levels of experience in the diagnosis and treatment of insanity stated their opinions as to Freeman's "present mental condition." Based upon "the testimony adduced on the trial, and also upon their personal examination of the prisoner," six doctors concluded that Freeman was presently insane, while seven reached the opposite conclusion.[20]

The attorney general began his summation at nine o'clock on the evening of July 3. After the court recessed, Van Buren resumed his argument on the July 4, concluding at noon. Seward then took the floor on behalf of Freeman, speaking "from 2 to 11 o'clock P. M., with but half an hour's intermission."[21] In the charge to the jury that followed, Judge Whiting appended language reminiscent of Shaw and Edmonds to a strict McNaughtan definition. He advised the jury that Freeman was insane and could not be tried if "some disease is the acting power within him which he cannot resist." If Freeman lacked "sufficient use of his reason to control his passions" and was "dispossessed of the free natural agency of his mind," he was to be considered presently insane.[22] Whiting concluded his charge at 11:55 P.M., and the court adjourned. The jury returned the following morning and announced that they stood eleven to one in favor of sanity.[23] Cyrus Davis, the lone dissenter, explained to Whiting that although it had been proved that Freeman had memory and knowledge of events, it had not been shown that he was able to reason properly. Whiting responded, "The main question for the jury to decide is whether the prisoner knows right from wrong." If Freeman did, the jury was to pronounce him sane for the purpose of standing trial. Whiting then told the jury that he did not believe Freeman was delusional since there was proof that convicts commonly claimed pay for being confined. The judge stated that since the jury's verdict was for the information of the court, and was not a final judgment as to guilt or innocence, the court had greater freedom to confer with them. Finally, he stated that it was the court's duty to keep the jury together until an agreement was reached.[24]

At 8:00 P.M. on the evening of July 5, the jury rendered a verdict that planted the seeds for tremendous controversy: "We find the prisoner sufficiently sane in mind and memory to distinguish between right and wrong." Freeman's counsel immediately asked the court to reject the verdict and to instruct the jury to answer the question demanded by the statute. Was Free-man sane or insane for the purpose of standing trial? Judge Whiting refused to resubmit the question to the jury and directed a verdict of sanity to be recorded. He added that the verdict rendered was "equivalent to a verdict of sanity, under the rule laid down in his charge." [25] The dissenting juror had entertained the possibility that Freeman, although in possession of certain mental faculties, could not reason properly. The first definition that Whiting recited left room for the argument that Freeman was morally insane, and therefore could not reason properly on the issue of compensation for wrongful imprisonment. Whiting's second set of instructions downplayed the possibility of delusion and presented a definition of sanity that was Mc-Naughtan without any of Shaw's modifications. Under this definition, Free-man stood no chance whatsoever of being found insane. The jury's verdict was a compromise that simply expressed what little was clearly known about Freeman: he possessed the intellectual ability to distinguish right from wrong in the abstract sense.

The conclusion can hardly be avoided that Whiting was anxious to see Freeman tried on the murder indictment. He narrowed the definition of sanity in his second charge, commented negatively on the merits of Freeman's insanity plea, and accepted a verdict that avoided the issue at hand. The preliminary trial was held in compliance with the statutory pro-vision prohibiting the trial of insane persons for crimes. "Sufficiently sane in mind and memory to distinguish between right and wrong" did not satisfy the statutory requirement of sanity, yet Whiting forged ahead as if the mat-ter had been settled. Seward remarked with understandable disgust that the end result was "a contemptible compromise verdict in a capital case." [26] At least one juror had recognized that Freeman's case was complex. Under the broader definition of insanity introduced by Shaw and Edmonds, Freeman's plea took on considerable merit. Whiting closed the gate by allowing the jury to focus on the black and white issue of intellectual capacity to distin-guish right from wrong. Even then, the jury's verdict reflected a lack of cer-tainty that possession of such intellectual capacity was equivalent to sanity. Whiting, however, could not be deterred.

Some observers interpreted the preliminary trial as having conclusively settled the issue of William Freeman's state of mind when the killings took place. "Though the defence of insanity, at the time of the commission of the offence, may yet be interposed, in behalf of the prisoner, it is not probable, considering the latitude of the inquiry already had, that it will be again persisted in," the *Albany Evening Atlas* concluded.[27] The *Cayuga Patriot* believed that since no one contested the fact that Freeman killed John Van Nest, one trial was sufficient. If Freeman "gave the usual manifestations of a diseased mind, any jury that could be obtained in this county would readily acquit him," the *Patriot* concluded. By "usual manifestations," the editors meant symptoms of mental illness as defined by Coke and Hale rather than Isaac Ray. One jury had already concluded that Freeman manifested a healthy exercise of his mental faculties, and that satisfied the *Patriot's* editors that he was legally responsible for his actions.[28]

On July 6, Freeman was once again arraigned. Seward again attempted to prevent the proceedings from going any further. Until the issue of Freeman's present state of mind had been properly settled, Seward argued, the court could not require him to plead in response to the murder indictment. Van Buren replied that although the jury had not found a verdict of sanity "in form," they had "in effect" and the court had accepted this decision. Whiting agreed that the court had been satisfied that Freeman should be tried and refused to pursue the controversy any further. It was for the court alone to say whether they were satisfied that the prisoner was sane, he declared. He added that the verdict of the preliminary trial, although not precisely a verdict of sanity "in form," was indeed a verdict of sanity "in substance."[29]

The dialogue that ensued between Freeman and the district attorney during the arraignment was remarkable. When Sherwood asked Freeman to answer the murder indictment, Freeman responded, "Ha!" Sherwood once again demanded to know how Freeman pled, and Freeman stated that he did not know. When Sherwood asked him if he was ready for trial and if he had counsel, Freeman responded "I don't know." The accused killer did not acknowledge any relationship whatsoever with Seward and his colleagues. Sherwood finally inquired, "Are you able to employ counsel?" Freeman responded that he was not.[30] David Wright, after witnessing the exchange, arose and informed the court that he could no longer consent to take part in a cause which "had so much the appearance of a *terrible farce.*" Seward was reported to have rushed from the courtroom, "perfectly overwhelmed with

his feelings." Both men were steadfast in their belief that Freeman was insane. Seward returned shortly thereafter, and pledged to "remain counsel for
the prisoner until his death." The court prevailed upon Wright to reconsider
his departure, and he once again agreed to bring his considerable abilities to
Freeman's defense.[31] The court directed a plea of not guilty to be entered in
Freeman's behalf, no other option being available in cases where insanity was
proposed as an excuse for criminal acts.[32]

As the trial on the indictment was set to begin, Seward made a motion
for its postponement to the next term of the court, "on the ground of the
state of public sentiment in the county." The outcomes of Wyatt's retrial and
Freeman's preliminary trial had done little to allay Seward's fear that public
vindictiveness prohibited a fair trial. The court refused the motion, and the
process of jury selection began immediately.[33] Seward moved to set aside the
array of jurors summoned, on the grounds that two men were stricken from
the list by the court because they were Quakers. The court once again refused. As they were active in the effort to abolish capital punishment, it is not
surprising that adherents to Quakerism were dismissed as unfit for jury service in capital cases. Given public sentiment regarding the role of antigallows
reformers in the first Wyatt trial and, by implication, the Van Nest killings,
the court's effort to eliminate a source of further controversy is understandable.[34] Out of the first panel of potential jurors, only three were selected,
forcing the court to direct the sheriff to summon a new panel of thirty.[35]
Four days later, after over five dozen men had been examined, a jury was finally in place and the proceedings began.[36]

Antebellum common law presumed every man to be sane until the contrary was proved, to the satisfaction of the jury. Then, as now, insanity was an
affirmative defense, a matter of fact that, if proved, was an excuse for a criminal act. The burden of persuasion rested clearly on the defendant.[37] The
crucial point that was contested in Freeman's main trial was the legal definition of insanity. All evidence relating to Freeman's appearance, character, or
actions eventually had to be weighed in the context of that legal definition.
The defense worked to broaden the jury's conception of what constituted
legal irresponsibility, introducing elements of the theory of moral insanity.
People suffering from moral insanity might possess the intellectual capacity
to distinguish between right and wrong generally but refuse to consider

their own immoral or criminal acts wrong.[38] The prosecution attempted to persuade the jury to accept a very narrow definition of insanity, predicated generally upon the defendant's ability to distinguish between right and wrong. Van Buren and Sherwood did not hesitate to warn the jury that the doctrines proposed by Freeman's counsel would greatly handicap the administration of justice.[39]

Freeman's counsel faced the likelihood that the jury would be impatient with legal excuses and unsympathetic to criminals in general. The nature of Freeman's actions on the night of March 12, 1846, rendered his prospects even more bleak. For reasons eternally difficult to determine, he butchered four members of a prominent Cayuga County family. Finally, his race would certainly be used against him in court. The only chance that Seward, Wright, and their colleagues had to spare Freeman a murder conviction rested in the jury's acceptance of moral insanity. Judge Whiting's jury charges in the two Wyatt trials gave Freeman's counsel reason to be hopeful that Shaw's innovations would be offered for the jury's consideration once again. The immediate difficulty rested in getting an unsympathetic jury to entertain the validity of the theory as an excuse for crime. Equally daunting was the task of overcoming all serious doubts that Freeman fit the description.

Seward attempted to demonstrate precedent for moral insanity excusing crime in New York. He detailed for the jury Judge Edmonds's handling of the murder trial of Andrew Kleim, in which the accused was acquitted and sent to the State Lunatic Asylum at Utica. The first notable feature in Edmonds's jury charge, according to Seward, was its spirit of humanity. Edmonds conceded that Kleim's acts were so brutal that it was understandable for the jury to possess "strong feelings of indignation against him." The jury must beware, however, the manner in which they permitted their anger to influence their judgment. The jury must "bear in mind that the object of punishment was not vengeance, but reformation" and general deterrence. Nothing "was so likely to destroy the public confidence in the administration of criminal justice, as the infliction of its pains upon one whom Heaven has already afflicted with the awful malady of insanity," Edmonds concluded. Seward likewise argued that nothing would energize the opponents of vindictive justice more than "the fact that a jury of the country, through ignorance or passion, or prejudice, have mistaken a madman for a criminal."[40]

Seward quoted specific passages from Edmonds's charge that incorporated Shaw's innovations. He recited Edmonds's comment that the "moral as well as the intellectual faculties may be so disordered by the disease as to deprive the mind of its controlling and directing power." The former governor drew the jury's attention particularly to Edmonds's description of the circumstances that rendered an accused criminal irresponsible: "If on the other hand, he have not intelligence enough to have a criminal intent and purpose; and if his moral or intellectual powers are either so deficient that he has not sufficient will, conscience, or controlling mental power; or if through the overwhelming violence of mental disease his intellectual power is for the time obliterated, he is not a responsible moral agent." Seward also made reference to certain aspects of Kleim's behavior that Edmonds deemed worthy of the jury's careful consideration. The jury needed to consider "the extraordinary and unaccountable alteration" in Kleim's "whole mode of life." Also important were the "inadequacy between the slightness of the cause and the magnitude of the offence" as well as the "stolid indifference" Kleim manifested during the trial upon which his life depended. Seward pressed the point that the similarities between Kleim's mental state and Freeman's were unmistakable.[41]

Seward and Wright were inhibited by circumstances best described by Judge Edmonds, when he acknowledged that "the law in its slow and cautious progress, still lags far behind the advance of true knowledge." Freeman's acquittal hinged upon his counsel's ability to use recent scientific advances to overcome widely accepted notions regarding the nature of crime. Seward attempted to persuade the jury that insanity "such as the Counsel for the People would tolerate, never did and never will exist." The prosecution "admit in the abstract that insanity excuses crime," he complained, "but they insist on rules for the regulation of insanity to which that disease can never conform itself." Derived "from Coke, Blackstone and Hale," these rules unrealistically required that "by reason of either natural infirmity or of disease, the wretched subject shall be unable to count twenty, shall not know his father or mother, and shall have no more reason or thought than a brute beast."[42] Wright reminded the jury that "all of the late cases upon the subject decided in this state, and also in Massachusetts" demonstrated that the legal definition of insanity was more inclusive than that proposed by the prosecution.[43] The fallaciousness of the prosecution's approach, Seward observed, was especially visible in the testimony of Dr. Thomas Spencer, professor of theory and practice at Geneva Medical College. In looking for insanity, Seward observed, Spencer demanded "an entire obliteration of all conception, attention, imagination, association, memory, understanding and reason." Seward argued that "the human mind is not capable, while life remains, of such complete obliteration."[44]

In addition to arguing in favor of a broader definition of insanity, Wright and Seward took great pains to assure the jury that if Freeman was found not guilty by reason of insanity, the law required that he be confined for life in the State Lunatic Asylum.[45] Freeman's counsel reminded the jury that Freeman faced four separate murder indictments before he could be considered fully acquitted. Even if he was acquitted in each instance, the jury could rest assured that Freeman would never again personally threaten society.[46] This assurance was crucial to Freeman's defense, given the emphasis that the prosecution placed on the role of the law in protecting society. Seward's counsel, however, could do little to allay doubts that the threat of confinement in an asylum deterred crime.

In order to convince the jury that Freeman suffered from moral insanity, his attorneys called upon witnesses that were familiar with recent advances in the study of mental illness. These experts were capable of diagnosing the variety of mental disease that Shaw and Edmonds provided for in their definitions of legal insanity. Crucial to the defense, however, was Seward and Wright's ability to convince the jury that these medical experts were competent witnesses and their testimony worthy of the most careful consideration.

Freeman's counsel turned once again to Edmonds for assistance. In the Kleim trial, Edmonds argued that the opinions of physicians "who had devoted themselves to the study of insanity as a distinct department of medical science, and studied recent improvements and discoveries" could never be "safely disregarded by Courts and Juries." Physicians with the added experience of personal care of the insane were especially competent witnesses. On the other hand, Edmonds cautioned, "the opinions of physicians who had not devoted their particular attention to the disease, were not of any more value than the opinions of common persons."[47]

Delivering the defense opening, David Wright warned the jury against what he perceived to be the danger inherent in the prosecutors' reasoning in regard to medical testimony. The district attorney had clearly expressed his distaste for the theory of moral insanity in his own opening remarks. He had then invited the jurymen to disregard any medical opinion that did not coincide with their own opinions regarding the proper conclusions to be drawn from the facts in the case.[48] Wright warned that Sherwood was asking the jurors to prejudice themselves against any medical testimony that contradicted the opinions that they held at the outset of the trial. The advance of scientific of knowledge was to have no impact on American criminal justice if juries were advised to disregard anything that contradicted their own preconceptions. For Wright, to let the point go without a fight was to not only surrender William Freeman to an unjust death, but to abandon American jurisprudence to the darkness of the old common law. Wright excoriated Sherwood, claiming that the learning of the medical witnesses employed in Freeman's defense was beyond the comprehension of the district attorney. Hence Sherwood found it necessary to ridicule these witnesses and to compare psychiatry, what Wright called "the most difficult in the range of human studies," with "the exploded errors of a barbarous age." In other words, the defense witnesses were quacks, worthy only of comparison to sorcerers and necromancers.[49]

Wright and Seward pleaded with the jury to give Freeman's defense a "fair and impartial scrutiny," which meant giving all witnesses a "fair and impartial examination." Since the theory of moral insanity postulated that changes in demeanor and appearance were among the clearest symptoms of derangement, the observations of witnesses that had known Freeman throughout his life were particularly important. Medical authorities, including Jean-Etienne Esquirol, James C. Prichard, and Isaac Ray, all agreed that people suffering from moral insanity underwent changes in personality as a result of disease. Happy individuals became morose and gentle ones became violent. Insomnia often set in, and facial expressions changed, resulting in foolish grins that were frequently accompanied by senseless laughter.[50]

Beyond having witnesses that were more familiar with recent advances in the diagnosis of insanity, the defense boasted of medical witnesses that were more closely acquainted with Freeman himself. For example, Dr.

Lansing Briggs, an Auburn physician and surgeon, had been acquainted with Freeman for close to a decade and could compare Freeman's present appearance and behavior with his demeanor before he entered the state prison. Furthermore, Seward considered Briggs to be superior in both learning and candor to his counterparts that testified for the People. Dr. Charles Van Epps, also an Auburn physician, had known Freeman since the latter was born. Like Briggs, Van Epps had followed the progress of Freeman's entire life. Only Freeman's relatives were at a better vantage point from which to observe changes in Freeman's appearance and behavior.[51] The prosecution, Seward pointed out, produced no medical witnesses with any recollections of Freeman prior to his incarceration in the state prison. The value of their professional opinions was depreciated by their lack of personal understanding of Freeman's history. At best, they relied upon the testimony of other prosecution witnesses, which, as we shall see, supported the theory that the crime was in keeping with Freeman's naturally ignorant, morose, and violent nature.[52]

If the jury accepted, as Seward and his colleagues certainly hoped, the expanded definition of legal insanity, the medical witnesses bore the responsibility of convincing the jury that the definition encompassed Freeman. Freeman's counsel could only hope that their entreaties had convinced the jury that expert medical opinions deserved careful and impartial consideration. Among these witnesses, Dr. Briggs addressed several key themes regarding moral insanity. Briggs compared Freeman to the young boy he once knew, and concluded that he "had less vigor or strength of mind—was less capable of reasoning, comparing, retaining, and associating ideas." Freeman had difficulty continuing a narrative of the events surrounding the killings without being continuously prompted by interviewers' questions. Most crucial in terms of Freeman's defense was Briggs's interpretation of Freeman's feelings regarding the killings. Although Freeman "is perfectly conscious of what he has done and was doing, he thinks and believes he has committed no crime," Briggs stated. Freeman undoubtedly knew that the penalty for murder was hanging, but he "thinks it should not be enforced in this case because he has done nothing but what is right." Briggs reasoned that Freeman "justifies himself under the delusion that he had been wronged, and that society owed him reparation—that it was rightfully his, and was due to him as an equivalent and satisfaction." Ultimately the doctor concluded, "This delusion, in my judgement, is an insane delusion."[53]

Likewise, Dr. Van Epps testified that Freeman had once been "as bright and intelligent as children generally," but he now appeared "not to have the intellect of a child of five years old." Freeman suffered from dementia, "or that species of insanity which is accompanied with a loss of the intellect," Van Epps told the jury. His general diagnosis illustrated, with unequaled clarity, the defense's case. Freeman "has been under an impression that he ought to have pay for the time that he was in prison, and that somebody owed him, and I have not been able to make him believe to the contrary," Van Epps asserted. Freeman suffered from "an insane delusion," and was driven to kill by the feeling that everybody was against him. Freeman "had nothing in particular against John Van Nest," Van Epps concluded, "yet insane people generally kill their best friends sooner than they will their enemies."[54] The defense denied that Freeman killed the Van Nests because they, in particular, had caused him harm. He labored under the delusion that he deserved, and should be granted, some form of compensation for the wrongful conviction that had robbed him of five years of his life. No one was able to convince him to the contrary. When Freeman attempted to obtain warrants against the people who testified at his grand larceny trial, he was told that he had no legal recourse. Unable to be reasoned out of the delusion, it took control of his mind, and he indiscriminately killed the Van Nests as compensation for the injuries inflicted on him by society.[55]

Following these local physicians, Freeman's counsel presented as witnesses the most distinguished scientific experts that could be persuaded to attend the trial. Dr. Charles B. Coventry, a Geneva Medical College professor and comanager of the State Lunatic Asylum at Utica, offered his opinion that Freeman's intellect had declined since March 12.[56] "Yet I don't believe, in reference to the act he committed, that he knew the difference between right and wrong," Coventry concluded. Insanity may exist where the patient can distinguish between right and wrong in regard to other things, Coventry added, yet not in regard to a particular act. Freeman had suffered "almost a total abolition of moral faculties" in addition to impairment of his intellect. According to Coventry, Freeman was under a delusion that he was entitled to pay and could obtain it by murder. Asked to comment on the prosecution's contention that it was common for prisoners to assert their innocence and to believe that they were entitled to pay for time lost, he claimed that prisoners did not generally believe that they could gain compensation through murder. Whether or not prisoners commonly felt entitled to compensation for wrongful imprisonment, Coventry asserted that Freeman's manner of seeking compensation was highly unusual.[57]

Coventry, along with other key medical witnesses, made much of Freeman's external appearance. To Coventry, Freeman's "whole appearance and manner" indicated insanity. Dr. John McCall, president of the Medical Society of the State of New York, concurred. He found Freeman's countenance and "the movement of the muscles of the face showing an idiotic laugh" to be indicative of "dullness of understanding or comprehension." Freeman appeared indifferent, McCall observed, his manner and deportment giving no indication of soundness of mind. Himself a resident of Utica, McCall drew upon experience gained by observing patients at the state asylum. Freeman's rigid and unnatural posture resembled that of numerous patients the doctor had observed.[58]

McCall also drew heavily upon phrenological theory to support the contention that Freeman was insane. He testified that Freeman's head, "in the region of the brain," was smaller than "that of persons of his age who are healthy." For that matter, Freeman's whole head was "smaller than a healthy man of his age" and failed to indicate the presence of "intelligence or moral qualities." McCall referred to the head sizes of Dr. Amariah Brigham and Attorney General Van Buren as examples of the appropriate size.[59] Taking his diagnosis a step further, the doctor concluded that Freeman's "head and countenance indicate signs of homicidal mania," a term used to describe one violent manifestation of moral insanity.[60] Drawing upon the theoretical aspects of phrenology, McCall testified that Freeman's environment had played an important role in the onset of moral insanity. Freeman, a man lacking in intellect, had spent five years in the state prison where "the propensities and passions are left unrestrained." McCall concluded that the uncontrolled exercise of these emotions predisposed Freeman to insanity.[61]

Ultimately, McCall concluded that Freeman "committed the murder under an insane delusion, and by impulse." The delusion about pay, the doctor testified, "gained an ascendancy" over Freeman's mind until it became "the predominant feeling." Freeman was a monomaniac, in that his mind brooded over one idea and could not be reasoned out of it. Freeman "believed that he was entitled to pay from somebody—that it was due him," McCall argued. Freeman labored under this delusion when he killed the Van Nests and still labored under it when McCall interviewed him prior to the trial.[62] The indiscriminate nature of the killings, in McCall's opinion, supported the theory of moral insanity. Freeman both denied having any personal vendetta against the Van Nests and indicated that he would have killed anyone else whom he might have met on that March evening. McCall concluded that the delusion resulted in an irresistible impulse, under the influence of which Freeman committed the acts in question.[63] Judge Edmonds, we recall, had instructed jurors that if "some controlling disease was in truth the acting power within [the accused], which he could not resist," he was not responsible. By McCall's estimation, Freeman certainly fit that description.[64]

Dr. Amariah Brigham, superintendent of the State Lunatic Asylum at Utica, agreed with McCall and Coventry as to the meaning of Freeman's external appearance. Freeman's "abject and demented appearance" and his inexplicable laughter, even in the gravest of circumstances, indicated mental disease.[65] Brigham also concurred with McCall regarding the influence of environment. Brigham concluded that in his youth, Freeman was of slightly less than average intellect as compared with other "colored persons of his age." He was left, however, to the "indulgence of his passions, without mental, moral, or religious culture." The indulgence of the passions, Brigham argued, "forms a character that cannot brook control, subjects them to violent emotions, and thus lays the foundation of insanity in the passions and affections." Brigham pointed to testimony that revealed Freeman's tendency, while in prison, to react violently to trivial provocations such as another convict moving his shoes without permission. Freeman had been allowed to overdevelop certain passions to the point where he could no longer control his violent reactions.[66] Brigham also introduced the hereditary element of phrenology to the trial by pointing out that insanity ran in Freeman's family. In doubtful cases, Brigham argued, prevalence of insanity in the person's family was "entitled to great weight." Like McCall, Brigham employed phrenological theory to buttress the argument that Freeman was morally insane.[67]

The defense's key witness, Brigham concluded that Freeman's mental illness commenced in prison and was "more of a derangement of the passions and feelings than of the intellect at first." Freeman's intellect "finally took up the delusion, and under that delusion he tried to get pay." When the community failed to compensate him for what he perceived to be wrongful imprisonment, Freeman was no longer able to control his emotions. "I cannot believe that a sane man, in the exercise of his intellect and moral feelings, could do such an act, unless the provocation was very great, or the motive very powerful and strong," Brigham testified. The doctor was unconvinced that any such provocation existed in Freeman's case. In addition, Brigham did not consider careful planning and concealment of wrongful acts incompatible with insanity. Freeman may have been aware that society would seek to punish him for the killings; that did not suffice to reason him out of the delusion that he deserved compensation for wrongful imprisonment and should seek it at any cost. Brigham theorized that Freeman feared detection because it would terminate his quest for compensation, not because he believed he was doing something wrong.[68] Freeman had, after all, told some interviewers that he had fled the crime scene only because the injury to his wrist prevented him from doing more killing. His intention had been to flee the county, wait until his injury healed, and "come back again."[69]

Brigham tried earnestly to impress upon the jury his medical opinion that insanity did not mean total obliteration of the mental faculties. Freeman was, in Brigham's opinion, childlike in his level of intelligence. His condition approached but could not be considered dementia, since Freeman retained some understanding and memory.[70] Working as he did with the insane, however, Brigham had seen many instances in which insane persons "exhibited as much intellect as any person in this assembly." Brigham employed insane persons to perform tasks at the asylum that required considerable patience, skill, and intelligence. "When I know these people are as deranged on certain subjects as any person ever was, the fact that [Freeman] remembers and repeats, does not carry conviction to my mind that he is sane," the doctor asserted.[71]

Lastly, Brigham offered the court his conclusions regarding Freeman's apparent indifference to the trial proceedings. Freeman answered questions readily but expressed no unsolicited interest in or concern for his legal case.

Brigham compared Freeman's lack of appreciation for the gravity of his own situation to that displayed by Andrew Kleim, with whom the doctor had become familiar since Kleim's confinement in the State Lunatic Asylum.[72] "I tried in various ways to ascertain if [Freeman] knew what he was to be tried for," Brigham reported, but "never could get a distinct answer." When Brigham asked Freeman if his counsel should say that he did not kill, Freeman replied, "No, that would be wrong; I did do it." When an accompanying interviewer asked if counsel should argue that Freeman was crazy, Freeman responded, "I can't go so far as that." Brigham asked Freeman what he could prove in his own defense, to which he responded, *"the jury* can prove that I was in prison five years for stealing a horse, and didn't steal it." By Brigham's estimation, even when facing trial for capital murder, Freeman's delusion still possessed such a grip on his mind that it overwhelmed any rational concern for his own fate or appreciation of his current circumstances. Freeman felt that he had done right, and that feeling dominated his understanding of the events surrounding him.[73]

In summarizing the defense's case for the jury, Seward took great pains to emphasize the conclusions put forth by these physicians. Dr. Brigham, supported by other defense experts, concluded that delusion prevented Freeman from believing that the law should or even would punish his particular act in the usual manner. Seward cited additional testimony that supported this evaluation. John Austin, for example, recalled that after Freeman's arrest, the killer had declared, "If they'll let me go this time I'll try to do better." Austin remarked that the statement reflected Freeman's "want of all rational appreciation of the nature and enormity of his acts," a conclusion which Seward deemed perfectly logical. No adult of sound mind, having killed four people, could suppose "that he would be allowed to escape all punishment by simply promising, like a penitent child, that he would 'do better,' " Seward proclaimed. Horace Hotchkiss, Freeman's instructor in the state prison Sabbath school, recalled asking Freeman what would become of him if he were convicted and executed. Freeman responded that he would "go to heaven because he was good," demonstrating, by Seward's estimation, a total lack of appreciation for the immorality of his particular act. The former governor asked the jury to believe that Freeman, irrespective of society's judgments, could not by any means be convinced that his own act was wrong.[74]

Given the importance of environment in the theory of moral insanity, Freeman's racial background became a crucial part of his defense. From the outset, outspoken reformers had used Freeman's race to explain why he became a killer. Freeman's criminal defense had to go one step further in order to spare him the gallows. Using society's mistreatment of nonwhites to explain why Freeman became vengeful and violent was not enough. Freeman's counsel had to convince the jury that society was partially responsible for depriving Freeman of his moral sense and his ability to control his emotional impulses. Society had rendered William Freeman morally insane.

In his opening remarks, David Wright proclaimed that Freeman had "been a brother man, made in the image of his Maker, and might have so continued but for brutal treatment received by him amongst this Christian community." Wright also spoke of Freeman's "want of opportunities for improvement" and of his "isolated position, by reason of the wicked and unchristian prejudice against him and all others of his kind, by reason of their color." Given the "wrongs [Freeman] had suffered, the hardships he had endured, and the cruelties which had been inflicted upon him," Wright found it amazing that "people should now hold up their hands in holy horror at the result of their own treatment of this 'unlearned, ignorant, stupid and degraded negro.'" In this instance and at every other available opportunity, Wright quoted this description of Freeman presented by the district attorney during his opening remarks. This practice was intended to demonstrate that even the courtroom did not offer William Freeman shelter from the mistreatment he had endured throughout his life.[75]

Wright also addressed the fundamental difference between the prosecution and the defense regarding Freeman's intelligence. According to the prosecution, Freeman's intelligence was natural for people of his race. "Our poor senseless client is so ignorant," Wright exclaimed, "it would almost appear, from the learned counsel's estimate of him, impossible that he ever could have changed for the worse, and without some such change argues the counsel, he cannot be insane." The prosecution averred that Freeman appeared before the court in his natural and constant state, his appearance and behavior bearing no markings of the recent onset of mental illness. The defense retorted that Freeman's intelligence could only be judged as normal for an adult male by means of a grossly perverted standard. The opposite con-

clusion, which the defense supported unflinchingly, was that Freeman's intellectual development began in the normal fashion, only to be stunted by
the lack of opportunities available to his race. Coping with the loss of five
years of his life and the brutal discipline of the state prison finally shattered
his underdeveloped mind.[76]

Several defense witnesses called the jury's attention to the social conditions in which Freeman was raised. John Austin, who expressed his feelings
so clearly under a pseudonym in the *Auburn Journal and Advertiser,* spoke out
openly on the witness stand. The prosecution cross-examined Austin in
order to expose his opposition to capital punishment and to cast doubt upon
the objectivity of his testimony. Austin freely admitted that his distaste for
the gallows heightened his interest in the case, but he denied that his personal convictions biased his evaluation of Freeman's behavior. Austin admitted that he had penned the articles attributed to "Justice" in the *Journal and
Advertiser* and reemphasized the conclusions he had drawn regarding
Freeman's race. "I said [the community] were, to a certain extent, responsible for the crimes committed in their midst, and I think they are, in some
degree," he testified. When asked if the killings were the legitimate consequence of the neglect of the colored people in Auburn, he responded that
neglect was indeed "one of the causes that led to it." The clergyman's words
were bold, but they fit in with the defense's attempts to convince the jury
that racism had played a role in Freeman's descent into insanity.[77]

The testimony of Freeman's brother-in-law John De Puy so moved Seward that he quoted it in his closing argument. Seward exclaimed that he
had heard the greatest of American orators, as well as Europeans Daniel O'-
Connell and Sir Robert Peel, but John De Puy had "excelled them all in eloquence." De Puy testified: "They have made William Freeman what he is, a
brute beast; they don't make anything else of any of our people but brute
beasts; but when we violate their laws, then they want to punish us as if we
were men." If any witness inspired a degree of self-consciousness among the
jury, it was John De Puy.[78]

As we have seen, Doctors Coventry and Brigham clearly expressed their
conclusions regarding the debilitating effects of Freeman's social environment. Although neither digressed into social commentary while under oath,
their references to Freeman's lack of mental, moral, and religious culture

clearly implied that Freeman suffered because of his race. Lack of positive moral influences resulted in the underdevelopment of Freeman's moral faculties and the overindulgence of his emotions. White society, through its neglect of the education and religious training of nonwhite children, destroyed Freeman's chances of growing to be a productive and law–abiding adult.

Seward devoted some of his most passionate remarks of the proceedings to the subject of racial prejudice and its impact on Freeman's mental state. "All writers agree, what it needs not writers should teach, that *neglect of education* is a fruitful cause of insanity. If neglect of education produces crime, it equally produces insanity." Freeman had been a bright and cheerful child, "entitled by the principles of our government to equal advantages for perfecting himself in intelligence, and even in political rights, with each of the three millions of our citizens. . ." However, Sally Freeman had been forced to send her son forth at the age of eight or nine years to employment in "menial service." Seward noted that reproaches were cast on Mrs. Freeman and on the white men with whom young Freeman lived and worked for not sending him to school. Such reproaches were all unjust, Seward exclaimed, for Sally Freeman, "poor degraded negress and Indian as she was," had no means to send her son to school. Likewise, there was no school to which Freeman's employers Warden and Lynch could have sent him had they so desired. Freeman's "few and wretched years date back to the beginning of my acquaintance here," Seward told the jury, "and during all that time, with unimportant exceptions, there has been no school here for children of his caste." Freeman's education could not but have been neglected, Seward concluded, because a "school for colored children was never established here, and all the common schools were closed against them." [79]

Becoming more blunt as he went on, Seward linked the Van Nest killings directly to the community's neglect of nonwhite children. "Here are the fruits of this unmanly and criminal prejudice," he declared. "A whole family is cut off in the midst of usefulness and honors by the hand of an assassin" who had been denied the ameliorative benefits of an education. Never afraid to appeal to the jury as fellow Christians, Seward attempted to arouse self-consciousness regarding the neglect of Freeman in his childhood. "You may avenge the crime," he warned, "but whether the prisoner be insane or criminal, there is a tribunal where this neglect will plead powerfully in his excuse, and trumpet-tongued against the 'deep damnation' of his 'taking off.' " Man might punish one of his own, who had been denied the benefits of moral culture and human benevolence, but God would ultimately judge who bore responsibility.[80]

Seward's choice of the word "unmanly" to describe the treatment of blacks in Auburn was perfectly consistent with his appeal to the Christianity of the jurors. In calling prejudice toward blacks "unmanly," Seward drew upon abolitionist images of Christian manliness. As mentioned earlier, abolitionists and other northern social reformers looked to Jesus Christ as the embodiment of the virtues that they associated with true manhood. Oppression of blacks either slave or free was certainly not consistent with this image of manliness. Gerrit Smith, for example, was lauded by fellow abolitionists as the "very best of men" and a "model man" because of the empathy he displayed for free blacks and slaves. Fearless political dissent, as also demonstrated, was viewed as a means of achieving the "political credibility" associated with manliness. In the political realm, Garrisonian abolitionists held that "the true man was an outspoken social reformer." Garrisonian publications praised reformers and northern congressmen for their " 'manly stand,' 'manly hostility,' and 'manly utterances' against slaveholders." Frederick Douglass, one publication proposed, "would make an admirable member of Congress—not according to the corrupt standards of the day, but rather, when 'manliness' was valued." [81] For abolitionists, vocal opposition to the oppression of blacks was manly both because it epitomized Christlike empathy, and because it was a righteous protest in the face of widespread hostility. Seward shared these views of manliness and hence described the social neglect of blacks as completely "unmanly." [82]

Seward and Wright, with the assistance of eloquent medical and lay witnesses, asked the jury to overcome deeply ingrained notions regarding both mental illness and race. This would have been a formidable challenge under any circumstances, let alone in the wake of one of the most brutal mass killings the community had ever witnessed. Bearing the burden of persuasion, the defense faced the overwhelming task of convincing a more-than-likely unsympathetic jury that the Van Nest killings were something more than premeditated acts of butchery. Freeman's counsel met the challenge with legal skill and powerful oratory. They were not afraid to appeal to the jury as Christians and as men. Their efforts on Freeman's behalf truly made this a case of trouble, as defined by Llewellyn and Hoebel. After all, Freeman's acts inspired fear and vengefulness rather than empathy, inquisitiveness, or even open-mindedness among most observers. He seemed to embody the worst attributes associated with African and Native Americans, and his acquittal threatened to send the message that the most violent of criminals were likely to escape punishment. The prosecution seized upon the emotions generated by the Van Nest killings and professed the best manner in which to prevent another William Freeman from harming the community.

5

The Tried Experience
and Security of Law

IN PROSECUTING WILLIAM FREEMAN, John Van Buren and Luman Sherwood repeatedly drew attention to what they regarded as a dangerous trend in criminal law. Driven to meet what many viewed as a serious challenge to the security provided by law, the prosecutors gave expression to commonly held values and commonly felt concerns. The more inclusive the legal definition of insanity became, the wider became the window through which dangerous criminals escaped. Only raving lunatics or imbeciles, the prosecutors maintained, truly lacked the intellectual ability to foresee the consequences of their actions. Mirroring public convictions regarding the nature of crime, prosecutors insisted that the Van Nest killings resulted from Freeman's depraved nature and not from disease. Freeman's ignorance, moroseness, and eccentricity were owing to his racial background rather than to mental derangement.

In his opening statement, District Attorney Sherwood traced the evolution of insanity jurisprudence and dubbed the McNaughtan rules "the test of insanity now the law of both England and the United States." Noticeably absent were any references to the Rogers or Kleim cases. Before a plea of insanity should be allowed, Sherwood submitted, *"undoubted* evidence ought to be adduced, that the accused was of diseased mind, and that at the time he committed the act, he was not conscious of right and wrong." The standard of proof required by the jury to consider Freeman insane was another matter, to be settled by Judge Whiting when he delivered his charge. The essential point to be noted is that Sherwood made no reference to irresistible impulse or moral insanity, choosing instead to impress upon the jury the need for a strict investigation of Freeman's ability to distinguish right from wrong. Many of his legal references were, in fact, to cases or treatises that defined insanity as nearly complete mental incapacity.[1]

Sherwood made plain his reasons for this approach. Referring to the defense of moral insanity, with which he had been forced to become familiar in light of Wyatt's trials and the preliminary trial of Freeman, the district attorney spoke of an affront to public safety and the law of the land. "These established maxims, which have for ages governed criminal trials in the country from which we have derived our laws, and which have been sanctioned and upheld by our own tribunals, and which have thus far preserved society and punished crime, are now sought to be overruled," Sherwood began. The threat was posed not by learned judges or the sages of the legal profession, but by the "new light of our learned adversaries, with the help of learned Doctors of Medicine, and speculative Theorists, upon the various and mutifarious divisions of insanity." Leaving the jury little doubt as to his opinion regarding the nature of Freeman's defense, Sherwood added, "It is proper that I should caution you against the adoption of such heresy to the law."[2]

Van Buren also spoke reverently of traditional legal doctrines regarding insanity and only tacitly recognized the contribution of Shaw. He proclaimed that "a reference to the simple and early tests of legal responsibility, under which well ordered communities have existed to this time, will show that no other has ever been furnished by the successive wisdom of ages or the humanizing spirit which has waited on this wisdom and pervaded criminal legislation." Emphasizing the fairness of the traditional doctrines, Van Buren noted that under these tests, "prisoners indicted for the highest crimes have been acquitted." He then took direct aim at Freeman's counsel, chastising him for characterizing the old common law as barbarous, severe, and oppressive. Seward's insistence that the community "reject the tried experience and security of law, and cleave to the subtleties of the asylum" was not justified by any "past evil or danger" in the history of English jurisprudence, the attorney general argued. The "enlightened liberty of the old common law" had dealt with insanity in a manner that neither punished the truly irresponsible nor endangered society by acquitting those who acted with malice.

The jury, Van Buren stressed, could feel secure knowing that traditional definitions of legal insanity both guaranteed the rights of the accused and protected the community.[3]

"The simple question for you to determine," Van Buren proclaimed, "is, had the prisoner, when he killed John G. Van Nest, sufficient capacity to judge whether it was right or wrong so to do?" The attorney general acknowledged that innovations in the common law allowed the jury to acquit if it was proved that disease divested Freeman of control over his actions. However, he encouraged the jury to adhere closely to the McNaughtan rules. "The only inquiry will be—had [Freeman] capacity to know the right, and physical ability to pursue it?" he declared. Moreover, the jury could take comfort in the security provided by the old common law, under which only clear cases of mental incapacity excused homicide.[4]

It is likely that the prosecution found in the jury kindred spirits on the subjects of law, order, and public security, given the sheer brutality of Freeman's acts. Linking a narrow definition of legal insanity to the protection of society certainly helped the prosecution's chances of gaining a conviction. Among Van Buren's final words to the jury during the main trial were references to security. "If crimes of this magnitude are to go unpunished, and thus to invite imitation, it is your hearthstones, not mine, that may be drenched in blood," he warned. In spite of the acquittal of Kleim, Van Buren noted that New York residents had thus far been reluctant to entertain legal excuses for malicious acts. Disturbingly, he added, in other jurisdictions, "the murderer may go at large as a somnambulist, an insane man, or a justifiable homicide." In New York, on the other hand, "the steady good sense and integrity of our juries, and the enlightened wisdom of our Judges, have saved our jurisprudence from ridicule, and firmly upheld law and order." The jury faced a very solemn responsibility, but Van Buren expressed his confidence that they would prove "that the jurors of Cayuga fully equal their fellow citizens of other counties, in intelligence to perceive, and independence to declare the guilt of a criminal."[5]

The element contained in the theory of moral insanity that most disturbed the prosecution was the tendency of proponents to view atrocities committed in the absence of adequate motives as themselves symptoms of insanity. Here was to be found the clearest link between the medical theory and Shaw's common-law innovations. Shaw had, after all, taken an interest in medical theories that linked *indiscriminate* acts of violence to insane delusion. He had worried that the McNaughtan rules ignored cases of mental disease that attacked the volitional-inhibitory system, so he had added a test for irresistible impulse. Absence of a motive that would adequately explain violent behavior indicated to certain physicians the presence of mental disease that "overwhelmed the reason, conscience, and judgement." Shaw agreed that in cases such as this, the behavior was not that of a voluntary agent governed by his own will. Medical advances had inspired recent challenges to the old common law and those very same medical innovations were being enlisted to defend Freeman. Under the circumstances, it is easy to understand why the prosecutors tried to turn the jury's attention to the common law previous to *Commonwealth v. Rogers.*[6]

Sherwood emphasized that "non-discovery" of a motive did not necessarily confirm its "non-existence." He chided Freeman's counsel for not allowing the jury to infer, once Freeman was proved to have killed John Van Nest, that "malice" prompted the act. This, Sherwood insisted, was what the jury was directed to do by the law. Sherwood cited cases where no reasonable motives were ever discovered for the commission of atrocious murders, and yet the perpetrators were held properly accountable. The theory of moral insanity assumed or implied, according to Sherwood, "that sane men never commit a crime without an apparent motive; and that an insane person never has a motive, or one of a delusive nature only, in the perpetration of a criminal act." This failed to explain crimes that had been committed "without any apparent motive by sane individuals, who were at the time perfectly aware of the criminality of their conduct." In addition, Sherwood observed, "lunatics, confined in a lunatic asylum, have been known to be influenced by motives in the perpetration of crimes." Sherwood cited instances where insane individuals killed their caregivers out of revenge for abusive treatment. Ultimately, he argued, if such "fallacies" as moral insanity were accepted by juries, society could "bid adieu to all hopes of punishing the atrocious crime of murder" until science enabled doctors to "enter the murderer's heart or analyze his mind and discover the influences by which it is operated."[7]

Van Buren emphasized the same theme in his closing argument. There was no way society could possibly expect to discover a motive that would adequately explain why a man brutally stabbed to death a pregnant woman, her two-year-old son, and her elderly mother. Yet this did not rule out the possibility that Freeman's act was willful and malicious, the attorney general declared. Van Buren drew the jury's attention to Dr. McCall's testimony as a glaring example of the type of reasoning that the jury should reject. McCall interpreted Freeman's choice of victims "against whom he could have no purpose of revenge, or discoverable motive for killing them all" as "strong evidence of insanity." The "murdering of a whole family and among them a little child" convinced McCall that Freeman "must have been insane." That Freeman took no money or possessions from the Van Nest residence further convinced McCall that the killings were motiveless. Plunder could not adequately explain Freeman's violent actions, Van Buren conceded. However, this inclination to view a criminal act itself, when perpetrated without a clear motive, as proof of insanity would place in "frightful jeopardy" the "property and the life of the citizen."[8]

In addition to noting the threat to public security, Van Buren employed legal reasoning in his attempt to dissuade the jury from accepting absence of motive as proof of insanity. "The motive of a criminal is important when there is no direct evidence that he has committed the crime," he advanced. Circumstantial evidence was "vastly strengthened by proof of a strong motive actuating the accused, and impelling him to the act with which he is sought to be charged." In cases such as Freeman's where the testimony was "direct and conclusive" that the act was performed by the accused, the attorney general asserted that motive "ceases to be material." Only the Almighty, and not man, had the capacity to search the heart of a fellow human being. "The illegal act being proved, the law declares the motive," Van Buren concluded, and that motive "is malice—a wicked, depraved heart."[9]

The prosecution, in arguing that proof of the act allowed the jury to infer malice, contradicted the common law with regard to criminal intent, or mens rea. In 1845, Chief Justice Shaw had helped to clarify the "old law" regarding criminal intent. In *Commonwealth v. York,* Shaw ruled that since the malicious state of mind can never actually be proved, malice could be implied from the facts proved by the whole evidence. Importantly in regard to Freeman's case, Shaw was careful to note that this rule applied only in cases where intentional homicide was proved and there was "no apparent excuse or justification for the crime." The prosecution attempted to downplay for the jury the relevant mitigating factor of Freeman's state of mind. Freeman's legal excuse was that he was incapable of exercising his will or committing a voluntary act of murder. However critical the prosecution was of the theory of moral insanity, in Freeman's case motive was highly relevant. The defense, we must remember, bore the burden of proving that Freeman was legally insane. The discovery of motive would cast doubt upon Freeman's specific defense, namely that his behavior was indiscriminate and the result of delusion. Whether plunder or revenge, if the prosecution convinced the jury that Freeman's actions could be plausibly explained by the existence of some real motive, the affirmative defense of moral insanity stood to falter.[10]

In light of the widespread public speculation that the killings were connected to the failure of the jury to convict Wyatt in February, the jurors in Freeman's trial probably were suspicious of the mode of defense used to defend both men. Regardless, the prosecution was not prepared to depend upon the jury's misgivings regarding moral insanity. Despite their denials of the relevance of motive, Sherwood and Van Buren were clearly aware of the damage that could be done to Freeman's defense should the jury accept the possibility that Freeman was actuated by real motives. Sherwood began this process, proclaiming that the prosecution would prove that shortly before Freeman was sentenced to state prison in 1840, he had resided upon the premises where the killings were committed. This coupled with proof that Freeman was at the house about a week previous to the killings would demonstrate that Freeman was certainly familiar with the layout of the Van Nest residence. The prosecution would also attempt to prove that Freeman was acquainted with the family and must have known them to be prosperous. Whether Freeman's object was plunder or whether he "took refuge in some *fancied wrong*," Sherwood promised the jury that they would hear ample evidence to cast doubt on the contention that the killings were motiveless.[11]

The prosecution expended considerable effort to establish the possibility that Freeman specifically targeted the Van Nests. Helen Holmes, the young survivor of Freeman's rampage, testified that she had seen Freeman at the Van Nest residence roughly one week prior to the crime. On that occasion, Freeman asked John Van Nest if he needed a laborer, to which Van Nest replied he did not. Freeman would not have encountered Cornelius Van Arsdale during that visit, Holmes testified, since Van Arsdale was yet to begin staying with the family. Mrs. Wyckoff was "a lady of wealth, and was in the habit of loaning money," Holmes added, while observing that John Van Nest "was also in good circumstances." [12] To this information was added the testimony of John Van Nest's mother, who also lived in the vicinity of Owasco Lake. She swore that she had seen a black man in her own yard between the hours of eight and nine on the night of March 12. The man had turned and went away toward her son's residence. [13] The prosecution hoped to establish by these witnesses that Freeman was familiar with the Van Nest residence, and knowing the family to be reasonably well off, he specifically chose their home to burglarize. Something such as unanticipated detection may have caused the burglary to go awry, inducing Freeman to turn to violence. Unaware that Van Arsdale resided with the Van Nests and believing that John Van Nest was the only adult male in the house, Freeman may have assumed that he would face minimal resistance should he be detected.

Van Buren focused on the evidence in the case that pointed to the possibility of revenge as a motive. "There is no doubt that he supposed that Van Nest was concerned in his [grand larceny] conviction," the attorney general proclaimed. [14] Nathaniel Hersey, an acquaintance, testified that Freeman told him, prior to the killings, that he had found and was going to kill the "folks that had put him in prison." Hersey swore that Freeman had specifically named the Van Nests. [15] Augustus Pettibone, sheriff of Cayuga County, testified that subsequent to his arrest, Freeman told an interviewer that he killed the Van Nests because "They swore me into prison." [16] Aretus Sabin, a longtime acquaintance, swore that Freeman confessed the same information to him in an interview conducted after Freeman's arrest. [17] Martha Godfrey, the woman whose horse Freeman was convicted of stealing in 1840, testified that she noticed horse tracks in her yard in Sennett the morning after the killings. [18] Just days prior to the killings, Freeman had asked a local magistrate for a warrant against Godfrey for swearing him into prison. [19] Auburn physician Sylvester Willard testified that Freeman admitted riding to Godfrey's house on the night of the Van Nest killings with the intention of killing her. According to Willard, Freeman claimed that his badly wounded wrist and the darkness of the location had prevented him from confronting Godfrey. [20]

Van Buren encouraged the jury, in light of this body of evidence, to entertain the possibility that Freeman was driven by a very real desire for revenge.

In addition to casting doubt upon the theory that the Van Nest killings were the indiscriminate product of Freeman's delusion, the prosecution still had to satisfy the jury that Freeman was not insane under the McNaughtan definition. The prosecutors also knew that despite their protests, the jury would most certainly be directed by the judge to decide whether Freeman's acts were the result of an irresistible impulse. Therefore, it was necessary to establish that Freeman possessed the requisite self-control to be considered a voluntary agent. Linked with possible motive, evidence of a criminal intent would render it exceedingly difficult for the defense to convince the jury that Freeman was legally irresponsible.

The prosecution claimed that Freeman's careful preparation and concealment of his intentions denoted criminal intent.[21] Two Auburn craftsmen buttressed this contention by noting the care and precision with which Freeman prepared the weapons that he eventually carried with him to the Van Nest residence. One blacksmith remembered asking Freeman if he wanted a knife for the purpose of killing somebody, to which Freeman responded, "It's none of your business, as long as you get your pay for it."[22] Dr. Leander Bigelow, an Auburn physician, testified that Freeman spoke of concealing his weapons under the woodpile at the house where he boarded.[23] Bigelow also recounted Freeman's confession that on the night of the crime, he had "stood around and thought about it, and didn't know whether it was best or not," but then decided to go anyway.[24] The prosecution presented this as evidence that Freeman understood the wrongful nature of his contemplated act, yet calmly and deliberately did it anyway. That Freeman committed the crime after dark was also presented as evidence of criminal intent. This degree of self-control and deliberation was deemed inconsistent with crime resulting from sudden, uncontrollable fury. The killing of John G. Van Nest and his family, the prosecution contended, was thoroughly calculated and carried out according to a specific plan.[25]

Furthermore, Freeman's flight and his evasiveness when first queried about the killings were presented as evidence that he knew he had done wrong and wished to conceal his actions. This evidence supported the prosecution's contention that Freeman was sane under the McNaughtan definition.[26] Alonzo Taylor, the constable who arrested Freeman at Gregg's Tavern in Oswego County, testified that Freeman initially denied any knowledge of the killings.[27] George B. Parker, who also assisted in the interrogation of Freeman at Gregg's, testified as to Freeman's reaction when the investigation was pursued further: "I shan't answer any more; if they can prove anything against me let them prove it."[28] To this, the prosecution added testimony revealing Freeman's feelings of guilt regarding the killings. Defense witness James H. Bostwick, justice of the peace in Auburn, testified under cross-examination that Freeman admitted it was wrong to commit the murders. When asked if he was sorry, Freeman told Bostwick, "I was sorry when I got to Syracuse."[29] Dr. Sylvester Willard testified that Freeman admitted regretting having "went up there" to the Van Nests'.[30] Defense witness William P. Smith, a foreman in the state prison dye house who had supervised Freeman years earlier, recalled asking Freeman if he thought it was wrong to kill the child. Freeman hesitated and finally answered, "Well, that looks kind o' hard."[31] Nathaniel Lynch also testified that Freeman told him that killing the family "looked hard."[32]

It is important to note at this point that more than a desire for justice and a speedy conviction lay beneath the prosecution's dissatisfaction with the mode of Freeman's defense. As demonstrated, the prosecution portrayed the incorporation of moral insanity within the common law as a dangerous legal innovation. Accompanying and reinforcing this antipathy was a general distaste for the physicians who inspired the innovation. Antipathy to professionalism in medicine was rooted both in traditional American attitudes toward healing and in the spirit of anti-intellectualism that was characteristic of the Jacksonian era.

While there was an active demand in the early nineteenth century for the services of well-qualified regular physicians, especially in cases of serious illness, many Americans continued to consult herb doctors, folk practitioners, apothecaries, and midwives. In addition, most people continued to rely upon health lore passed down through generations and on their favorite health handbooks.[33] Botanics, hydropaths, Thomsonians, and eclectics, who were "somewhat more systematic" in their methods than the aforementioned healers, also practiced "widely among the general population." All of the foregoing, known collectively as "irregulars," coexisted uneasily with the "formally educated and scientifically oriented 'regulars,' who dominated most medical schools, controlled most formal medical societies, and considered themselves at the top of their profession."[34] In the 1820s, medical societies sought to monopolize medical practice for formally trained physicians who, as Joseph F. Kett notes, "constituted only a fraction of the total number of medical advisors."[35] The American public became actively involved in the debate over medical exclusivity by expressing opposition to licensing proposals that would "diminish their traditional choices of healers."[36] By the early 1840s, over thirty thousand people in New York had signed petitions opposing any form of exclusive control over the practice of medicine.[37]

Traditional American attitudes toward medicine were, as James H. Cassedy notes, "enhanced by the developing trends toward political and social democracy and economic laissez faire."[38] As popular democracy became a stronger current in American life, it "reinforced the widespread belief in the superiority of inborn, intuitive, folkish wisdom over the cultivated, oversophisticated, and self-interested knowledge of the literati and the well-to-do." The Democratic Party was responsible for the first infusion of anti-intellectual rhetoric into American politics. The Jacksonian movement's distrust of expertise, disdain for centralization, desire to "uproot the entrenched classes," and its "doctrine that important functions were simple enough to be performed by anyone," amounted to a repudiation of "the special value of the educated classes in civic life." Opposition to monopoly in the professions perfectly complemented the Jacksonian antimonopolistic position on economic matters.[39] As James C. Mohr astutely points out, the assault on medical licensure took place during the same years that President Andrew Jackson was waging "political and ideological war on the 'monster' Bank of the United States."[40]

It was not merely Jacksonianism that was egalitarian, however, but the nation itself. Perry Miller, in his discussion of hostility to the legal profession, concludes that there can be "no worse falsification of American history than to suppose that this antilegalism of the early nineteenth century was merely 'Jacksonian,' merely the expression of a party." Opposition to professionalism was something "more pervasive than either of the parties could control," reflecting a widespread fear among Americans that the law was "an artificial imposition on their native intelligence."[41] By 1840, the competitive nature of the Second Party System had forced the Whig Party to adopt the rhetoric of populism. The appeal of democratic rhetoric was so broad that Whigs were forced to "swallow their distaste" for it and learn its methods. Both parties eventually became vehicles for what Richard Hofstadter calls an "anti-intellectualist populism" that rejected "the specialist, the expert, the gentleman, and the scholar."[42]

As sociologist Karl Mannheim has argued, the "democratic ideal in the sphere of knowledge calls for the greatest possible accessibility and communicability." By the early nineteenth century, American popular opinion "reflected an extreme form of rationalism that demanded science be democratic." Paul Starr concludes that it had become "an article of faith in America that every sphere of social life—law, government, religion, science, industry—obeyed principles of natural reason that were intelligible to ordinary men of common sense." Antebellum Americans viewed the appearance of complexity as "an imposition by a self-interested class," more the result of "mystification and deception" than of any "intrinsic difficulty." The seeming complexity of medicine, according to this view, was artificially imposed in order to place its practice beyond the reach of the average citizen.[43]

The prosecution in the Freeman case, led by one of New York's most prominent Democrats, responded to popular revulsion against the professions and their attempts to establish exclusive privileges. Medical licensure was widely viewed as yet another form of licensed monopoly, merely a means by which medical societies and boards of censors closed the ranks of the profession to all except individuals chosen for political or personal reasons. The public did not view medical licenses as evidence of "objective skill" in the field of medicine. In fact, widespread skepticism existed as to the effectiveness of medicine practiced by formally educated "regulars." Public opinion in antebellum New York was so fervently opposed to licensing that juries seldom if ever convicted anyone of unlicensed practice. Furthermore, the testimony of licensed physicians was "received with suspicion and disfavor by juries" in these cases. By 1844, New York State law no longer forbade the unlicensed practice of medicine. However, with the recent legal innovations regarding moral insanity, experienced medical professionals stood to gain exclusive privileges in the courtroom. If insanity, as an excuse for crime, were defined in a manner corresponding to the complicated theories of medical professionals, then their diagnoses and not the common sense of the jury would ultimately decide guilt or innocence. The prosecution in the Freeman case vigorously defended the ability and the right of ordinary citizens, sworn as jurors, to decide whether one of their peers acted contrary to the law.[44]

While antebellum lawyers defended the right of ordinary citizens to decide criminal guilt or innocence based on intuitive sense, they also feared a direct encroachment on their own professional realm by doctors. In trials involving medical issues such as insanity, certain physicians entered the courtroom with the heightened status of "professional expert." Lawyers feared the level of influence that these physicians' reputations would command with juries. That fear was not always justified, since jurors weighed expert testimony against their own conceptions of mental illness, which were, in many cases, drastically different. However, the lengths to which antebellum lawyers went to "thoroughly and relentlessly" demolish expert witnesses under cross-examination demonstrate the depth of their uneasiness. Lawyers feared medical experts for their ability to damage otherwise straightforward cases with "medical ambiguity and technicality." The legal profession even feared that cases involving medical issues might someday be heard by physicians instead of being tried in court in the traditional manner. If ordinary juries were deemed unfit to decide such cases, and juries of experts were convened in their place, the "adversarial principles upon which the American legal structure was ultimately based" would be forsaken. "Lawyers," Mohr concludes, "had no intention of surrendering power, real or symbolic, to rival professional collectives." When doctors entered the courtroom, the legal profession demanded that they did so under rules "established, interpreted, and administered by lawyers."[45]

As we have seen, Luman Sherwood vexed Freeman's counsel by urging jurors to determine for themselves the knowledge or empiricism of medical witnesses based on the facts of the case.[46] In *Commonwealth v. Rogers,* Shaw had indeed ruled that it was for the jury to decide whether the facts presented in the case were satisfactorily proved. Medical experts were not to judge the *truth* of facts testified to by other witnesses. The professional *opinions* of physicians, "who have long been conversant with insanity in its various forms," were regarded by Shaw as competent evidence even if based upon the testimony of other witnesses rather than direct examination.[47] Sherwood encouraged the jury to be far more skeptical, however, inviting them to employ their own common sense when evaluating the testimony of medical experts.

Van Buren likewise declared in his closing remarks that insanity, "as constituting legal incompetency or irresponsibility, must be within the comprehension of any ordinary man of fair capacity." The attorney general vehemently criticized "the theory of the professors, who have made insanity their peculiar study, that an ordinary man can't comprehend it." He encouraged the jury to be aware that the theory of moral insanity, "which substitutes the testimony of a physician, as to legal responsibility, for the law of the land," expelled the judge from the bench and the jury from the box. He hoped the jury shared his distrust of any theory that "overturns the government, and places the property, liberty, and life of any citizen in the hands of the trustees and superintendents of lunatic asylums." He feared that medical experts, such as Dr. Brigham, were acquiring privileged status in American courts. If questions of legal responsibility were transferred to "men of scientific pursuits," the constitutional right of trial by jury would be denied. "Our institutions are founded on the capacity of jurors to determine intelligently every question presented to them," Van Buren proclaimed.[48]

Specifically, medical experts could confuse jurors with theories and interpretations beyond the capacity of laymen to understand, only to offer totally different and yet equally complex theories on subsequent occasions. The best manner in which to keep criminal irresponsibility where it belonged—a question of law to be determined by a jury—was to define it in such a manner that the jury could render a decision based on a common-sense examination of the facts. If the McNaughtan definition was used, the jury could simply decide whether Freeman understood that the murder of John G. Van Nest was a wrongful act, prohibited by law. Based on the evidence presented regarding Freeman's effort to conceal the crime and his admission of remorse, the prosecution believed with good reason that this decision would be an easy one. If moral insanity was allowed to excuse crime, juries would repeatedly encounter medical experts such as Dr. Brigham, who mystified Van Buren by insisting that every trait used to describe a sane man could in certain cases also describe an insane man. The prosecutors' praise of the old common law and emphasis on the intellectual test of responsibility embodied in the McNaughtan rules stemmed both from a legitimate desire to preserve public safety and a jealous desire to protect their own professional turf.[49]

What held true for the jury was also deemed to be valid for witnesses as to Freeman's state of mind. "Insanity, unless occasioned by some sudden injury, is generally if not always preceded by some marked change, altering the habits or conduct of the patient," Sherwood argued. This change, he continued, was "as readily discovered by a man of ordinary astuteness and sense as by the man of extensive learning, and more likely to be first discovered by the most intimate friends and acquaintances of the diseased." Echoing popular opinion that science was rational and conformed to the laws of nature, the district attorney voiced his unwillingness "to concede that vast learning is necessary in detecting the mental aberrations of our intimate acquaintances." Men of common sense who were well acquainted with Freeman could more easily and legitimately detect insanity than medical experts who had only met him after a plea of insanity had been interposed. Of course, laymen's observations bore much more weight under the tests of insanity used prior to *Commonwealth v. Rogers*. It did not necessarily take a psychiatrist to ascertain whether Freeman understood that he acted wrongly.[50]

Laymen witnesses for the prosecution contradicted the defense's contention that Freeman underwent profound changes in appearance and behavior while in state prison. It is highly probable that the jury, given the climate of opinion at the time regarding professional medicine, accepted the judgments of these laymen as competent. The theory of moral insanity could not be sustained if the facts upon which it rested were contested by credible witnesses. Added to the prosecution's efforts to establish motive and criminal intent, evidence that Freeman's demeanor remained unchanged rendered the moral insanity defense increasingly untenable.

Among these witnesses, Freeman's uncle testified that his nephew had been "rather wild" as a boy and always possessed the same smile and "down look" that the defense presented as evidence of insanity. The uncle, Aaron Demun, added that Freeman "talked as rational" with him on the day of the murder as he ever he had.[51] Abraham A. Vanderheyden, a constable who had known Freeman since the latter was a boy, testified as to Freeman's history of petit and grand larceny. He also noted that Freeman's facial expression remained unchanged from his youth. Furthermore, Vanderheyden asserted that the taciturnity, identified by the defense as a symptom of insanity, was part of Freeman's natural demeanor. Both witnesses were convinced that Freeman was sane.[52]

Thomas F. Monroe, a second law enforcement officer that had observed Freeman since boyhood, testified that Freeman's countenance was unchanged. Monroe also noted that Freeman had been ugly tempered even in childhood, throwing stones at and beating other boys in the streets. Monroe had never observed anything in Freeman's behavior or appearance that he regarded as indicative of insanity. He knew of no one else who had even broached the subject until after the Van Nest killings.[53] Jefferson Wellington likewise testified that Freeman was "pretty ugly" in temperament as a boy and physically appeared "much the same as now." Wellington recalled one altercation in which he whipped Freeman for failing to return a borrowed umbrella. According to Wellington, Freeman retaliated by throwing a flat-iron at him and threatening to kill him.[54] Other prosecution witnesses testified that Freeman's sleeping pattern was perfectly normal; this contradicted the defense's contention that Freeman suffered from insomnia, a symptom of insanity, at the time of the crime. Both the owner of the house where Freeman boarded at the time of the killings and the keeper of the jail where he was taken upon his arrest testified that Freeman slept well.[55]

In thus casting doubt on the contention that Freeman underwent a change in character, the prosecution further reduced the likelihood that the jury would accept the theory of moral insanity in Freeman's case. In spite of his often-mentioned moroseness and ignorance, Freeman certainly did not fit the "wild beast" image that most laymen associated with insanity. To credible laymen testimony, the prosecution added its own medical witnesses. Physicians, most of whom were generally lacking in specific experience treating mental illness, were called to demonstrate that Freeman possessed enough intellectual faculties to be considered responsible. This would cap the prosecution's effort to convince the jury that Freeman was sane under the McNaughtan definition.

Dr. Jedediah Darrow, a local physician and surgeon with little experience in the field of psychiatry, testified that Freeman's memory was intact. Freeman recalled events from his childhood in minute detail, indicating to Darrow that he was not insane.[56] Dr. David Dimon, who also lacked experience in the treatment of mental illness, testified that Freeman was "ignorant and depraved" yet demonstrated no disturbance in his mental faculties or indications of insanity in his general manners or appearance.[57] Leander Bigelow, physician to the state prison, had observed mentally ill inmates but was by no means a specialist in the field. He concluded that Freeman recollected recent as well as remote events equally well and answered "readily and pertinently" all questions that he "seemed to understand."[58] Professor Thomas Spencer of Geneva Medical College presented a complicated theory regarding the operation of and relationship between the mental faculties. His level of complexity smacked of the very mystification of science that antebellum Americans in general, and Jacksonian Democrats in particular, rebelled against. Yet in the end he testified that Freeman exhibited reason, attention, perception, imagination, association, and memory, among other faculties. Simply because Freeman exercised his faculties in absurd ways, Spencer argued, did not mean that he was insane.[59]

Medical witnesses for the prosecution testified that Freeman's ignorance did not preclude the operation of his faculties or abrogate his ability to understand the nature of his actions. The murder of John G. Van Nest, by their estimation, was the willful act of a depraved individual. If the nature of the act itself did not confirm this for the jury, the prosecution was confident that Freeman's racial background would alleviate all doubt. Arguments similar to those that appeared in the press in the wake of the killings were presented once again in the courtroom. The prosecution insisted that Freeman was depraved, violent, unintelligent, and intemperate but not insane. Every opportunity was taken to link these character flaws to Freeman's racial background, in effect negating the defense that his environment had corrupted what began as a normal, healthy life.

Although he deemed Freeman "an *unlearned, ignorant, stupid and degraded negro,*" Sherwood doubted that Freeman could convince "those who have known him and been familiar with his history and habits" that he was insane. The crucial implication was that those who were familiar with the history and habits of the black community would readily see that Freeman's behavior was normal. Sherwood cautioned the jury that the doctors employed by the defense "may be deceived by converting natural imbecility and taciturnity into strong *'symptoms'* of mental derangement." Freeman's behavior, Sherwood maintained, was natural for someone descended from both African and Native American peoples. His aversion to conversation was a product of his lack of education and a natural character trait of Native American peoples. Freeman's demeanor and appearance were not, as the defense insisted, evidence of recent mental derangement brought on by the harsh discipline of the state prison. On the contrary, Sherwood declared, Freeman's "attitude and the expression of his countenance are the same [as prior to his entering prison], and both hereditary." Freeman's "moroseness is natural to him, and, you will observe, is a trait in the natural character of his maternal ancestry," the district attorney concluded.[60]

The defense witnesses, Sherwood added, made another important mistake in the manner in which they attempted to assess Freeman's mental state. Clergyman and doctors, having had no contact with Freeman prior to the trial, "attempted to converse with this unlettered and ignorant negro upon theology, physiology, moral philosophy, and those higher branches that pertain more appropriately to the schools than the cell or the cabin." From these conversations, Sherwood lamented, the defense witnesses concluded that Freeman was "in such a state of dementia as to be unconscious of the commission of a crime." The district attorney maintained that it made little sense to test Freeman's intelligence on subjects to which he had never been exposed in the first place, given his race and level of education. The prosecution, on the other hand, focused on the common events of Freeman's past and the "subjects of which he has acquired any knowledge" in order to test his mind and memory. From such examinations, the prosecution concluded that Freeman's mental capacity had not deteriorated due to disease but had remained at its originally low level.[61]

Norman Dain, a student of the development of psychiatry in the United States, observes that in the Freeman trial many witnesses "used standards for insanity that they regarded as valid only for Negroes, Asians, and Indians." A reading of the trial testimony bears out Dain's contention and serves to illuminate antebellum impressions of the relationship between race and intelligence. The prosecution began with the assumption that the average intelligence of members of the nonwhite races was far beneath that of Caucasians. Prosecution and defense witnesses alike testified that Freeman was childlike in intellect. Numerous prosecution witnesses, as well as certain defense witnesses to the detriment of the insanity plea, failed to view this low level of intellect as indicative of mental derangement. The testimony of witnesses who employed racist standards for insanity generally buttressed the argument that Freeman's marked deficiency in intelligence, as compared to whites, was normal given his race. In doing so, however, the prosecution came dangerously close to portraying Freeman as the intellectual equivalent of the "infant, brute or wild beast" deemed insane even in the eighteenth century.[62]

For example, defense witness James Tyler, a keeper in the state prison, testified that he once struck Freeman on the head with a board in self-defense. Seward attempted to use Tyler's testimony to establish that a sharp blow to the head had likely caused physical damage to Freeman's brain and rendered him deaf. Not so helpful to the defense were Tyler's words, "It never occurred to me that he was insane, but a person of small understanding, below the mediocrity as compared to blacks." To Tyler, Freeman's intelligence was somewhat deficient as compared to the normal degree of intelligence associated with blacks. If Freeman had been white, his "small understanding" would have made much more of an impression. However, Tyler expected little mental ability of blacks, so Freeman did not appear to be peculiar.[63]

Among the many other prosecution witnesses that conformed to the pattern described by Dain was the aforementioned Thomas F. Monroe. Monroe testified that he did not think Freeman's appearance was "as intelligent as that of colored people generally," but that Freeman was "as intelligent as the middle class."[64] Monroe also stated that he "never saw anything of insanity" in Freeman, "nor never heard anything of the kind until since the murder."[65] Freeman's intelligence was rated as average, or even slightly below average for his race. Yet Monroe's expectations were so low for black intelligence in general that nothing in Freeman's demeanor or appearance seemed abnormal. Another example was Stephen S. Austin, a former assistant keeper at the state prison. Under oath, Austin denied having once said that Freeman "was a fool, or that he knew less than a dog." Although he did not believe Freeman could "roll over as quick as a bull terrier," Austin thought that Freeman knew "more than either of my dogs." He firmly stated his belief that the accused murderer was not insane.[66] William Freeman's intellectual capacity inspired unfavorable comparisons with animals, but because of his racial background, it did not convince these witnesses that he was insane.

Dr. David Dimon was among the medical witnesses that assisted the prosecution in attempting to demonstrate that Freeman's mental capacity was typical for his race. Dimon stated that Freeman had "a very low grade of intellect" and was "very ignorant," but then denied that this constituted insanity. Dimon doubted that Freeman had "as much intellect as an ordinary child of fourteen years of age," and concluded that in some respects he would "hardly compare with children of two or three years."[67] Dimon believed that Freeman had not suffered impairment of his mental faculties due to the onset of disease, but rather had always been of low intelligence bordering on imbecility. The defense, Dimon argued, had created the opposite impression using black witnesses whose opinions were "easily biased." Black witnesses, Dimon observed, had considered Freeman to be "as smart as other boys" before he entered prison. White witnesses who knew Freeman in his youth testified to the contrary, terming him "stupid" and "dull." Whites, according to Dimon, were better able to ascertain and interpret Freeman's intellectual capacity because they appreciated the limits of black intelligence. Dimon himself judged Freeman sane despite offering a diagnosis that nearly placed Freeman within the "infant, brute or wild beast" standard of insanity used in the eighteenth century English cases cited by the prosecution.[68]

Freeman's counsel attempted to portray Freeman's behavior in the months and weeks prior to the killings as highly unusual and irrational. The jury heard testimony that Freeman danced and sang in his room in the middle of the night. The prosecution attempted to explain this behavior, as well as account in part for the violence unleashed upon the Van Nest family, by portraying Freeman as being fueled by alcohol. In a manner sometimes direct and other times more subtle, the prosecution linked intemperance to Freeman's racial background. Nathaniel Hersey, a black prosecution witness, swore that Freeman once threatened to kill his own brother-in-law John De Puy because De Puy had told village tavern owners not to let Freeman have liquor.[69] Stephen S. Austin, a white man, recalled asking John De Puy about

Freeman's state of mind once word spread that Freeman would plead not guilty by reason of insanity. According to Austin, De Puy replied that Freeman was "no more crazy than you or I except when he is drunk, and then he is an ugly little devil." [70] De Puy denied ever having made such a statement under cross-examination by the prosecution. [71] A second white witness, however, also contradicted De Puy, prompting the attorney general to ask the jury to disregard De Puy's testimony and to ask the court to commit De Puy for "gross and willful perjury." [72]

In addition, the prosecution called on a tavern keeper, referred to in the trial reports either as Henry Sumkins or Harry Lampkin, to testify that William Freeman had made several visits to his establishment. The tavern keeper testified that Freeman came in the company of "three other black fellows," at least once on the Sabbath, and drank beer and very likely whiskey as well. This by no means proved Freeman to be an abuser of alcohol, but it did display him drinking with other members of his race. It served as additional evidence in support of the prosecution's contention that Freeman was morally corrupt and depraved, rather than insane. [73]

Defense witness Adam Gray, a black man with whom Freeman boarded the winter prior to the killings, testified that Freeman sang, was restless, made noise that sounded like dancing, and "hallooed" during the middle of the night. In the process, however, Gray admitted that Freeman appeared at least once to have been drinking. The prosecution pressed Gray on this point, and he attempted to retreat by claiming that Freeman's behavior merely resembled that of someone intoxicated. He insisted that he did not mean to give the impression that he knew for certain that Freeman was "drunk." [74] The damage had been done, however, for the prosecution was able to cast doubt on the defense's argument that mental derangement caused Freeman's nocturnal behavior. In his closing argument, Van Buren chided Dr. Brigham for his eagerness to equate restless nights with insanity. Brigham, Van Buren protested, would not "sit still till the cross-examination shows that the true entry should be 'Negro Frolic—Rum.' " [75] In other words, Freeman was engaging in intemperate behavior, typical of members of his race, and this in no way signaled insanity.

Furthermore, the prosecution aimed at establishing a pattern of intemperance in Freeman's family, with accompanying references to race. Sally

Freeman's race and her vice were drawn together, playing upon stereotypical images of Native Americans and alcoholism. Nathaniel Lynch, a long-term acquaintance, testified for the prosecution that Freeman's mother was "a drinking woman, and was reputed to be part squaw."[76] The attorney general likewise observed that Freeman's mother "is part Indian, and is, and always was intemperate."[77] Dr. Van Epps admitted under cross-examination that Freeman's mother had lived with him for some time and was "an intemperate woman."[78] Dr. Bigelow concluded that it was not insanity that ran in Freeman's genes as the defense contended, but intemperance. Bigelow had known Sally Freeman for nearly twenty years, and, although she was "a hardworking woman," she was "subject to intemperance." Although the defense claimed that Jane Brown, Freeman's aunt, "died a lunatic," Bigelow had never seen "anything to indicate insanity in her, except intoxication."[79] Both Freeman's father and grandfather were intemperate, the prosecution alleged, Freeman's father having "drank himself to death." The prosecution contended that Sidney Freeman, the defendant's uncle, was the sole relative generally acknowledged to have been legitimately insane.[80]

A corollary to this assault on Freeman's character by means of his race was the prosecution's effort to portray black witnesses as untrustworthy and immoral. As we have seen, a central element of Freeman's defense was the idea that his demeanor and appearance changed. The defense expended considerable effort attempting to prove that Freeman was drastically different when he emerged from prison. It was logical for the defense to call upon those who knew Freeman best, his friends and his family, to demonstrate these marked changes. The prosecution attacked this aspect of the insanity defense on the grounds that it depended so heavily upon black and Native American witnesses. For example, Freeman's mother testified that after her son came out of prison, "he didn't act like the same child—he was changed and didn't appear to know anything." Under cross-examination, the prosecution made it a point to bring out her Native American ancestry. This, coupled with other testimony that revealed Sally Freeman's intemperance, both cast a dark shadow on her son's character and reduced her own credibility as a witness.[81]

John De Puy testified that although Freeman had been an "active, smart boy," his demeanor was markedly different when De Puy observed him several times in the state prison. Freeman "didn't appear as he did before he went to prison—appeared stupid—don't think he knew me," DePuy claimed.[82] As noted earlier, however, white witnesses contradicted other portions of his testimony, prompting accusations of perjury. Given that De Puy was contradicted "in every important fact he swears to," Van Buren urged the jury to completely discount his testimony.[83] There is reason to believe that observers took these charges of dishonesty seriously, despite Seward's efforts to prove that De Puy had not been allowed to completely explain his remarks.[84] David Dimon, editing the trial testimony for publication a quarter century later, wrote, "The testimony of this witness was fully proved to be perjured, and is omitted in consequence."[85]

Lastly, Deborah De Puy, common-law wife of John De Puy's brother, testified that she observed changes in Freeman's intelligence, appearance, and behavior after his release from prison. An acquaintance of Freeman's prior to his imprisonment, De Puy faced invasive cross-examination by the attorney general aimed at illuminating her relationship with Hiram De Puy. Van Buren demanded that she tell the court the date she was married, or who performed the marriage ceremony. When she refused, and Judge Whiting ordered her to answer, De Puy admitted that she could not provide these facts.[86] Van Buren subsequently warned the jury that Seward's medical experts relied upon discreditable witnesses for evidence that Freeman changed. "When asked if he relies on an unchaste black," Van Buren quipped, Dr. Brigham replied "with charming ingenuousness, 'I do believe Deborah.' "[87]

Van Buren urged the jury to note that there was "but one white witness who ever suspected Freeman of insanity before the murder!" In the very community where Freeman was born and raised, and where such a thorough search had been made for testimony, there was "but a single witness on whom you will place any sort of reliance, that swears he suspected [the] prisoner of insanity before the murder," the attorney general proclaimed. He asked the jury to disregard the testimony of witnesses who shared William Freeman's racial background, since these witnesses proved themselves to be intemperate, dishonest, and immoral.[88] At least one local newspaper believed that the prosecution's efforts to discredit these witnesses was effective. The *Cayuga Patriot* reported:"Doct. Brigham placed great stress on the *wakefulness* of Freeman, previous to the murder, which is allowed to be strong proof of insanity, and which was sworn to by some of the colored witnesses, whose testimony may not have been fully credited by the jury." [89]

When time came to synthesize the prosecution's case for the jury, Van Buren reemphasized the implications that the prosecution drew from Freeman's race. William Freeman was "an ignorant and degraded criminal" who was "vicious and intemperate in his habits; of a race socially and politically debased," the attorney general began. In dramatic fashion, he admonished Reverend John Austin for bringing a bible to Freeman in his cell. In Van Buren's opinion, a morally depraved black that could not even read had little use for a book of scriptures. "If the Rev. Mr. Austin knew the natural disposition of the negro as well as I do, and his clerical duty as well as I hope he does, he would have taken Freeman a jewsharp, instead of a Testament to play on!" the attorney general exclaimed. The "natural disposition of the negro" being profligacy and ignorance, Van Buren concluded that religious training was a waste of time. Freeman's demeanor was inalterable, and his actions, including the Van Nest killings, were in character for those of his kind. [90]

The prosecution's use of different standards to detect insanity in non-white peoples caused Seward to fear that Freeman was not receiving a fair and impartial hearing. "Those who seek the extreme vengeance of the law, will, if successful, need all the consolation to be derived from the sanity of the accused, if, at the age of twenty-three, he be thus imbecile in mind and barren in knowledge," he exclaimed during his closing remarks. "An inferior standard of intelligence has been set up here as standard of the negro race, and a false one as a standard of the Asiatic race," he added. Freeman's lineage was divided, Seward noted in romantic prose: "On the paternal side his ancestry is lost among the tiger hunters on the gold coast of Africa, while his mother constitutes a portion of the small remnant of the Narragansett tribe." Therefore, Seward concluded, "it is held that the prisoner's intellect is to be compared with the depreciating standard of the African, and his passions with the violent and ferocious character erroneously imputed to the aborigines." The end result was that indications of "manifest derangement, or at least of imbecility, approaching to idiocy" were set aside on the ground that they harmonized "with the legitimate but degraded character of the races from which he comes." [91]

Seward once again appealed to the Christianity of the jury in pleading that Freeman be treated fairly. "You, gentlemen, have or ought to have, lifted up your souls above the bondage of prejudices so narrow and so mean as these," he exclaimed. The color of Freeman's skin and the form of his features were not impressed upon "the spiritual, immortal mind which works beneath." Freeman was the child of the same heavenly father worshipped by all, and bore "equally with us the proudest inheritance of our race—the image of our Maker." Justice demanded that the jury exact of Freeman "all the responsibilities which should be exacted under like circumstances if he belonged to the Anglo-Saxon race, and make for him all the allowances, and deal with him with all the tenderness" they would expect for themselves. "Hold him to be a man," Seward implored.[92]

Seward acknowledged that the insanity defense was "universally suspected," and since it offered one final possibility of acquittal for the guilty, it was "too often abused." That danger, however, lurked where money, influence, and popular sympathy buoyed the defense. The community had "never seen a poor, worthless, spiritless, degraded negro like *this,* acquitted wrongfully." He encouraged the jury to prove that "such an one can be acquitted rightfully" and to demonstrate that the legal rights of citizens were guaranteed regardless of race. He punctuated his closing argument with a vitriolic denunciation of the state for prosecuting Freeman in spite of his imbecility. "There is not a WHITE man or WHITE woman," he declared, "who would not have been dismissed long since from the perils of such a prosecution, if it had only been proved that the offender was so ignorant and so brutalized as not to understand that the defence of insanity had been interposed."[93]

The prosecution's attack upon the character and credibility of nonwhite witnesses also inspired an impassioned response from the former governor. Seward conceded that in cases where the life, liberty, or property of whites was involved, blacks were forbidden to testify. In New York, and even in slave states, however, blacks were allowed to be witnesses for and against "persons of their *own* caste." Indeed, there was no legal reason to discredit testimony of blacks in Freeman's trial. This issue having been addressed, Seward proceeded to defend individual witnesses from attacks that focused on dishonesty, immorality, and intemperance.[94]

The prosecution denounced John De Puy as an example of the inherent dishonesty of black witnesses. Seward, on the other hand, portrayed him as a heroic defender of the black race. "John De Puy is a colored man, of vigorous frame and strong mind, with good education," Seward argued, insisting that De Puy's testimony was both intelligently given and conclusive. "He claims your respect as a representative of his people, rising to that equality to which it is the tendency of our institutions to bring them," the former governor added. Furthermore, Seward admonished the prosecution for insinuating that De Puy was Freeman's accomplice and had instigated the Van Nest killings. This conjecture stemmed from De Puy's involvement, twelve years earlier, in a financial dispute with John Van Nest's late father-in-law. True, Seward admitted, Peter Wyckoff's widow and daughter were among Freeman's victims, but Wyckoff himself had been dead for six years. John Van Nest was yet to join the Wyckoff family when the financial dispute occurred. Seward argued that this charge was part of a sustained effort by the prosecution to portray De Puy as a depraved and untrustworthy witness. Ultimately, the former governor labeled the perjury charge "persecution," a clear indication of his own belief that race had rendered De Puy vulnerable to attack.[95]

Seward portrayed John De Puy as one who succeeded, in spite of the obstacles placed in his path by racial prejudice. To defend the character and credibility of De Puy's sister-in-law Deborah, Seward focused once again on the community's neglect of nonwhites. Although never formally married, DePuy's fidelity to her husband and children was unquestionable, Seward asserted. It was inappropriate for the prosecution to label her "unchaste" since the securities of marriage were still denied blacks "over more than half this country." If De Puy had been a white woman, Seward admitted, he himself would have regarded her testimony "with caution." In this case, however, the jury must consider the history of blacks in New York. "It is within our own memory that the master's cupidity could divorce husband and wife within this state, and sell their children into perpetual bondage," Seward exclaimed. "Since the Act of Emancipation here," he demanded, "what has been done by the white man to lift up the race from the debasement into which he had plunged it?" Whites, Freeman's counsel maintained, must first "impart to negroes the knowledge and spirit of Christianity, and share with them the privileges, dignity and hopes of citizens and Christians, before we expect of them purity and self-respect." Deborah De Puy should not be condemned as immoral, Seward admonished, when white society had done little to cultivate the morality her race. Remember, he exhorted, "Let him that is without sin cast the first stone."[96]

Van Buren and Seward both treated informal or common-law marriage as if the majority of antebellum whites regarded informal unions as illegitimate and immoral exceptions to common practice. For Van Buren, this approach made it easy to label blacks such as Deborah De Puy "unchaste." Seward, while defending the character and honesty of blacks, somewhat paternalistically apologized for their failure to conform to the moral standards of the white community. His statement that common-law marriage *would* detract from the credibility of a white witness betrayed his belief that informal marriage was an understandable moral lapse given the treatment of blacks in white society.

The treatment of common-law unions by American courts in the early nineteenth century suggests a different reality from that portrayed by Van Buren and Seward. In order to prevent women and children from becoming public charges in the event of the death of a common-law husband, the courts in a majority of American states legitimized the position of these surviving family members for inheritance purposes. The courts granted legal validity to a customary practice because they believed that preventing pauperism was in the best interest of the community.[97] Although some commentators criticized the courts for not upholding the law as the "guardian of the morals of the people," judicial practicality indicates that informal marriages were by no means exceptional among antebellum whites.[98] Judicial recognition of common-law marriage in the United States commenced in New York with the 1809 decision in *Fenton v. Reed*. James Kent, Chief Justice of the New York Supreme Court, ruled that marriage, like any other civil contract, depended for its validity solely on the free consent of the parties. "The consent of the parties may be declared before a magistrate, or simply before witnesses, or subsequently confessed or acknowledged, or the marriage may even be inferred from continual cohabitation, and reputation as husband and wife," Kent wrote.[99] Both Seward and Van Buren seem to have downplayed the history of informal marriage to their own ends. Deborah De Puy's choice of lifestyle was far from exceptional in antebellum American society and was supported, first and foremost, by the law.[100]

The final witness that Seward defended was Sally Freeman, who was accused of alcoholism by the prosecution and deemed unworthy of the jury's confidence. "No woman ever appeared with more sobriety, decency, modesty, and propriety, than she has exhibited here," he exclaimed. If Sally Freeman succumbed to vice, Seward urged the jury to recognize that society was responsible. "The white man enslaved her ancestors of the one race, exiled and destroyed those of the other, and debased them all by corrupting their natural and healthful appetites," he proclaimed. Yet, he admonished, when Mrs. Freeman came to court to testify that she recognized a change in her own son, whom she knew in the way only a mother was able to know her children, "the white man says she is a drunkard!" Appealing once more to the Christianity of the jury, Seward asked heaven to "forgive the white man for adding this last, cruel injury to the wrongs of such a mother!" Not only was white society responsible for placing Sally Freeman in a position where she was susceptible to vice but now also for denying her the right to speak on her son's behalf. The jury could make a small gesture in atonement for society's failures, Seward pleaded, by evaluating her testimony with impartiality.[101]

By the close of testimony on July 21, sixty-five witnesses had been called. Many testified for the second time, having previously appeared before the court during the preliminary trial. As in the preliminary trial, the medical witnesses were evenly divided; this time nine testified that Freeman was insane and eight to the contrary.[102] Seward's closing argument lasted twelve hours, finally drawing to a close on the afternoon of July 22. Van Buren spoke for the remainder of that day's session, with Judge Whiting charging the jury the following day.[103]

As Seward and his colleagues hoped, Whiting spoke to the jury in language that once again reflected Shaw's influence. Since men varied in their opportunities to acquire knowledge, the defendant's knowledge of subjects other than the alleged crime was irrelevant. The only uniform test of responsibility was "knowledge of right and wrong as to the particular act charged." This was a turnaround from the final hours of Freeman's preliminary trial, when Whiting invited the jury to view a general knowledge of right and wrong as satisfactory. Furthermore, a responsible agent had intelligence to know that the act he was about to commit was wrong as well as the ability to remember that punishment would accompany such an act. Responsibility also required reason and will which enabled the individual to compare and choose between the gratification to be obtained from the criminal act and the immunity from punishment to be secured by abstaining.[104]

Whiting once again added an irresistible impulse test to the McNaughtan definition. "If some disease was the acting power within him, which he could not resist, or if he had not sufficient use of his reason to control the passions which prompted the murder, he is not responsible," the judge instructed. If Freeman's "moral and intellectual powers were so deficient that he had not sufficient memory, will, conscience, or controlling power, or if, through the overwhelming violence of mental disease, his intellectual power was for the time obliterated," he was not to be considered a responsible moral agent. By including the irresistible impulse test and the stipulation that Freeman must understand the wrongful nature of his specific act, Whiting invited the jury to consider the theory of moral insanity.[105]

The power of "passions" or emotional forces to overcome the controlling power of intelligence, memory, reason, and will was at the heart of the theory of moral insanity. Like Edmonds, Whiting feared that acts resulting from "mere impulses of passion" would be mistaken for irresistible impulses.[106] Hence he included the stipulation that the jury must be satisfied that there was "a dispossession, by disease, of the free and natural agency" of Freeman's mind. Excusing all crimes resulting from emotional impulses would place society in tremendous danger. Acquittal was only justified when disease, manifested typically by delusion, overwhelmed the individual's ability to accept society's judgment that a particular act was wrong. Whiting never employed the term "moral insanity," nor did he demand that the jury classify Freeman's mental status in the manner employed by "learned men." The jury was only required to determine, based on the facts of the case, if Freeman was sane or insane according to the definition presented.[107]

As noted, the burden of producing evidence and of persuading the jury that a defendant was insane clearly rested upon the defense. However, the standard of proof that the defense was required to meet was not well established. In *Commonwealth v. Rogers*, Chief Justice Shaw advised the jury that "if the preponderance of the evidence were in favor of [Rogers's] insanity—if its bearing and leaning as a whole, inclined that way—they would be authorized to find him insane." Yet in August 1846, Chief Justice Joseph C.

Hornblower of New Jersey ruled that "the proof of insanity, at the time of committing the act, ought to be as clear and satisfactory as the proof of committing the act ought to be in order to find a sane man guilty." In other words, insanity of the accused had to be proved beyond a reasonable doubt, which was then and still remains the most stringent legal standard of proof.[108]

Shaw's approach to insanity jurisprudence was innovative, but as Hornblower's charge demonstrates, there were certainly dissenters. Hornblower rendered the defense's task of proving insanity extremely difficult when he ruled that the jury should be convinced beyond a reasonable doubt that the defendant was insane. In cases such as Freeman's, where moral insanity was presented as the mode of defense, it was exceedingly difficult to meet this standard. Freeman's case depended heavily upon the argument that his actions were prompted by an insane delusion that overwhelmed his intellectual ability to reason. There was no way to prove beyond a reasonable doubt that this was the case. No one could ascertain, with that degree of certainty, William Freeman's thoughts when he killed the Van Nests. If, as was the case in the Freeman trial, the prosecution presented evidence of possible motive and remorse, the jury was likely to convict. Shaw's approach at least allowed defense counsel the opportunity to convince the jury that it was more likely than not that the defendant was insane. In Freeman's case, especially if the charge to the jury included an irresistible impulse test or other elements of moral insanity in the definition of irresponsibility, Shaw's approach raised the possibility of acquittal.

Whiting chose a middle ground between the two extremes represented by Shaw and Hornblower. He employed far less specific language, stating merely that to acquit by reason of insanity, it had to be "clearly proved, to the satisfaction of the jury" that the accused was insane according to the definition provided. The language "clearly proved, to the satisfaction of the jury" did not imply that the jury needed to be convinced beyond a reasonable doubt. Whiting's language did imply that the jury should hold the defense to a more stringent standard than a preponderance of the evidence. The phrase "clearly proved" most closely resembles the standard known as clear and convincing evidence, which is generally employed in civil cases. This standard has been defined in various ways, the most useful being that the "jury must be persuaded that the truth of the contention is highly probable." Slightly greater room was left the jury for doubt under this standard than the standard advocated by Hornblower. Still, the jury was invited to convict unless fairly certain that Freeman was insane. This did not bode well for Freeman, since the chances were slim that any antebellum jury would be so intensely captivated by the theory of moral insanity as to excuse the slaughter of a family.[109]

On the highly relevant subject of expert medical witnesses, Whiting was somewhat ambivalent. To the benefit of the defense, he took the heart of his remarks on this subject directly from Shaw and Edmonds.[110] Yet he added some cautionary comments that were inspired by the context of the Freeman trial. He noted, first of all, that medical opinions in cases involving insanity were "competent evidence" and were entitled in many instances "to great consideration and respect." He also included a nearly verbatim recitation of Shaw's remarks regarding questions that were "beyond the scope of the observation and experience of men in general" but which were frequently under the consideration of certain professionals. Since many of the medical witnesses had never observed Freeman prior to the Van Nest killings, Whiting sought guidance directly from *Commonwealth v. Rogers*. He advised that "the opinions of witnesses who have been conversant with insanity in its various forms, and who have had the care and superintendence of insane persons" were competent evidence even though these witnesses had not examined the defendant at the time of the alleged insane act.[111]

Whiting instructed the jury that experience was the key factor to consider when evaluating expert testimony. The opinions of "persons of great experience, and in whose correctness and sobriety of judgement just confidence can be had" deserved "the respectful consideration of a jury." Such witnesses were of great assistance to the jury in weighing the influence of facts and circumstances that ordinary persons were not prepared to interpret. The opinions of persons "not educated to the profession, but who have been so situated as to have given particular attention to the disease, and to patients suffering under it" were also competent evidence. Such opinions were not to be valued as highly, however, as those of medical professionals possessing specific experience treating the insane. The opinions of medical men of small experience in the field of mental illness deserved very little consideration, however. Yet again echoing Shaw, Whiting cautioned the jury that medical witnesses were not to "judge of the credit of the [other] witnesses, or of the truth of the facts testified to by others." It was the jury's responsibility to decide which facts were satisfactorily proved. If certain facts were accepted as proved, the jury should then ask the medical witnesses to offer opinions based on those facts as to Freeman's mental state when the crime took place.[112]

The judge's downplaying of the opinions of inexperienced professionals certainly applied more readily to the prosecution's medical witnesses than it did to Dr. Brigham and his counterparts for the defense. But Whiting also responded to the prosecution's misgivings over the intrusion of complex medical theories into the realm of law. He cautioned the jury against the opinions of medical professionals who had "crude or visionary notions" or who had "some favorite theory to support."[113] Of the prosecution witnesses, only Dr. Spencer and his complex theory of mental faculties could have fallen under such a classification. This comment probably encouraged the jury to receive the opinions of Seward's medical professionals, especially Dr. Brigham, with caution. Given popular suspicion of medical professionals in and out of the courtroom, even such a tacit warning probably went a long way. Moral insanity, if accepted as part of the definition of legal insanity, depended heavily upon the testimony of experienced medical professionals. Whiting, although influenced by Shaw and Edmonds, was not entirely prepared to allow these professionals an overwhelming degree of influence in the realm of the law. The common man could benefit from medical professionals' interpretation of human behavior, but the law must reserve for the jury the right and the ability to determine legal responsibility. Given the enormity of the alleged crime and public desire for an affirmation of the law's power to protect, Whiting's remarks most likely limited the impact that expert medical testimony had upon the jury.

After Whiting concluded on July 23, the jury deliberated for two hours before rendering a verdict of guilty. The following morning at 6:30, Judge Whiting sentenced William Freeman to hang on the afternoon of Friday, September 18, 1846.[114] Facing a steep uphill battle from the start, Seward and his colleagues failed to convince twelve Cayuga County residents that Freeman should be spared criminal punishment. The brutality of Freeman's act coupled with a perceived laxity in the administration of justice rendered the chances of acquittal remote from the outset. The purely legal challenges that Freeman's counsel confronted in attempting to clearly prove insanity further increased the likelihood of conviction. Legal tradition, popular conceptions of insanity, and suspicions of medical professionals made it exceedingly difficult for Freeman's counsel to introduce moral insanity as an excuse for criminal acts. Prosecutors were able to convincingly portray Freeman as a responsible agent according to the specifications of the McNaughtan rules. The rules closely paralleled popular convictions regarding the nature of crime, and it is reasonable to conclude that the jury felt considerably more comfortable with the prosecution's approach than with that of the defense.

Furthermore, Freeman's racial background amplified his demonic image in the eyes of the jury. Even if the jury acknowledged that society had failed to temper Freeman's innate depravity and ignorance, he was not absolved of responsibility for such a heinous crime. Freeman's race aside, John G. Van Nest's killing was regarded as the willful act of a wicked heart. Perhaps society's neglect of nonwhite children limited Freeman's choices in life, but it is doubtful that the jury entertained the possibility that society rendered Freeman incapable of resisting violent urges. This would have required acceptance of an environmental explanation of criminal behavior, something that was unlikely in the antebellum United States. The McNaughtan definition championed by the prosecution reflected the public's conviction that only raving lunatics or imbeciles were unable to choose good over evil. All that legal guilt required was the knowledge that murder was wrong.

Nevertheless, the legal and moral challenges mounted by Seward and his colleagues made the Freeman case a "case of trouble." The enormity of the Van Nest killings, coming as they did on the heels of the failure to convict Wyatt, guaranteed that Freeman would be vigorously prosecuted. The odds, as we have seen, certainly favored the prosecution, but recent trends in criminal justice worried a significant portion of the public. The issues raised by the defense and Freeman's supporters among the public at large forced the prosecution to call upon the jury's innate sense of justice and natural desire to feel safe in their own community. Seward and his colleagues invested a tremendous amount of time and energy in Freeman's defense and truly made the trial a venue for a heated debate concerning principles of criminal punishment, legal definitions of insanity, theoretical criminology, and antebellum race relations. Although no legal precedent was established, so much was as stake and so controversial were the issues that social and legal patterns were revealed in sharp detail. This is precisely why the trial deserves our attention.

6

Aftermath

WHEN WILLIAM FREEMAN WAS SENTENCED on July 24, another significant exchange took place that cast doubt upon the verdict rendered in the case. Speaking very loudly, in order that Freeman could hear him, Judge Whiting asked the convicted murderer if he remembered John G. Van Nest. Freeman nodded assent and did the same when Whiting asked him if he knew he had killed Van Nest. "You have been tried for killing him, do you understand that?" the judge then inquired. Freeman replied, "Don't know." Whiting pressed for some evidence that Freeman understood his current situation, once again demanding, "the jury say you're guilty; that you did kill him—do you understand that?" Freeman again responded, "Don't know." Finally, when the judge asked Freeman if he understood that he was about to be sentenced to hang for killing Van Nest, the response was "yes." The last question Whiting asked Freeman was whether or not he had anything to say against his pending sentence. His ultimate fate about to be determined, Freeman said nothing more than "I don't know." [1]

Whiting had endeavored to see Freeman at least stand trial for the murder of John G. Van Nest. He had then encouraged the jury to consider, with extreme caution, the theory proposed by the defense. His charge to the jury in the trial on the indictment certainly reflected the influence of Shaw and Edmonds in a case where public anger hardly encouraged the inclusion of a broader definition of insanity. In sentencing Freeman, Whiting employed language that reflected popular expectations of the law. "While we give full effect to the plea of Insanity as an excuse for crime," he proclaimed, "we learn with great satisfaction that there is in the community, intelligence enough to discriminate between acts originating in moral depravity and ignorance, and those which proceed from the impulse of disease." The rule by which man must be judged, he added was "whether he had knowledge of right and wrong in regard to the act for which he is on trial." By that rule Freeman had been tried and convicted, Whiting noted, "and whatever theories learned men may create, there is no other which can be safely introduced into a court of justice."[2]

Whiting trumpeted the fairness of the proceedings but openly acknowledged that race had indeed been an issue. By virtue of the statutory prohibition of the trial of insane persons, Freeman had been given "the benefit of two verdicts." The jury in the preliminary trial found him sane, enabling him to be tried on the indictment for the murder of John G. Van Nest. Insanity constituted Freeman's "whole defense" in the trial on the indictment, and a second panel of twelve men found him sane and therefore guilty of murder. Whiting hoped that those who doubted Freeman's sanity would "yield to an opinion thus carefully formed and solemnly expressed." That this "degraded, ignorant felon, who has consummated his wickedness by these atrocious murders" had received the benefit of two verdicts, left no ground for the charge that "the administration of justice is partial or prejudiced by reason of his color, his social degradation, or his monstrous crimes." The slow and tedious nature of the proceedings was a testimony to the fairness of the criminal justice system, Whiting proclaimed. In conclusion, he expressed his confidence that "in the minds of all reflecting men, a confidence will arise in the power of the laws to protect the rights of our fellow citizens, and that the result will reflect honor upon the institutions and laws of the country." This statement was highly relevant given community concern that antigallows reformers and proponents of the insanity defense were sabotaging the justice system.[3]

After stating clearly his belief that Freeman had been given the full protection of the law, Whiting addressed the issue of race and social responsibility. "The lessons to be drawn from this tragic event are many," he noted, the most impressive being "that there is a duty upon society to see to the moral cultivation of the colored youth, now being educated for good or evil in the midst of us." This was "so obvious that it needs no comment," Whiting proclaimed. Brief and to the point, Whiting acknowledged that there was truth in the social criticism offered by commentators from as diverse backgrounds as John Austin, Horace Greeley, William Lloyd Garrison, John De Puy, Amariah Brigham, David Wright, and William H. Seward. Whether or not most people admitted it, society bore a share of the responsibility for the immorality and criminality of blacks. This did not, however, alter the fact that Freeman had been judged legally responsible for the killings at Fleming. Nothing regarding the circumstances of his childhood or adolescence could mitigate that judgment.[4]

Several journals enthusiastically received Freeman's conviction as an indication of the limited influence of medicine in the courtroom. The *Daily Cayuga Tocsin* expressed the opinion that the evidence presented by the medical witnesses for the defense, as well as their professional status, struck "at the very foundation of society." Society was destined to become "one vast asylum of lunatics," the *Tocsin* warned, if the law was "to be clouded by their theories, and to be made to bend to the influence which official station has given them, to speak as oracles." These were indeed the very same concerns expressed by the prosecution during the trial. Also echoing the prosecution, the *Tocsin* voiced its alarm at the defense's theory that atrocious acts themselves, committed in the absence of adequate motive, signaled insanity. The *Tocsin* regarded Freeman's conviction as evidence that there was "an enlightened public opinion which puts its foot upon [such] visionary theories" and which would "uphold the law" against assault by "modern lunatic theorists." The editors of the *Tocsin* encouraged that "enlightened public opinion," in hopes of limiting "the mischief of such *experts*, who would exalt the dreams of medical research above the common law, and above common sense, and common understanding." The *Albany Argus* agreed wholeheartedly with these sentiments. "The *Tocsin* speaks," the *Argus* observed, "with a just reprobation of the extraordinary (or rather, ordinary) defence of insanity, and the grounds taken by some of the medical witnesses, for the prisoner."[5]

The *Cayuga Patriot* was pleased that the jury in Freeman's main trial heeded Whiting's warning against allowing medical witnesses to "judge of the credit of the witnesses, or of the truth of the facts testified to by others."[6]

The *Patriot* congratulated the jury for having the common sense to disregard the opinions of "medical theorists" if those opinions were not based upon clearly established factual evidence. Upon many contested facts, the editors observed, the "very intelligent jurors would judge for themselves, without regard to the opinions of medical men, who appeared not to have listened very attentively to the evidence." The *Patriot* charged that the expert medical witnesses for the defense based some of their conclusions solely upon facts attested to by other defense witnesses. The members of the jury, the editors remarked with satisfaction, were astute enough to weigh these conclusions against the whole of the evidence. In some cases, the *Patriot* concluded, "very credible witnesses" contradicted the premises upon which the defense's expert opinions were based. In the end, the jury "heard all of the evidence, gave it their strict attention," and, in the opinion of the *Patriot,* "came to the right conclusion." The editors were gratified that the jury did not allow the sheer stature of the defense's medical witnesses to inflate the value of their testimony. The *Patriot* perceived that common sense, much as the prosecution had hoped, carried the day with these twelve men.[7]

Satisfaction with the conviction was far from unanimous, however. In the wake of Freeman's trial, the preeminent legal journal of the day criticized the manner in which American courts determined legal responsibility. The editors of the *Law Reporter* were dismayed by what they viewed as "remarkable disregard of established scientific facts" in recent judicial decisions and popular discussions regarding insanity. It is interesting to note that the attitudes that most alarmed the editors were, in fact, those very same attitudes demonstrated by the prosecution in the Freeman trial. The *Law Reporter* was incensed by the frequency with which the courts treated insanity "as if it were susceptible of none of those improvements which the progress of knowledge is constantly effecting in every other branch of science." The nation's courts anachronistically looked to the authority of Lords Hale and Coke rather than to the most recent scientific developments in the study of mental illness. Lord Hale himself, the *Law Reporter* observed, "was obviously desirous of making his views faithfully reflect the knowledge of his times" and therefore freely consulted medical authorities. Hale's approach, the editors suggested, exemplified the ideal relationship between law and science. Had Hale's successors "manifested any of the great jurist's endeavors to shape his opinions by the light of science, instead of thoughtlessly reechoing his principles," the editors lamented, "we should have been spared a host of decisions equally discreditable to jurisprudence, to medical science, and to humanity." The Freeman trial certainly fit the editors' description of a prosecution and decision based upon the rejection of recent medical advances in the study of mental illness.[8]

The *Law Reporter* also criticized the legal system for its inconsistencies in dealing with insanity and for its failure to adequately protect the insane in cases where mental illness was not easily diagnosed. The editors noted that in cases where the insanity of the accused was "manifest to the most superficial observer," acquittals were not unusual. The same held true, they claimed, for cases in which the alleged offense was minor or the assistance of "powerful friends and eminent counsel" was forthcoming. William Freeman clearly did not appear insane to all observers and his offense was far from minor. His counsel was highly capable, and Freeman did have a few influential "friends" among antigallows reformers. By and large, however, the Freeman case more closely fit the editors' description of the typical case in which justice was denied. When the insanity of the accused required "some time and investigation to discover" or popular feeling was aroused against him, demanding a victim, protection of the law was often withdrawn. While Freeman's state of mind at the time of the Van Nest killings was enigmatic, the public vehemently desired retribution and an affirmation of the law's ability to protect. The talents of Freeman's counsel and the fortitude of his small cadre of advocates only intensified the desire for swift and severe justice. By the *Law Reporter's* estimation, Freeman's chances of acquittal were never more than marginal.[9]

Ultimately, the *Law Reporter* concluded that the McNaughtan rules exemplified the legal system's shortcomings in addressing insanity as a legal excuse. In the rules, the editors claimed, the House of Lords sought "a general expression of the law capable of embracing every possible case, and working injustice to none." In the *Law Reporter's* opinion, the rules fell woefully short of that intended goal. Those in the community "who are best acquainted with the phenomena of the diseased mind," the editors argued, confirmed that nine-tenths of the inmates of insane asylums were able to distinguish right from wrong "with all their original acuteness." The insane, while recognizing the illegality of their acts, often considered themselves "absolved from the obligations of the law." Medical authorities testified that the insane "deliberately commit acts, knowing them to be contrary to the law and followed by punishment which, perhaps, they are ready to receive, in order to obtain some fancied good." In some cases, the motives for this behavior were "too vague and indefinite to be understood by others." The insane, the *Law Reporter* said, "move in a sphere beyond the reach of the ordinary motives of human conduct, and are a law unto themselves." The editors at length concluded that the McNaughtan rules were inadequate because they were based on the uninformed assumption that the insane reasoned as logically as the mentally healthy. The insane were unjustly punished simply because they failed to logically apply the abstract concept of socially approved/prohibited behavior to their own actions.[10]

The *Law Reporter*'s conclusions regarding insanity were much akin to those that Freeman's counsel tried to impress upon the jury in both of his trials. The editors protested that the tests of responsibility that generally guided the courts made no reference to the "undeniable" scientific fact that the moral or affective faculties were "generally, and often exclusively impaired in insanity." Seward and Wright clearly expressed their lack of confidence in the capacity of the McNaughtan rules to encompass all relevant forms of insanity. Freeman's counsel assailed the prosecution for advocating a legal definition of insanity that exclusively tested the knowing powers of the accused. At the same time, Seward and his colleagues labored painstakingly to convince the jury that moral insanity should excuse criminal acts. The *Law Reporter*'s dismay sheds plenty of light on the manner in which mental illness was dealt with in antebellum courts.[11]

The *New York Journal of Medicine and the Collateral Sciences* voiced similar dissatisfaction with the McNaughtan definition of legal insanity. Following Freeman's conviction, the editors remarked that Freeman was "tried by a rule which is unsound and cannot hold." The difficulty with McNaughtan, they argued, was that it was a "test of *knowledge* not of *power*." The knowledge of right and the power to do it, they insisted, were "as distinct as science and art," since a criminal act presumed "knowledge, motive, and will." If the motive for the killings was the product of delusion, and the will was "incapable of obeying any but the insane impulse," criminal responsibility should be annulled. Ultimately they concluded that the more practical approach to legal insanity, in Freeman's case and those similar to it, was that taken by Lord Erskine in the 1800 trial of Hadfield. Erskine postulated, and the editors agreed, that legal responsibility was annulled if the act in question was proved to be the "immediate unqualified offspring" of insane delusion. The editors were convinced that Freeman was "laboring under some delusive notions," there being no rational motive for the killings. The extent of Freeman's knowledge of right and wrong, in the "legal, or moral and religious sense," was problematic.[12]

Like their counterparts at the *Law Reporter,* the editors of the *New York Journal of Medicine and the Collateral Sciences* commented extensively on what they believed to be the true nature of insanity. "Every person conversant with insanity knows, that many insane persons have committed acts which they knew to be wrong, and of the criminality of which they were at the time perfectly conscious," the journal remarked. Cases had been documented in which insane persons killed others purposely "in order to receive the punishment of death at the hands of the law." All of the standard writers on medical jurisprudence, including Alfred Swaine Taylor, Isaac Ray, Amariah Brigham, and T. R. Beck, repudiated the McNaughtan definition, the editors observed. These authorities agreed that "a knowledge of the law, whether human or divine, does not imply the control of the *will.*" Those conversant with the nature of insanity, the editors concluded, agreed that the "possession of conscience does not prove that instinctive impulses may not be too powerful to resist." Although Whiting had invited the jury to consider moral insanity in Freeman's main trial, the editors felt that the spirit of McNaughtan, so aggressively advocated by the prosecution, had held sway. After all, their editorial noted, in the "mind of the masses—the great body of the community—the idea of *crime* is always associated with those of injury and wrong, no matter what the state of mind of the individual may have been who committed the wrong."[13]

The course and outcome of Freeman's trials likewise did little to alter the opinions of those that truly and consistently believed he was insane. People that shared Seward's sympathy for the mentally ill lauded his efforts on behalf of Freeman. Dr. John McCall praised Seward for his "unremitted labors . . . in the cause of truth and humanity." McCall encouraged the exhausted Seward to conserve his strength since his efforts might be "required to be put forth, in behalf of suffering humanity, at some future day." [14] The abolitionist Gerrit Smith wrote Seward, "If the people are saved from the crime of murdering this idiot, it will be owing, under God, to yourself." [15]

In August 1846, a pamphlet produced from the trial notes of Seward's law partner Samuel Blatchford was published. *Argument in Defense of William Freeman* drew tremendous attention both to Seward's ability as a lawyer and to the merits of Freeman's case. Seward recognized that his efforts on behalf of Freeman were beginning to bring the financial rewards that he had sought at the start. "The argument in Freeman case is doing wonders for me professionally, and bids fair to secure me business of that better kind which is most profitable and least unpleasant," he wrote Weed. [16] Even some pro-capital-punishment journals, which had joined in the outcry for retribution, acknowledged Seward's ability and were forced to give some credence to the defense employed on Freeman's behalf. For example, the *New York Courier and Morning Enquirer* praised Seward for "the superiority with which he presents his facts and his arguments and for the zeal with which he enforces them upon his hearers." Seward was heralded for his "love of justice, his great humanity, his philanthropy, and his unquestionable abilities." [17] The Democratic *Daily Cayuga Tocsin* also reacted positively to Seward's pamphlet, calling Seward's work "a noble instance of the devotion which professional men often make for the wretched outcast of society." The editors were so impressed that they disparaged any effort to attribute Seward's devotion to "unworthy motives" in order to weaken its "apparent force and beauty." [18]

Horace Greeley's *New York Daily Tribune,* sympathetic to Freeman's cause from the start, was particularly moved by one passage in the pamphlet. Seward, acknowledging public outrage at his role in the Wyatt and Freeman trials, lamented at one point that his own remains would someday lie "unhonored—neglected—spurned!" Perhaps one day, Seward added, when "passion and excitement" had subsided, "some *Indian* —some *Negro*—may erect over them an humble stone, and thereon this epitaph—'HE WAS FAITHFUL!' " The *Tribune* appended the following: "Wherever the tidings of this strange trial shall be wafted, throughout the civilized world, there the name SEWARD will be embalmed as a sacred treasure, in the hearts of all lovers of humanity—of all who sympathize with the degraded and enslaved

Ethiopian." In Greeley's opinion, it was a measure of the former governor's humanity that he had defended "this forsaken, pitiable, son of Africa," who possessed no resources with which to pay for legal services. Seward, according to the *Tribune,* was among the few who had responded with humanity to this unfortunate soul.[19]

The pamphlet's publication by no means satisfied all of Seward's critics or convinced the public that Freeman had been wrongfully convicted. The *Albany Evening Atlas* quipped that Seward had carefully edited the pamphlet prior to publication. Even those that remained critical, however, were unable to deny the publicity generated by the Freeman trial. The *Atlas* editors grudgingly conceded that "the reputation of the counsel engaged," as well as the "singular character of the defence," would likely "give the published speech a multitude of readers." Publicity notwithstanding, public desire for swift and severe justice had not abated.[20]

All efforts to reverse Henry Wyatt's conviction and to delay his execution failed. After he mounted the gallows, Wyatt begged the community not to censure his counsel. "They have done all they could for me," he exclaimed, which to many in the community was precisely the problem. On the afternoon of August 17, "the drop fell, and Wyatt instantly passed into eternity, without a struggle!" Although the *Daily Cayuga Tocsin* called the execution a "tragic event," the editors could scarcely mask their satisfaction.[21] Still, Freeman's lawyers were undeterred in their efforts on his behalf, their conviction that he was insane never wavering. The day of Wyatt's execution, Seward wrote a letter to Governor Wright asking him to pardon Freeman. "I believe him absolutely and hopelessly insane, sinking from monomania into dementia," Seward stated. Freeman was "a lunatic, and committed his crimes under the influence of an insane delusion," Seward wrote, the jury having overlooked the evidence that supported this conclusion. For the governor's edification, Seward enclosed a copy of his *Argument in Defense of William Freeman.*[22]

Silas Wright was by no means unsympathetic to the mentally ill. Upon Wright's death in September 1847, the *American Journal of Insanity,* published from the State Lunatic Asylum at Utica, spoke in terms of highest praise for the late governor. "At different periods he had relatives and acquaintances as patients at this institution, and, without exception, no one has ever shown so

great an interest in the welfare of friends here, as the late Gov. Wright exhibited," the obituary stated. By the "simplicity of his manners, his kindness
and true genuine sympathy with the suffering and afflicted," Wright was said
to have "won the affections of all who saw him."[23] Wright's sympathy extended to the criminally insane. In July 1846, Wright commuted to life imprisonment the sentence of Abram Wilcox, convicted for the murder of
Samuel McKinster in Saratoga County. An insanity plea had been interposed on Wilcox's behalf, and after a careful review, Wright determined that
the case "admitted of so wide a difference of construction" that he felt "con-
strained to lean to the side of mercy."[24]

Wright studied Freeman's case with equal care, reading Seward's pamphlet as well as reports from Judge Whiting and other materials connected
with the proceedings. On September 7, the governor wrote to Seward expressing his regrets. "The case is a painful one in every aspect of it," Wright
explained, "and yet it would have been pleasant to my feelings to find it in
my power, consistently with my sense of duty, to save this man from the
awful fate impending over him." However, the governor discovered nothing
in the trial records that in his opinion warranted the overruling of "the verdicts of the two juries, finding the fact of sanity." Wright, like other observers, interpreted the preliminary verdict as conclusive regarding
Freeman's state of mind. The verdict in the main trial merely reiterated that
which had already been determined, namely that Freeman was a responsible
agent. Seward and his colleagues disagreed, and they turned to their next recourse, the Supreme Court of the State of New York.[25]

Sympathetic members of the community assisted Freeman's attorneys in
their continued efforts on his behalf. In mid-September, a petition "signed
by some of our most eminent Jurists, Physicians and others" was sent to the
governor, pleading for the commutation of Freeman's sentence "on the
ground of his insanity."[26] In the meantime, Seward submitted a bill of exceptions covering issues raised by both the preliminary trial and the trial on
the indictment. Most importantly, Seward argued that the definition of insanity proposed by the prosecution and prescribed by the court in its charge
to the jury in the preliminary trial was erroneous. The trial court advised the
jury to focus on Freeman's ability to distinguish right from wrong, instead of
his capacity to stand trial. Seward also argued that the preliminary verdict

"was defective, in not finding the fact to be tried" under the requirements of the statute. Lastly, Freeman's counsel charged that in the trial on the indictment, the court improperly allowed the prosecution to introduce the preliminary verdict as conclusive evidence of Freeman's present sanity. The defense was prohibited from presenting any evidence to the contrary, produced by examinations of Freeman after the date on which the preliminary verdict was rendered. The issue of Freeman's present sanity had been settled, the trial court ruled, and was not open to argument before the jury in the trial on the indictment.[27]

On September 14, just four days before Freeman was to be executed, Justice Samuel Beardsley, after consultation with the Chief Justice of the New York State Supreme Court, allowed a writ of error in Freeman's case. The writ of error also operated as a stay of execution, eliminating the immediate fear that Freeman would go to the gallows.[28] In November, the parties convened in Rochester to argue the bill of exceptions before Justices Greene C. Bronson, Samuel Beardsley, and Freeborn G. Jewett. Van Buren once again attended, lending his legal acumen to the effort to sustain Freeman's conviction.[29] Seward argued the exceptions on behalf of Freeman who "remained in chains in the jail of Cayuga County."[30] In January 1847, the Supreme Court reversed the decision of the Cayuga County Court of Oyer and Terminer and granted Freeman a new trial.[31]

The higher court voiced its dissatisfaction with both Whiting's charge and the verdict in Freeman's preliminary trial. Justice Samuel Beardsley, writing for the court, offered the common law interpretation of the statute prohibiting the trial of insane persons. Sanity for the purpose of being tried was equated with capability of understanding the nature and object of the criminal proceedings, comprehension of one's own condition in reference to such proceedings, and ability to conduct one's defense "in a rational manner." Derangement or unsoundness of mind on subjects unrelated to the proceedings at hand was irrelevant. Beardsley recognized that mental illness could affect the ability of the accused to appreciate the immorality of his particular act. The accused might possess "a very just perception of the moral qualities of most actions" and yet labor under an insane delusion that extended to the alleged crime or the contemplated trial. If such were the case, the accused was not "in a fit condition to make his defence, however sound his mind may in other respects be." By furnishing a single criterion of sanity, namely a general capacity to distinguish between right and wrong, the trial court invited the jury to pronounce sane an individual who was not competent in mind to make his defense in a rational manner.[32]

The higher court ruled that the proper instructions would have been that Freeman was to be deemed sane "if he had a knowledge of right and wrong in respect to the crime with which he stood charged."[33] Even in the first set of instructions, in which Whiting included elements of the irresistible impulse test, he did not emphasize that knowledge of right and wrong should extend specifically to the alleged criminal act. We cannot say with any certainty that if Whiting had charged the jury differently, Freeman would have been found insane and hence incapable of standing trial. Freeman was certainly not rational on the subject of seeking redress for wrongful imprisonment. He did not seem to genuinely believe that his particular act was wrong, and he did not betray any appreciation for the gravity of the circumstances in which his act had placed him. When asked to explain his actions, he generally stated that he had been wrongfully imprisoned and had to get "his pay." Yet Freeman did seem to understand that killing, in general, was wrong under the law and punishable by death. Furthermore, he did express some degree of guilt over his actions and did flee the crime scene, which may have convinced the jury that he knew his own particular act was wrong. What is clear, however, is that the prosecution had little difficulty establishing that Freeman possessed a general knowledge of right and wrong.[34]

The higher court ruled that the preliminary verdict was defective in that it "did not directly find any thing, and certainly not the point in issue, but evaded it by an argumentative finding." The trial court was faulted for failing to require the jury to "pass directly on the question of insanity." This finding "would be objectionable in a civil procedure," Beardsley concluded, "and in a criminal case should not be allowed."[35] Judge Whiting essentially ruled that William Freeman was to be tried on a murder indictment without first having been pronounced sane for the purpose of standing trial. The community's desire for vengeance and concern for its own security may very likely have motivated the judge to see that Freeman at least went to trial. He certainly was not willing to interpret statutory or common law in such a manner as to open windows through which Freeman could escape trial altogether.

Furthermore, the higher court held the Cayuga County Court of Oyer and Terminer's interpretation of the preliminary verdict to be erroneous. During Freeman's main trial, the prosecutors paid lip service to the fact that the preliminary verdict meant nothing more than that Freeman was in a "suitable condition to be tried."[36] However, when Freeman's counsel attempted to present medical witnesses who had not interviewed Freeman until after the preliminary verdict was rendered, the prosecution objected. When Seward called Doctors Thomas Hun and James McNaughton, professors at Albany Medical College, the attorney general inquired as to what Seward intended to prove by their testimony. Seward replied that these doctors, through their conversations with Freeman, observations of his personal appearance, and interpretation of the trial testimony, would offer their opinions that Freeman was presently insane and was so on March 12, 1846. Van Buren argued that the verdict in the preliminary trial was conclusive as to Freeman's present sanity and could not be contradicted by evidence. The attorney general demanded that the two medical professors refrain from delivering testimony based on anything derived from personal examinations of Freeman after the date on which the preliminary verdict was rendered.[37]

The trial court sustained Van Buren's objections. The doctors were instructed that they were allowed to offer opinions as to Freeman's sanity at the time of the crime but that such opinions were to be based only upon facts within their knowledge before the sixth of July or upon the personal appearance of the prisoner. They were not to deliver testimony based upon any information gained through conversations with Freeman since July 6 or based upon the trial testimony.[38] Seward was outraged by the ruling and perceived accurately that the trial court founded upon the preliminary verdict "a judicial statute of limitations, and denies [the defense] all opportunity to prove the prisoner insane, after the sixth of July." He astutely argued that the preliminary verdict had neither been pleaded nor proved during the trial on the indictment. Yet Freeman's present state of mind was certainly relevant to the circumstances surrounding the events of March 12. Why, Seward demanded, should the jury be forced to accept Freeman's current sanity as a proven fact, when it had not even been argued before them in the trial on the indictment?[39]

The higher court accepted Seward's reasoning. Beardsley wrote that the trial court's decisions clearly showed that it regarded the preliminary verdict as "absolutely conclusive for all purposes, in this case, that the prisoner on and after the sixth of July, was in a sane state." The trial court accepted the prosecution's contention that the issue of Freeman's present mental capacity had been settled. Since Freeman was considered legally sane from July 6 forward, no evidence to the contrary was to be presented in court. Even if medical experts believed, based on interviews conducted afterwards, that Freeman was unquestionably insane, they were forbidden from saying so in court. Beardsley affirmed that the preliminary trial was only meant to determine whether Freeman was sane for the purpose of standing trial. That verdict was not before the trial court nor was it material to the trial on the indictment. However, since Freeman's state of mind at the time of the trial was a relevant fact in the trial on the indictment, the trial court had no legal right to prohibit Freeman's counsel from presenting evidence in relation to that fact. The prosecution attempted to use the preliminary verdict as an established fact in the main trial without conceding to the defense its right to present evidence contradicting that fact.[40]

Beardsley emphasized that a murder indictment was "not to be tried piecemeal, but at one time, and by a single jury." Facts that were relevant to the guilt or innocence of the accused were to be argued in front of the jury, and the jury was to decide which facts had been adequately proved. Beardsley could not help feeling that medical opinions based on Freeman's behavior in July were relevant to the issue of his state of mind the previous March. "It will sometimes, undoubtedly be found, and perhaps not infrequently, that the mental malady is such that an examination would disclose beyond all peradventure to a skilful physician, what must have been the condition of the patient for months or years before," the Supreme Court opinion stated.[41]

The higher court in effect recognized that the prosecution had successfully turned a verdict that failed even to settle the issue of Freeman's competency to stand trial into a pronouncement that Freeman was incontrovertibly sane from July 6 forward. The trial court's approval of this approach makes sense only in the context of public outrage and desire for justice. Freeman's defenders were denied the opportunity to produce new evidence that had not been presented in the preliminary trial. That trial, of course, had gone poorly for Freeman, and the defense desperately needed something new. The trial court limited the defense's options and left Freeman's counsel only to hope that twelve new faces would view the same old evidence in a new light. Plus the prosecution's contention that the defendant sitting in court was presently sane was certainly not lost on the jury. Whiting's approval signaled to the jury that Freeman was, in truth, presently sane, rendering it exceedingly difficult for the defense to argue convincingly that Freeman had been insane just a few months earlier.[42]

Judge Bowen Whiting displayed chameleon-like qualities at Freeman's two trials. Obviously a student of Justices Shaw and Edmonds, he introduced elements of moral insanity and irresistible impulse for the juries to consider. Yet he seems to have bowed to public pressure in taking pains to make sure that Freeman stood trial for the murder of John G. Van Nest. Furthermore, his interpretation of the preliminary verdict clearly benefitted the prosecution by barring the testimony of two additional medical witnesses for the defense. His remarks during sentencing also seemed to play to the public at large, praising the McNaughtan rules as the only means of testing for insanity that protected society. He lectured his audience on the community's neglect of nonwhite peoples, but he did not give any indication that this neglect should serve as an excuse for crime. Overall, at least publicly, he steered a safe course in order to mollify an angry public. He was drawn into the firestorm brought on by the first Wyatt trial, the Van Nest killings, and Freeman's controversial defense.

The *New York Journal of Medicine and the Collateral Sciences* was thoroughly satisfied with the higher court's ruling in *Freeman v. the People*. In their introduction to an abstract of Beardsley's opinion, the editors claimed that the opinion "will be found to coincide with the views advanced in this Journal at the time of the former trial of Freeman."[43] It is understandable that medical writers, influenced in their conception of insanity by the likes of Isaac Ray and Amariah Brigham, would feel vindicated by the reversal of Freeman's conviction. The editors' reaction is perplexing, however, when viewed in light of the fact that the higher court actually affirmed that the McNaughtan definition was the "undoubted rule of common law" in cases where insanity was interposed as a defense to an indictment. The accused, Beardsley wrote, "may be deranged on other subjects, but if capable of distinguishing between right and wrong in the particular act done by him, he is justly liable to be punished as a criminal." As noted, the editors voiced concern the previous fall that the McNaughtan definition led to many unjust convictions, and they lamented the influence of the McNaughtan rules upon Freeman's trial. The reversal of Freeman's conviction resulted from several errors by the lower court, including both Whiting's charge and acceptance of the verdict in the preliminary trial. Yet Whiting made no error, according to the higher court, in charging the jury in the main trial.[44]

At first glance, the reaction of the *New York Journal of Medicine and the Collateral Sciences* to the reversal of Freeman's conviction and the granting of a new trial seems like a startling about-face. It seems highly unlikely, however, that the editors would have gained an affinity for the McNaughtan test over the winter of 1846–47. More likely, they were distracted by Beardsley's remarks regarding Whiting's charge in the preliminary trial. As noted, the higher court found that Whiting defined insanity in a manner that was too narrow for the purpose of determining competency to stand trial. The higher court objected to Whiting's failure to require that the accused possess knowledge of right and wrong specifically with regard to the act in question. This was an acknowledgment by the State Supreme Court that an otherwise rational person could be delusional on a specific topic. If the accused did not appreciate the criminality of his actions, he could hardly be considered competent to assist in his own defense. The higher court's ruling offered the protection of the law for defendants that clearly did not appreciate the wrongful nature of their actions. This viewpoint understandably would have been favorably received. Still, this was no more than another reiteration of McNaughtan. The editors failed to appreciate how truly difficult it had been to determine Freeman's capacity to distinguish right from wrong in regard to the Van Nest killings. The prosecution might still have presented enough evidence to convince the jury that Freeman understood that his actions were criminal and was therefore competent to stand trial.

The *Law Reporter* interpreted the higher court's rejection of the preliminary verdict as an acknowledgment that the trial court should have abided by the New York statute. Since the statute prohibited the trial of an "insane person" for any crime or offense, a finding of "sufficient" sanity was deemed inadequate. The editors found this perfectly satisfactory but then wondered why the statute was completely abrogated in the trial on the indictment. After all, the statute also forbade punishment for any act done by "a person in a state of insanity." Judge Whiting, the editors charged, failed to "define insanity in contradistinction from sanity," opting instead to describe the variety of mental disease that annulled legal responsibility. The editors took this as an implication that there was "an insanity that does not annul criminal responsibility," even though in their opinion the statute "conveys no such idea." The higher court, the editors observed, actually affirmed the McNaughtan stipulation that only insanity in respect to the act in question annulled responsibility. Although Whiting went beyond the McNaughtan definition, as had Shaw and Edmonds, the *Law Reporter* desired a literal interpretation of the statute. An insane person, the editors maintained, should be excused from legal responsibility even if the alleged criminal act was not directly traceable to his insanity. This was precisely the type of reasoning about which Van Buren and Sherwood warned the jury. Acts of malice would be excused simply because medical professionals considered the perpetrator to be "insane," for whatever obscure reason.[45]

"The decision in Freeman's case excites wonder and indignation," Seward informed Weed following the Supreme Court ruling. "The Harpies shout for blood, but they will be disappointed," he added, betraying both the enduring public desire for retribution and his own everlasting confidence in the righteousness of his efforts to save Freeman.[46] As we have seen, personal antipathy to the criminal punishment of the insane and a need to enhance his reputation as an attorney motivated Seward. Public hostility rendered it unlikely that the Freeman case would serve any useful political purpose. Limited partisan squabbling did occur in the wake of the trial, however. Thurlow Weed's *Albany Evening Journal* printed numerous favorable reviews of Seward's *Argument in Defense of William Freeman* and noted that Seward's reputation had certainly been enhanced. Weed's paper called Seward "as eminent for his devotion to principle and right, as for brilliancy of genius and cultivation of mind." The pamphlet would strengthen the opinion that Seward was "one of the first men of our country," the *Evening Journal* asserted.[47] When the State Supreme Court reversed Freeman's conviction, Weed and other political associates of Seward became bolder in their defense of the former governor. Weed heralded Seward for battling "day and night against Judicial oppression and popular indignation."[48]

The *Albany Evening Atlas,* however, thought that Weed implied that the "popular indignation" was the work of the Democrats. The *Atlas* lashed back that "Freeman has had the question of his sanity passed upon by two consecutive juries, selected with great care, and *composed almost wholly of warm political* and personal friends of Gov. Seward." For instance, the editors noted, the first jury included Samuel Bell, "Whig member of the last and present house of Assembly from Cayuga, and as intelligent and fair a man as is or was in either house." It was a fact that no less than sixty-five jurors were examined prior to the trial on the indictment, and that the jury in the preliminary trial was selected with equal care. The *Atlas* certainly exaggerated the degree of sympathy between the juries and Seward, but the editors' point was plain: the Freeman trial was not tainted by partisan politics. There were Whigs on the juries before which Freeman was tried, the *Atlas* averred, and these juries were most competent. The *Atlas* was emphatic that the decision of the higher court not be portrayed as vindicating a former Whig governor who persevered in the face of *partisan* attack. Given the bipartisan indignation at Freeman's crime and the defense interposed on his behalf, the *Atlas* was justified in resenting the *Evening Journal's* implications.[49]

The *Auburn Daily Advertiser,* a Whig journal associated with the *Auburn Journal and Advertiser,* also drew criticism for reporting that the higher court's decision fully sustained "Gov. Seward in the course he pursued as Freeman's counsel." The *Cayuga Patriot* responded that it could discover "no approval or even allusion to Gov. Seward" in the higher court's decision. "All the Supreme Court has decided," the *Patriot* exclaimed, "is, that decisions made by the Court of Oyer and Terminer of this county, during the progress of the trial, were erroneous, and in consequence of those errors, they awarded a new trial." The editors resented the effort of the local Whig paper to somehow link the efficient functioning of a multifaceted judicial process to one man: William Henry Seward. As did the *Atlas,* the *Patriot* feared that Seward was being trumpeted for standing up to a hostile and partisan judicial system, when in fact that was not the case.[50]

The *Patriot's* position is illustrated even more clearly by its response to the remarks of a Whig legislator on the floor of the New York State Assembly. William Cornwell, a "Sewardite from Cayuga County," gushed with praise for the former governor. "When it was scarcely safe to convey the prisoner to prison—when (I blush to say it) foul play was apprehended from an excited mob," he proclaimed, "Gov. Seward was the man who dared to stand up like a man, and defend a fellow being, in accordance with the law of the land and the law of humanity, notwithstanding the scorn and contumely which was heaped upon him by the excited multitude." The *Patriot* responded angrily to Cornwell's generalizations, again fearing that the Whigs, as a party, were taking credit for Seward's personal courage. The *Patriot* pointed, as did the *Atlas,* to the fact that the "most active and efficient individual on the jury" in Freeman's preliminary trial was the Whig Samuel Bell. The editors claimed that Bell had intimidated a fellow juror by threatening to expose him to the "excited mob" if he refused to cooperate in finding Freeman "sufficiently sane" to stand trial. The *Patriot* strongly implied that this "excited mob" that had wanted to lynch Freeman was comprised of Whigs, whereas the officers that had guarded his life were Democrats. The *Patriot* even accused local Whigs of attempting to tamper with the jury by providing the sheriff with a list of individuals unsympathetic to Freeman. The *Patriot* invited the community to clearly identify the parties that had "shouted for blood," a move that would have nullified Whig efforts to parlay the Supreme Court decision into partisan propaganda.[51]

The *Patriot* commended Seward for doing "his whole duty to his miserable client" and denied Whig charges that the former governor was being treated "unfairly and harshly" in its columns. Many, if not all, of Seward's harshest critics, the editors claimed, were "his own political friends." Seward's own perceptions of the public mood, as portrayed in court and in the Seward-Weed correspondence, support the *Patriot's* claims. The Supreme Court's decision seemed to embolden some Whigs to claim partisan credit for a burden that Seward had shouldered with little support from political associates. The editors of the *Patriot* deeply resented this effort to reap political advantage from the "horrid butchering of a family" and worked diligently to prevent any public misconceptions.[52]

The fact remains, however, that the devotion of a handful of reformers, including Whig editor Horace Greeley, never wavered. After the Supreme

Court's decision, the *Tribune* once again acknowledged that Freeman's race had helped to fuel the fire of public indignation. The popular desire for punishment and popular disaffection with Seward for defending Freeman were augmented by the fact that Freeman was both black and Native American. Seward was praised in the columns of the *Tribune,* which claimed, "Whether popular or unpopular he has not feared to be right." Seward's sympathies, the *Tribune* reported, "have not been confined to one class of the population, but extended to all." [53]

Gerrit Smith observed Seward's defense of Freeman's legal rights with interest and enduring satisfaction. "I rejoice," he wrote Seward in February 1847, "that you have obtained a new trial for poor Freeman." [54] In an 1855 letter, in which Smith admonished Seward for failing to aggressively attack slavery in the District of Columbia, the abolitionist still praised the U.S. senator for his defense of Freeman. "There are passages in your life, of great beauty—of great power—of true sublimity," Smith began. "Were I to single out the one which most exalted you in my esteem," he continued, "it would be the identification of yourself with the loathed and execrated William Freeman." In Smith's opinion, nothing "short of a high-souled devotion to the cause of justice" could account for that "unpopular and self-denying identification." Although Smith did not always agree with Seward's political approach to the slavery question, he never ceased to regard Seward's defense of Freeman as an example of the former governor's humanity and empathy for the African race. [55]

Like Smith, fellow immediatist abolitionist Wendell Phillips gained profound respect for Seward. Nearly fifteen years after the Freeman trial, Phillips still found it extremely difficult to criticize Seward, given the lengths to which he went in defending Freeman. During the secession crisis in February 1861, Phillips hurled harsh words at northern politicians for contemplating compromise in what he viewed as an effort to appease the South. "The cowardice that yields to threats invites them," Phillips told an overflow crowd at the Music Hall in Boston. "Seward would *swear* to support the Constitution, but not keep the oath," Phillips claimed, admonishing the U.S. senator. Yet, Phillips added, it was "always with the extremest reluctance I bring myself to see a spot on the fame of that man, who, at his own cost, by severe toil, braving fierce odium, saved our civilization from the murder of the idiot Freeman."[56]

Black abolitionists, on the other hand, were not so easily convinced of Seward's devotion. The black abolitionist and physician James McCune Smith informed Gerrit Smith that he did not share his white associate's respect for or faith in Seward. "My spiritual quarrel with Seward began in the very act for which you commend him," he wrote. In defending Freeman, James McCune Smith complained, Seward "used an expression about 'inferiority of race' which I can forgive in no man." Ultimately, he informed his fellow abolitionist, "I gave up all hope of [Seward] when I read that sentence, because no man can fight the true Anti-Slavery fight who does not believe that all men are equal *socii*."[57] In drawing the jury's attention to the absence from the proceedings of the defendant's family members, Seward did in fact state that Freeman's father died "a victim to the vices of a superior race."[58] The remark was calculated to inspire sympathy for Freeman by illustrating that white society gave freely of its vices, in this case alcohol abuse, while withholding its virtues. Coupled with his references to blacks as "degraded," however, this remark supports the conclusion that Seward regarded blacks as morally and socially inferior to whites.[59]

The editor of *The Black Abolitionist Papers* notes that "evidence of a commitment to racial equality was the litmus test for black abolitionists." Black leaders believed that "the battle to destroy American prejudice required vigilance," which occasionally "compelled them to reprimand their friends." James McCune Smith was critical of Seward because Seward "advocated civil and political equality for blacks, while rejecting the idea of racial equality."[60] Gerrit Smith's admiration for Seward, while disturbing to James McCune Smith, makes sense when viewed in the context of paternalism among white abolitionists. Lawrence J. Friedman describes the manner in which white immediatist abolitionists constantly encouraged free blacks to "learn to practice self-help virtues with diligence and morality and thus rise from their lowly status." Immediatists, including Gerrit Smith, clearly implied that "free blacks were different from, indeed inferior to, their middle-class and devout white" sponsors. Immediatists believed that with "diligent missionary endeavor," they could "educate and uplift the innocent black child and gradually extinguish his savage crudities." By the mid-1840s, Gerrit Smith had developed a "remarkable capacity" to empathize with blacks and to understand their despair. Nevertheless, he continued to display the "pervasive immediatist ethnocentric missionary perspective under which pious whites felt duty bound to set standards for unenlightened blacks." Seward, while not an immediatist, shared with Gerrit Smith both an intense hatred of slavery and a paternalistic attitude toward blacks. It is not surprising that their relationship was generally one of mutual respect and admiration.[61]

Silas Wright was defeated in his bid for reelection as New York's governor in November 1846 by the Whig John Young. Although of a different political party, the new governor, like his predecessor, took Freeman's case very seriously. Young directed Van Buren's successor as attorney general to participate in the prosecution of William Freeman. The new trial was slated to commence on the second Monday of March pending an examination of Freeman by the circuit judge in order to ascertain his present mental condition.[62] Judge Whiting visited Freeman in his cell and found him "in a decline of health and strength," as unconcerned about his fate as his defenders had asserted he had been during the trial. Whiting concluded that Freeman was not in a condition to be tried, and he refused to conduct a new trial in his jurisdiction.[63] The village magistrate, who attempted to take Freeman's recognizance for a new trial, concurred. Justice Payne certified to the fact that he "totally failed to make the miserable wretch understand what he wanted." At that point, the criminal proceedings against William Freeman ceased.[64]

Freeman's condition only worsened after the authorities visited him that spring. In June, a physician was called to attend Freeman when he complained of discomfort in his left ear. The ear "discharged pus profusely," a condition that persisted for what remained of Freeman's life. Freeman also displayed symptoms of tuberculosis and had difficulty breathing. His vision began to fail, and the left side of his face soon became paralyzed. He never gave his doctors any verbal indication that the remedies they prescribed offered him any relief. By mid-August, his condition was so grave that the chain that bound him to the masonry of his cell was removed. He never again left the Cayuga County jail before his death on August 21, 1847.[65]

A postmortem examination left little doubt that tuberculosis was the direct cause of William Freeman's death. His lungs were found to be "an almost entire mass of disease," with tuberculous matter "interspersed with abscesses throughout the whole organ." Conclusive evidence was also found to support the contention that Freeman was partially deaf. Doctors found Freeman's "membrana tympani, with the internal structure of the ear, mostly obliterated." The bones of the middle ear were severely diseased, fetid pus being observed that had "no perceptible connection with the external ear." The condition of the ear was determined to be chronic, predating the Van Nest killings by "some months." The attending physicians postulated that the condition was likely the result of head trauma, lending support to Freeman's own account of the onset of his deafness. When interviewed prior to his trial, Freeman claimed that one of the assistant keepers at the state prison struck him on the head with a board, damaging his hearing. The physicians also theorized that the injury to Freeman's ear resulted in disease "which ultimately involved the whole brain."[66]

In death as in life, however, the condition of Freeman's brain was a subject of controversy. The examination of the brain was conducted at night, with Doctors Brigham and McCall arriving from Utica to assist in that portion of the process. The main group of physicians that participated in the postmortem examination prepared and published a statement to the effect that Freeman's brain showed "the appearance of chronic disease." They stated that "the arachnoid membrane was somewhat thickened and congested" and that the medullary substance of the brain was "of an unnatural dusky color, and in places harder than natural, as if parboiled." The left temporal bone in the vicinity of Freeman's auditory nerve was described as "carious and much diseased," the dura mater at that point also showing signs of disease.[67]

With the exception of Dr. Charles A. Hyde, all of the physicians who signed the postmortem report regarding Freeman's brain had testified for the defense in Freeman's trials. Besides Doctors Brigham and McCall, these included Blanchard Fosgate and Lansing Briggs. Dr. David Dimon, a prosecution witness who attended the autopsy of the brain uninvited, disagreed with the findings as published by the group. He also took issue with the fact that of the prosecution witnesses, only Dr. Hyde was asked to attend the postmortem. The findings, Dimon charged, reflected a self-interested desire on the part of the group for validation. No portion of Freeman's brain indicated to Dimon "any decided marks of disease." In Dimon's opinion, any irregularities observed in Freeman's brain could more likely "be attributed to other maladies which were the cause of death, and about which there was no doubt and no difference of opinion." Dimon even charged that the symptoms of chronic disease observed in Freeman's brain were further exaggerated in later reports published by members of the group.[68]

It is highly unlikely that this group of doctors collectively misinterpreted the physical condition of William Freeman's brain. Dr. Dimon's charges of self-interest on the part of the medical witnesses for the defense must be received with some caution. Having testified for the prosecution, Dimon himself could just as easily have been charged with attempting to validate his assessment of Freeman. Given the scope of their professional lives, Doctors Brigham and McCall were far more likely than their colleagues to have performed previous postmortem examinations on individuals generally considered to have been mentally deranged. Their familiarity with the pathology of the human brain was far greater than that of the average antebellum physician. True, it may have been self-validating, but their approval of the postmortem report lends to it substantial credibility. Nevertheless the dispute over the postmortem report epitomizes the degree of controversy inspired by the Van Nest killings. It is fitting that the William Freeman case continued to be a "case of trouble" even after Freeman's death.

Conclusion

THE WILLIAM FREEMAN CASE was a "case of trouble." Nothing transpired, nor was any precedent set, that altered the course of history, yet the issues raised were so controversial that the case yields a wealth of information regarding antebellum society and culture. In this one remarkable venue, conflicting attitudes regarding crime, punishment, mental illness, legal responsibility, and race are all revealed in explicit detail. Popular opinions and concerns were voiced with intensity in direct response to the challenges posed by advocates of social and judicial reform. Freeman's supporters, in and out of the courtroom, expressed ideas that were perceived as threatening the safety of the community. The attitudes and practices that carried the day reflected, above all else, a desire to protect society from people like William Freeman.

In the context of Wyatt's first trial, the Van Nest killings inspired fear and outrage in Cayuga County and beyond. Prosecutors played upon these feelings of insecurity in conducting the Freeman trial. They invited the jury to conclude that anyone that understood the wrongful nature of his contemplated act and did it anyway demonstrated an evil heart. Prosecutors claimed that efforts to broaden the definition of legal insanity merely invited the depraved to commit heinous crimes under the pretense of mental derangement. Furthermore, prosecutors warned, incorporation of moral insanity within the common law meant that medical experts would exercise substantial power over guilt or innocence. Van Buren and Sherwood insisted that the common sense of ordinary members of the community was the best guarantor of public security. The common law as embodied in the Mc-

Naughtan rules allowed the community to exercise this common sense in determining legal responsibility.

William Freeman was convicted despite the defense's insistence that he was unable to apply abstract legal and social concepts to his own behavior. The trial court, while incorporating elements of the theory of moral insanity in its charge, severely handicapped the defense's ability to convince the jury that Freeman was not legally responsible. Freeman's sanity at the time of the trial was asserted, and the jury was encouraged to be skeptical regarding the new scientific theories upon which Freeman's life depended. In the end, the trial court advised the jury to demand a standard of proof that was extraordinarily difficult for the defense to satisfy. The court responded to public concerns regarding the administration of justice by affirming that insanity excused crime only when "clearly proved." There was simply no manner in which defense attorneys and expert medical witnesses could "clearly prove" that Freeman, or any other violent individual, was driven by inner forces that could not be controlled.

Essentially, the prosecution's approach to insanity more closely coincided with popular feelings regarding crime, mental illness, and the limits of legal responsibility. The killings so incensed and frightened the community that it seems as though only someone infantile in intellect or literally raving like a wild beast would have stood a chance of acquittal. Freeman's behavior leaves little doubt that he was mentally ill. His violent actions simply outweighed any impression that his overall demeanor made upon the jury. Although Freeman's conviction was overturned, the higher court expressed no reservations regarding the McNaughtan definition of legal insanity. The trial verdict illustrates the triumph and endurance of the conviction that crime resulted from human depravity. Crime was the willful act of a wicked heart. Furthermore, the community feared they were imperiled unless all but the totally insane or idiotic were held accountable for their actions.

Public response to the Van Nest killings and Freeman's mode of defense provides tremendous insight into antebellum perceptions of the link between punishment, crime, and religion. The events in Auburn during the early months of 1846 took place in the context of a heated debate over capital punishment. Commentators from both major political parties seized upon the killings as evidence of the evil that antigallows reformers were cultivating in American society. The death penalty, these journals argued, was the only manner of punishing murderers that deterred violent crime and reflected human instinct. Furthermore, they insisted that God explicitly sanctioned the death penalty as the appropriate method of punishing murderers. These commentators regarded the insanity defense as a legal ploy, used at the urging of the antigallows reformers, to save Freeman from just punishment. They pointed to the first Wyatt trial as an example of a case in which this ploy had worked.

The reformers rebelled against this climate of vindictiveness, citing the New Testament in support of their argument that Christ's teachings repealed the law of retribution. Also representing both parties, reformers praised the advance of medical science and insisted that Freeman deserved full protection of his legal rights. Although not strictly opposed to the gallows, William Henry Seward undertook Freeman's defense largely because he objected to vindictive punishment of the insane. Seward and the reformers, in their vocal objections to the widespread desire for vengeance, also challenged popular images of manhood. Their words demonstrate that certain segments of northern society looked to Christ as a shining alternative to belligerent and competitive masculinity. Their actions also demonstrated their conviction that righteous protest, in the face of anger and reprobation, was an affirmation of manhood. In their opponents' opinion, this protest seemed to strike at the very heart of the values upon which the peace and security of society was based.

Despite the involvement of major political players from rival parties, Freeman's case was not a venue for any extensive partisan machinations. The case reveals much more about antebellum attitudes concerning the nature of criminals and the appropriate means of punishment. The majority of public responses to the Van Nest killings reflected the same popular conceptions of crime and criminals that came to the fore in Freeman's trial. Freeman was regarded as a depraved individual upon whom the reforming mission of the penitentiary had had no positive effect. The Van Nest killings proved to many observers that the death penalty was the only means of deterring the depraved from taking human life. The connection between the public debate and Freeman's conviction is undeniable. Suspicion of the insanity defense and the need to demonstrate that the law protected society were the dominant themes in the press leading up to the trial. Before a single juror was sworn, it was clear that the larger community had lost its patience with efforts to excuse crime or forestall retribution. Freeman's conviction demonstrates the depth of community concern regarding the perceived laxity in the administration of justice.

Freeman's racial background clearly added to the controversy surrounding his case, making it that much more a "case of trouble." The case presents an outstanding opportunity to investigate the links that antebellum northerners perceived between race and violence, insanity, intemperance, and immorality. Numerous commentators traced the Van Nest killings, in part, to what they considered to be the natural inclinations of African and Native American peoples. Freeman's racial background made it easier for the community to demonize him. In addition, supporters of the gallows alleged that Freeman's race enhanced the sympathy he received from "misguided philanthropists." The reformers did indeed hold society partially responsible for the killings due to its neglect and mistreatment of nonwhite peoples. They resented, however, the implication that Freeman killed the Van Nests with complete confidence that the reformers would save him from the gallows. A black man, the reformers protested, had no reason to expect that his life would be spared for the killing of four members of a prominent white family.

During the trial, both sides explicitly used race to buttress their arguments. The prosecution attempted to explain Freeman's violent demeanor using the same racial arguments employed earlier in the press. Prosecution witnesses, in turn, expected such little mental ability from blacks that Freeman's childlike intelligence was interpreted as normal given his race. The prosecution extended its attack on nonwhite peoples to Freeman's family and friends, who were portrayed as dishonest, immoral, and intemperate people unfit to testify in a court of law. Seward and his colleagues echoed the reformers' insistence that society was implicated in the Van Nest killings. Society's neglect and mistreatment of blacks, Seward advanced, contradicted Christian notions of manliness. Taking the argument a step further, however, Freeman's counsel asserted that society, by virtue of its failure to educate Freeman as a moral being, had rendered him morally insane. Seward pleaded with the jury to evaluate Freeman's mental capacity according to the standards applied to healthy adults irrespective of race. He also vigorously, if somewhat paternalistically, defended the character of nonwhite witnesses.

Race was clearly a contributing factor in Freeman's conviction. It amplified the passions that inevitably would be inflamed and the fear that would be inspired by a crime of such violence. Coupled with the popular desire to neutralize the insanity defense and affirm the law's ability to protect society, Freeman's race made his acquittal unlikely. As demonstrated by the white man Wyatt's conviction and execution for a crime far less heinous, antebellum New Yorkers were impatient with efforts to excuse crime and deny retribution. It is highly unlikely that environmental explanations of crime would have carried much weight with the jury in this context. The prosecution played upon popular fears and prejudices regarding free blacks and coupled them with the perceived laxity in the administration of justice. Freeman's execution was to be a signal to blacks and whites that justice would be served. George J. Mastin astutely perceived as much when he envisioned Freeman's ultimate fate.

In the end, it is the controversial nature of the Freeman case that renders it such an appropriate subject for historical inquiry. All of the key issues involved in the case have continued to be debated in the more than one hundred and fifty years since the Van Nest killings. The Freeman case demonstrates that certain views were predominant in antebellum America. We must constantly recognize, however, that consensus did not exist on these issues. Defining legal responsibility, appropriately punishing criminals, and explaining criminal behavior challenged the most gifted minds of William Freeman's day. Harmony proved to be elusive, and each succeeding generation witnessed impassioned debates concerning the same difficult questions. For example, throughout the nineteenth century, most American jurists rejected the inclusion of irresistible impulse tests within the legal definition of insanity. They feared that ultimately it would be impossible to distinguish between those individuals that lacked the will to resist an impulse and those that consciously refused to resist. Still, Dr. Isaac Ray continued into the 1860s to convince certain judges, most notably Associate Justice Charles Doe of the Supreme Court of New Hampshire, that the McNaughtan definition of insanity was grossly deficient.[1]

Each generation has attempted to define the point at which legal responsibility terminates. Americans have continued to struggle with their desire to avoid punishing the mentally ill while still effectively deterring crime and satisfying the innate desire for retribution. Equally perplexing has been the problem of appropriately punishing convicted criminals, most notably murderers. The death penalty has been debated on criminological and philosophical grounds by every generation up to and including the present. Instinctive desire for retribution, the need to deter violent crime, and religious objections to "legal homicide" figure just as actively in the debate today as they did in the 1840s.

In short, every generation of Americans has debated the nature of crime. Social, environmental, and biological explanations have been and continue to be advanced in explanation of criminal behavior. The imposition of criminal punishments and the nature of penal institutions have varied as different explanations of crime have held sway. The connection between race and criminal behavior continues to interest social scientists, clergy, and historians. The manner in which the American criminal justice system deals with minorities has also captured the interest of generations of scholars and conscientious laymen. In sum, the issues raised by the Van Nest killings and the Freeman trial are American issues. They are no less relevant in the twenty-first century than they were in the 1840s. For many Americans, the prevailing undercurrent continues to be the protection of their families, their persons, and their hearths.

Notes

—⁓—

Bibliography

—⁓—

Index

Notes

Introduction

1. Official press release, September 1, 1954, marking the opening of an exhibit featuring Mastin's paintings at the Farmers' Museum in Cooperstown, George J. Mastin Collection, New York State Historical Association, Cooperstown, New York.

2. Original broadside promoting Mastin's traveling exhibit, Mastin Collection. The actual spelling of the victims' surname was Van Nest, although early press reports of the killings did refer to them as the "Van Ness" family. Given the amount of press coverage that the killings and Freeman's subsequent trial received, it is surprising that Mastin continued to employ the incorrect spelling.

3. Official press release, September 1, 1954, Mastin Collection.

4. James Taylor Dunn and Louis C. Jones, "Crazy Bill Had a Down Look: Quaint Pictures and a Grim Story Tell of Prejudice and Mob Passion in Upstate New York of the 1840's," in *Stories of Great Crimes and Trials from American Heritage Magazine* (New York: American Heritage Publishing Company, 1973), 27.

5. Original broadside, Mastin Collection. The original lecture is also part of the Mastin Collection. The original paintings are now the property of the New York State Historical Association.

6. Unpublished manuscript material, Mastin Collection.

7. Official press release, September 1, 1954, Mastin Collection.

8. Ibid.; John Wilmerding, ed., *The Genius of American Painting* (New York: William Morrow, 1973), 127, 129.

9. John I. H. Baur, *American Painting in the Nineteenth Century: Main Trends and Movements* (New York: Frederick A. Praeger, 1953), 22–23.

10. Wilmerding, 129.

11. Ibid., 127, 129.

12. Baur, 22.

13. Reprints of the paintings depicting the Van Nest killings can be found in Dunn and Jones, 26 and 29, and also in Sheila Saft Tucker, *The Township of Fleming, Cayuga County, New York, 1823–1973* (Auburn: Brunner the Printer, 1973), 45, 47.

14. Manuscript of Mastin lecture, Mastin Collection.

15. Ibid.

16. Ibid.

17. *Rochester Daily Advertiser,* March 25, 1846.

18. Manuscript of Mastin lecture, Mastin Collection.

19. Ibid.

20. K. N. Llewellyn and E. Adamson Hoebel, *The Cheyenne Way: Conflict and Case Law in Primitive Jurisprudence* (Norman: Univ. of Oklahoma Press, 1941), 20–29. Michael Grossberg also reminds us of the value of studying "singular exemplary events," which demonstrate that culture is the product of "innumerable individual experiences." Examinations of controversial cases, he adds, reveal aspects of past cultures that are obscured in studies of a larger scope. Moreover, highly publicized legal events "help construct popular images of social relations," thus becoming "active shapers of a culture, not merely its reflections." See *A Judgement for Solomon: The D'Hauteville Case and Legal Experience in Antebellum America* (New York: Cambridge Univ. Press, 1996), x–xv.

21. Earl Conrad, *Mr. Seward for the Defense* (New York: Rinehart and Co., Inc., 1956).

22. See in particular Glyndon G. Van Deusen, *William Henry Seward* (New York: Oxford Univ. Press, 1967), 93–97; see also John M. Taylor's more recent work, *William Henry Seward: Lincoln's Right Hand* (New York: Harper Collins, 1991), 65–69. Wayne Reynolds Merrick's *A Study of William Henry Seward, Reformer* (Ph.D. diss., Syracuse Univ., 1957; Ann Arbor: University Microfilms, Inc., 1963) is a more focused work, yet it still follows the general pattern of the other biographies in reference to the Freeman trial.

1. The Van Nest Killings

1. Elliot G. Storke places the population of Auburn at 8,500 in 1848. See *History of Cayuga County, New York, with Illustrations and Biographical Sketches of Some of Its Prominent Men and Pioneers* (Syracuse: D. Mason, 1879), 151.

2. *New York Daily Tribune,* June 8, 1846.

3. Conrad, 3–4; Dunn and Jones, 27. For a history of Auburn State Prison, see W. David Lewis, *From Newgate to Dannemora: The Rise of the Penitentiary in New York, 1796–1848* (Ithaca: Cornell Univ. Press, 1965).

4. Conrad, 28–29.

5. Henry Hall, *History of Auburn* (Auburn: Dennis Bro's, 1869), 150, 280.

6. Henry Mott Allen, *A Chronicle of Auburn from 1793 to 1955, Being a Chronicle of Early*

Auburn, and Chronicle of Auburn Consolidated (Auburn: Henry M. Allen, 1955), 22, 39. Leon F. Litwack notes that even many white abolitionists, although in favor of full citizenship for blacks, were hesitant about social intercourse with blacks on equal terms. He also recognizes the widespread existence in the antebellum North of conditions similar to those described here in reference to Auburn. See *North of Slavery: The Negro in the Free States, 1790–1860* (Chicago: Univ. of Chicago Press, 1961), 139, 215, 263.

7. "Defence of William Freeman," in *The Works of William H. Seward*, vol. 1, ed. George E. Baker (New York: Redfield, 1853), 471; *Auburn Journal and Advertiser*, March 18, 1846.

8. Wyatt's first trial is detailed in *Report of the Trial of Henry Wyatt, a Convict in the State Prison at Auburn, Indicted for the Murder of James Gordon, Another Convict Within the Prison* (Auburn: J. C. Derby, 1846).

9. Earl Conrad astutely draws this conclusion in *Mr. Seward for the Defense*, 18; the other legal references, which will be discussed in detail in later chapters, are to the trials of Abner Rogers and Andrew Kleim.

10. *Albany Evening Journal*, March 13, 1846. Fleming lies to the south of Auburn. As noted in the introduction, early news reports referred to the victims as the "Van Ness" family. The actual spelling of the name, as it appeared in later reports and in all published materials relating to the Freeman trial, was Van Nest.

11. *Auburn Daily Advertiser* quoted in *Albany Evening Journal*, March 14, 1846. Despite the spelling of the name as "Wykoff" in early reports, later news articles and the published accounts of the Freeman trial verify that the proper spelling was "Wyckoff."

12. *Auburn Daily Advertiser* quoted in *Albany Evening Journal*, March 14, 1846.

13. Ibid.

14. *Daily Cayuga Tocsin* quoted in *Albany Evening Atlas*, March 14, 1846.

15. *Auburn Daily Advertiser* quoted in *Rochester Daily Advertiser*, March 16, 1846. From the start, numerous newspapers repeatedly referred to Freeman as the "murderer." Little effort was made to differentiate between "killing" and "murder" as defined in criminal law. As this book goes on to demonstrate, in the eyes of many commentators, Freeman's act itself was proof enough of murder.

16. This telegraph report appeared in the *Albany Evening Journal* on March 14, 1846, and in the *Albany Argus* on March 15, 1846.

17. *Auburn Daily Advertiser* quoted in *Albany Evening Journal*, March 16, 1846.

18. Ibid.

19. *Daily Cayuga Tocsin* quoted and its report paraphrased in the *Morning Courier and New York Enquirer*, March 19, 1846.

20. Ibid.

21. *Auburn Daily Advertiser* quoted in *Albany Evening Journal*, March 16, 1846.

22. *Albany Evening Journal*, March 16, 1846.

23. *Daily Cayuga Tocsin* quoted in *Albany Evening Atlas*, March 14, 1846.

24. *Rochester Daily Advertiser*, March 18, 1846.

25. *Albany Evening Journal,* March 17 and 19, 1846; *Rochester Daily Advertiser,* March 17, 1846.

26. *Albany Evening Journal,* March 17, 1846.

27. The Van Nest's elder son was not identified by name in the press reports of the crime. The only reference to him by name appears in Tucker, 44.

28. *Rochester Daily Advertiser,* March 25, 1846.

29. Such reports appeared in the *New York Daily Tribune,* March 20, 1846; *Albany Argus,* March 16, 1846; and *Rochester Daily Advertiser,* March 17, 1846.

30. *Rochester Daily Advertiser,* March 17, 1846.

31. *Albany Argus,* March 16, 1846.

32. *Albany Evening Journal,* March 16, 1846.

33. *Rochester Daily Advertiser,* March 19, 1846.

34. Ibid.

35. *New York Daily Tribune,* March 20, 1846.

36. *Rochester Daily Advertiser,* March 19, 1846.

37. The testimony taken before the coroner's inquest was printed in the Auburn papers, and excerpts were reprinted in other papers around the state. The excerpts quoted here appeared in the *Albany Evening Journal,* March 17, 1846. Rumors abounded that Freeman had not acted alone and even that additional arrests had been made. A telegraph report from Utica, dated March 19, 1846, attempted to set the record straight. "There is no question but Freeman committed the murders alone," the wire stated, and all reports of additional arrests were "entirely unfounded." Mrs. Wyckoff was, in fact, the only witness to the crime that spoke of a second intruder. Telegraph report published in *Albany Evening Journal,* March 19, 1846.

38. Ibid., March 17, 1846. Dr. Pitney made reference here to one of the broken sections of blade recovered at the crime scene.

39. Ibid.

40. Ibid.

41. *Auburn Journal and Advertiser,* March 18, 1846. The *Syracuse Star* attempted to link William Freeman to a man named Dan Freeman who had recently been executed for murder in Syracuse. The *Star*'s report was cited in the *Albany Evening Journal,* March 19, 1846, and also in the *New York Daily Tribune,* March 20, 1846. The details of Freeman's 1840 grand larceny conviction are sketchy at best. We do know that a horse was stolen from the property of Martha Godfrey in the town of Sennett, which is situated several miles to the north of Auburn. Apparently, Freeman was found in possession of the horse but denied having acquired it illegally. Another African American, Jack Furman, was suspected in the theft and was arrested in addition to Freeman. Furman turned state's evidence, and it was essentially his testimony that led to Freeman's conviction. After the Van Nest killings, Freeman's sympathizers claimed that Furman, the actual thief, had convinced the unsuspecting Freeman to use the stolen horse to "ride an errand." The prosecutors at Freeman's murder trial, however, fer-

vently denied that Freeman's grand larceny conviction was wrongful. See "The Trial of William Freeman for the Murder of John G. Van Nest, Auburn, New York, 1846," in *American State Trials*, vol. 16, ed. John D. Lawson (St. Louis: Thomas Law Book Co., 1928), 326, 338, 485–86; see also *New York Daily Tribune*, March 20, 1846.

42. *Auburn Journal and Advertiser*, March 18, 1846. William Freeman was indeed punished while in state prison for "striking a convict with a board" and for "quarreling in the dye house" where he labored. See Daily Punishment Reports, 1836–1846, Auburn Prison, Record Series A0780–80, New York State Archives, Albany, N.Y.

43. Conrad, 107–15.

44. *Auburn Journal and Advertiser*, March 25, 1846.

45. Conrad, 107–15.

46. *Rochester Daily Advertiser*, March 17, 1846.

2. Human Depravity vs. Environmentalism: The Public Response to a Tragedy

1. Louis P. Masur, *Rites of Execution: Capital Punishment and the Transformation of American Culture, 1776–1865* (New York: Oxford Univ. Press, 1989), 141.

2. Ibid., 119–21, 157; Philip English Mackey, *Hanging in the Balance: The Anti-Capital Punishment Movement in New York State, 1776–1861* (New York: Garland Publishing, 1982), 239.

3. Mackey, 239. Interestingly, Mackey suggests that the Van Nest killings may have influenced reformers in the state legislature to wait until April, when the legislative session was nearly finished, to submit a bill to abolish the death penalty. This explanation of the reformers' lack of confidence is unconvincing, since word of the Van Nest killings did not spread throughout the state until the middle of March. The legislative session was already well under way when the details of the killings became known, and no bill had been introduced. Certainly, the killings did nothing to boost the reformers' confidence, but other factors had already rendered them extremely cautious. Mackey does explore other possible explanations for the reformers' unwillingness to introduce a bill before April. I merely suggest that these other explanations do more to account for the reformers' behavior during the bulk of the 1846 legislative session. The Van Nest killings occurred so far into the session that they could have done little to set the overall tone. See Mackey, 219–24.

4. Registers of Male Inmates Discharged, 1817–1949, Auburn Prison, Record Series B0068–77, New York State Archives, Albany, N.Y.

5. *Report of the Trial of Henry Wyatt*, 7, 11, 21–23, 31. Chapter 302 of the Laws of 1835 allowed assistant keepers at state prisons to punish prisoners at their discretion provided that they reported their actions in writing to the prison's agent or deputy keeper. On July 31, 1844, it was recorded that Henry Wyatt was given "twenty-eight blows with the cat for having in his cell a knife and an auger with intent to effect his escape with Smith (another convict)." The "cat" is a reference to the "cat o' nine tails," although the weapon used to deliver lashes to Wyatt was reported to have had five or six leather strands rather than nine. The above

citation of the law, as well as the punishment entry recorded for Wyatt, are found in *Daily Punishment Reports, 1836–1846*.

6. *Daily Cayuga Tocsin* quoted in *Albany Evening Atlas,* March 14, 1846.

7. *Daily Cayuga Tocsin* quoted in *Auburn Journal and Advertiser,* March 18, 1846.

8. Michael F. Holt, *The Rise and Fall of the American Whig Party: Jacksonian Politics and the Onset of the Civil War* (New York: Oxford Univ. Press, 1999), 163–64, 333–34.

9. *Cayuga Patriot,* July 8, 1846.

10. *Albany Argus,* March 16, 1846.

11. *Report of the Trial of Henry Wyatt,* 3–7.

12. For a discussion of the political struggle between conservative Whig journals (including the *Morning Courier and New York Enquirer* and the *New York Morning Express*) and more progressive Whig leaders such as Seward, Thurlow Weed, and Horace Greeley, see Glyndon G. Van Deusen, *Thurlow Weed: Wizard of the Lobby* (Boston: Little, Brown, 1947), 143–45. Michael F. Holt also notes that the conservative wing of the Whig Party was "spearheaded by Greeley's great editorial rival, James Watson Webb of the New York *Courier and Enquirer.*" Conservative New York Whigs were critical of progressive Whigs' support of black suffrage, support of the Anti-Rent movement, sympathy for immigrants, and desire for constitutional reform. See Holt, 227, 240–43.

13. *New York Daily Tribune,* March 16, 1846.

14. *Report of the Trial of Henry Wyatt,* 3–7, supports the claim that reservations regarding the death penalty played a crucial role in bringing about the rejection of jurors who expressed such concerns.

15. The relationship between the *New York Herald* and O'Sullivan is detailed in Mackey, 153. For a discussion of the career and political ideology of John L. O'Sullivan, see Masur, 141–59.

16. *New York Herald,* July 23, 1846. Fourierism refers to the variety of utopian socialism associated with the Frenchman Charles Fourier. It is interesting to note that Horace Greeley, among the foremost opponents of the death penalty, was also a supporter of Fourierism. See Andie Tucher, *Froth and Scum: Truth, Beauty, Goodness, and the Ax Murder in America's First Mass Medium* (Chapel Hill: Univ. of North Carolina Press, 1994), 132–33.

17. *New York Morning Express,* March 21, 1846.

18. Stewart E. Tolnay and E. M. Beck, *A Festival of Violence: An Analysis of Southern Lynchings, 1882–1930* (Chicago: Univ. of Illinois Press, 1995), 18; see also W. Fitzhugh Brundage, *Lynching in the New South: Georgia and Virginia, 1880–1930* (Urbana: Univ. of Illinois Press, 1993), 101.

19. *Morning Courier and New York Enquirer,* March 23, 1846.

20. Ibid.

21. *Albany Argus,* March 18, 1846.

22. Quoted in *Auburn Journal and Advertiser,* March 25, 1846.

23. Masur, 146–50, 152.

24. Mackey, 214, 217.

25. Sermon quoted from Tucker, 46. The Sand Beach Church was organized on December 8, 1810, under the name Reformed Protestant Dutch Church at Owasco Outlet. The official church minutes for the year 1812 referred to the congregation as "Reformed Protestant Dutch Church of Sand Beach." See "Historical Designation for Sand Beach Church," *Auburn Citizen-Advertiser,* October 12, 1974, as well as unpublished manuscript material available at the Seymour Public Library, Auburn, New York.

26. *Morning Courier and New York Enquirer,* March 24, 1846.

27. *New York Express,* March 21, 1846. The Biblical reference is to Genesis 9:6, as indicated in Masur, 67.

28. *New York Herald,* March 31, 1846.

29. *New York Morning Telegraph* quoted in the *New York Daily Tribune,* March 20, 1846.

30. *Morning Courier and New York Enquirer,* March 20, 1846.

31. Ibid.

32. *New York Morning Telegraph* quoted in the *New York Daily Tribune,* March 20, 1846.

33. During Freeman's trial, Austin affirmed that he was "Justice." See Benjamin F. Hall, *The Trial of William Freeman, for the Murder of John G. Van Nest, Including the Evidence and the Arguments of Counsel, with the Decision of the Supreme Court Granting a New Trial, and an Account of the Death of the Prisoner, and of the Post-Mortem Examination of His Body by Amariah Brigham, M.D., and Others* (Auburn: Derby, Miller, and Co., 1848), 253. Upon cross-examination, Austin admitted to having taken "a deep interest" in the case and having "written about this case and published letters in religious papers." Austin noted that his letters contained "matter in opposition to capital punishment." See "The Trial of William Freeman," 366–69. *The Prisoner's Friend,* an anti-capital-punishment weekly published in Boston, printed extended excerpts and noted that they were written, "as we think, by a clergyman formerly of Massachusetts." The reference was to Austin. See *The Prisoner's Friend,* April 8, 1846.

34. Mackey, 202.

35. Masur, 129–32, 153–54.

36. *Auburn Journal and Advertiser,* March 18, 1846.

37. Ibid.

38. Ibid., April 1, 1846.

39. Cynthia Griffin Wolff, " 'Masculinity' in *Uncle Tom's Cabin,*" *American Quarterly* 47 (1995): 599. See also E. Anthony Rotundo, *American Manhood: Transformations in Masculinity from the Revolution to the Modern Era* (New York: Basic Books, 1993), 25.

40. Wolff, 599–601.

41. Ibid., 602.

42. Rotundo, 22–23, 25.

43. Wolff, 599–602.

44. Mackey notes that Universalists, Unitarians, and Quakers all took active roles the in the anti-capital-punishment movement in New York and elsewhere. Although differing on

certain specific theological questions, the common thread linking them was the rejection of orthodox Calvinism. See pp. 214, 217.

45. *New York Daily Tribune,* March 18, 1846.

46. Ibid., March 25, 1846. The New Testament reference is to Matthew 5: 38–39.

47. Ibid., March 18, 1846.

48. *Auburn Journal and Advertiser,* March 18, 1846.

49. Ibid., April 1, 1846.

50. Ibid., March 18, 1846. Austin expressed the same theme in his article of April 1, 1846.

51. *New York Morning Telegraph* quoted in *New York Daily Tribune,* March 20, 1846.

52. *New York Daily Tribune,* March 20, 1846.

53. *Auburn Journal and Advertiser,* March 18, 1846. For a discussion of the goals and ultimate failure of the Auburn system of prison discipline, see Lewis, and Scott Christianson, *With Liberty for Some: 500 Years of Imprisonment in America* (Boston: Northeastern Univ. Press, 1998). David J. Rothman also discusses the environmental conception of deviance that led to failed efforts to create disciplinary institutions in *The Discovery of the Asylum: Social Order and Disorder in the New Republic* (Boston: Addison Wesley Educational Publishers, 1971).

54. Holt, 227.

55. *The Liberator,* March 27, 1846.

56. "Trial of William Freeman," 326.

57. *Syracuse Journal* quoted in the *Morning Courier and New York Enquirer,* March 20, 1846.

58. *Syracuse Star* quoted in the *Albany Evening Journal,* March 19, 1846, and also in the *New York Daily Tribune,* March 20, 1846.

59. *Auburn Daily Advertiser* quoted in the *Albany Evening Journal,* March 19, 1846.

60. *Cayuga Patriot,* March 25, 1846.

61. *Albany Argus,* March 18, 1846.

62. Lee Benson discusses the attitude of the New York Democratic Party toward blacks in *The Concept of Jacksonian Democracy: New York as a Test Case* (Princeton: Princeton Univ. Press, 1961), 304.

63. Winthrop D. Jordan examines the effect of emancipation on northern whites in *White over Black: American Attitudes Toward the Negro, 1550–1812* (Chapel Hill: Univ. of North Carolina Press, 1968). He concludes that a lost sense of control inspired whites to portray free blacks as depraved, violent, and dangerous in order to justify limiting their participation in American society. See pp. 410, 579.

64. Calvinist views on the depravity of man and need for restraint are discussed in Masur, 152–54.

65. *Rochester Daily Advertiser,* April 2, 1846.

66. Ibid., June 5, 1846.

67. Use is made here again of Jordan's argument in *White over Black,* 410, 579.

68. *New York Express,* March 21, 1846; Masur discusses the distaste expressed by support-

ers of capital punishment for environmental explanations of the origins of crime in *Rites of Execution,* 154.

69. *Albany Evening Atlas,* July 24, 1846.

70. Phyllis F. Field, *The Politics of Race in New York: The Struggle for Black Suffrage in the Civil War Era* (Ithaca: Cornell Univ. Press, 1982), 60–61.

71. See Masur, 9–19, 154. Masur uses the case of Washington Goode, a black sailor tried for the murder of a fellow black seaman in 1848, as an example of the manner in which the antigallows reformers approached this issue. Goode was convicted and hanged for the murder of Thomas Harding despite the efforts of reformers including Horace Greeley, John Spear, Wendell Phillips, and William Henry Channing.

72. *Auburn Journal and Advertiser,* March 18, 1846.

73. Ibid.

74. Ibid., March 28, 1846.

75. *New York Daily Tribune,* March 20, 1846.

76. Ibid.; Masur observes that young, black, and foreign criminals tended to be executed at higher rates in the early American republic than offenders from other social groups. Among the arguments offered by those protesting the hanging of Washington Goode was that race had been a determining factor in his execution. See pp. 6, 15.

77. *The Liberator,* March 27, 1846. As noted earlier, Garrison joined Greeley and Austin in criticizing vindictive justice and the death penalty. For a detailed discussion of the membership, characteristics, and activities of the Boston clique of immediatist abolitionists, see Lawrence J. Friedman, *Gregarious Saints: Self and Community in American Abolitionism, 1830–1870* (Cambridge: Cambridge Univ. Press, 1982), 43–67. Interestingly, the *National Anti-Slavery Standard* (the organ of the clique-dominated American Anti-Slavery Society) barely mentioned the Van Nest killings. The case was never touched on in the journal until mid-July, when it finally printed brief details of Freeman's trial. Even these reports failed to include any editorial commentary regarding the case. See the *National Anti-Slavery Standard,* July 16, July 23, and August 6, 1846.

3. Mental Illness in Antebellum America: Science, the Public, and the Courts

1. "Defence of William Freeman," 410.

2. *Rochester Daily Advertiser,* March 20, 1846.

3. "Trial of William Freeman," 327–28.

4. *Auburn Journal and Advertiser,* June 3, 1846.

5. 2 New York Revised Statutes 697, Section 2.

6. Daniel N. Robinson, *Wild Beasts and Idle Humours: The Insanity Defense from Antiquity to the Present* (Cambridge: Harvard Univ. Press, 1996), 145–53.

7. Leonard W. Levy notes that McNaughtan killed the secretary of British prime minis-

ter Sir Robert Peel, mistaking him for Peel. McNaughtan's acquittal, on an insanity plea, "occasioned the debate in the House of Lords which resulted in the House propounding their questions to the Judges." See *The Law of the Commonwealth and Chief Justice Shaw* (Cambridge: Harvard Univ. Press, 1957), 211n. For an in-depth discussion of McNaughtan's life, crime, and trial, see Richard Moran, *Knowing Right from Wrong: The Insanity Defense of Daniel McNaughtan* (New York: Free Press, 1981).

8. Levy, 211, 214.

9. Ibid., 209, 212.

10. Norman Dain, *Concepts of Insanity in the United States, 1789–1865* (New Brunswick: Rutgers Univ. Press, 1964), 73–74; Gerald N. Grob, "Origins of DSM-I: A Study in Appearance and Reality," *American Journal of Psychiatry* 148 (1991): 422. Dain notes that although the study of mental illness had developed into a recognized specialty field of medicine by the 1840s, the terms "psychiatry" and "psychiatrist" were not widely used until the twentieth century. He employs the terms as a matter of convenience to refer to the branch of medicine and those physicians specifically concerned with mental illness. I have found it convenient, at certain points in this book, to do the same. See Dain, 56, 193.

11. Michael Perlin, *The Jurisprudence of the Insanity Defense* (Durham: Carolina Academic Press, 1994), 81–82, 84.

12. Thomas Maeder, *Crime and Madness: The Origins and Evolution of the Insanity Defense* (New York: Harper and Row, 1985), 48.

13. Levy, 216.

14. Maeder, 49–51; Robinson, 161.

15. Dain, 155–57, 198. Evangelical Protestantism played an important role in turning antebellum public opinion against the theory of moral insanity. "Evangelical religion," Dain observes, "stressed that immorality was the natural condition of mankind." Man committed immoral acts because of an evil heart, all the while possessing free will to do otherwise. Only extreme cases of mental incapacity, either congenital or resulting from disease, excused crime. See Dain, 192–93.

16. David Brion Davis, *Homicide in American Fiction, 1798–1860: A Study in Social Values* (Ithaca: Cornell Univ. Press, 1957), 114, 117–18.

17. *Albany Argus,* March 16, 1846.

18. *Morning Courier and New York Enquirer,* March 23, 1846.

19. *Rochester Daily Advertiser,* June 5, 1846.

20. James C. Mohr, *Doctors and the Law: Medical Jurisprudence in Nineteenth-Century America* (Baltimore: Johns Hopkins Univ. Press, 1993), 143–44.

21. For this discussion of Ray's approach to mental illness and legal insanity, I am further indebted to Mohr, 145–47.

22. Dain, 61.

23. Robinson, 162.

24. Dain, 61; Robinson, 162.

25. John D. Davies, *Phrenology, Fad and Science: A Nineteenth Century American Crusade* (New Haven: Yale Univ. Press, 1955), 95–96.

26. Dain, 76–77.

27. Conrad, 218–19, 245; Dain, 162.

28. Davies, 47, 56, 60. The lives and careers of the Fowler family are detailed in Madeleine B. Stern, *Heads and Headlines: The Phrenological Fowlers* (Norman: Univ. of Oklahoma Press, 1971). In their defense, Stern notes that the Fowlers worked diligently to increase understanding of insanity in the United States and to reform the methods of treatment of the insane.

29. Levy, 213. For background information regarding Shaw's motivations and influences in the Rogers trial, see Levy, 214–17.

30. "Medical Jurisprudence of Insanity: Review of George Tyler Bigelow, and George Bemis, *Report of the Trial of Abner Rogers, Jr., indicted for the murder of Charles Lincoln, Jr., late Warden of the Massachusetts State Prison; before the Supreme Judicial Court of Massachusetts; holden at Boston, on Tuesday, January 30, 1844* (Boston: Charles C. Little and James Brown, 1844)," *American Journal of Insanity* 1 (1845): 268. James C. Mohr calls Isaac Ray's *Treatise on the Medical Jurisprudence of Insanity* "a virtual manifesto in behalf of the innocent insane, a category of defendants whom Ray considered all too often the victims rather than the beneficiaries of American legal procedure." See Mohr, 146.

31. "Medical Jurisprudence of Insanity," 268–69.

32. "Homicidal Insanity. Court of Oyer and Terminer, City of New York. Before Judge Edmonds and Aldermen Henry and Seaman.—M. C. Paterson, Esq., District Attorney. May 21, 1845.—Case of Murder. (Trial of Andrew Kleim for Murder of Catharine Hanlin, December 23, 1844)," *American Journal of Insanity* 2 (1846): 264–65.

33. *Report of the Trial of Henry Wyatt*, 39.

34. *Auburn Journal and Advertiser*, July 15, 1846.

35. Field, 37; Merrick, 240.

36. Van Deusen, *William Henry Seward*, 94.

37. Field, 46–47.

38. The New York constitutional convention and the issue of black suffrage are also discussed in Holt, 227, 229, 240; Glyndon G. Van Deusen, *Thurlow Weed*, 143–44; and John L. Stanley, "Majority Tyranny in Tocqueville's America: The Failure of Negro Suffrage in 1846," *Political Science Quarterly* 84 (1969): 412–35.

39. The conservative Whig position on the suffrage question is discussed in Holt, 227.

40. *Rochester Daily Advertiser*, April 2, 1846.

41. Seward to Alvah Worden, March 22, 1846, Thurlow Weed Papers, Univ. of Rochester, Rochester, N.Y.

42. Seward to Weed, March 28, 1846, Weed Papers.

43. Van Deusen, *William Henry Seward*, 94.

44. Stanley, 417; Holt, 240.

45. Van Deusen's conclusions regarding Seward's decision to defend Freeman are detailed in *William Henry Seward,* 93–94.

46. Seward to Weed, May 29, 1846, Weed Papers.

47. Ibid.

48. Ibid., July 13, 1846.

49. Ibid., June 10, 1846; Seward to Weed, July [n.d.], 1846, William Henry Seward Papers, Univ. of Rochester, Rochester, N.Y.

50. Seward to Weed, June 10, 1846, Weed Papers.

51. Ibid., August 29, 1846.

52. Seward to James Bowen, September 15, 1846, Seward Papers.

53. Van Deusen, *William Henry Seward,* 93–94.

54. Registers of Male Inmates Discharged, 1817–1949.

55. *Report of the Trial of Henry Wyatt,* 11.

56. Conrad, 7, 157. Despite his failure to document his account, Conrad demonstrates a very thorough familiarity with the leading characters and events in Auburn during the years 1846 and 1847.

57. See various newspaper accounts of the Van Nest killings and the Wyatt and Freeman trials in 1846.

58. *Albany Evening Atlas,* July 24, 1846.

59. Taylor, 301. In a letter to Salmon Portland Chase dated August 4, 1845, Seward stated his reasons for remaining loyal to the Whigs as opposed to joining the Liberty Party. Efforts to increase the ranks of the Liberty Party by tapping antislavery elements of the Whig Party, according to Seward, would merely waste valuable time and energy. Seward believed that the cause of antislavery would be better served by efforts to move the Whig Party further in the direction of opposition to slavery. See J. W. Schuckers, *The Life and Public Services of Salmon Portland Chase* (New York: D. Appleton and Co., 1874), 72.

60. *New York Daily Tribune,* March 20, 1846.

61. Seward to Weed, July [n.d.], 1846, Seward Papers.

62. Mackey, 131–35.

63. Van Deusen, *William Henry Seward,* 84, 93. Conrad also concludes that sympathy for the insane played a far more important role in Seward's decision to defend Freeman than did political considerations based upon Freeman's race. See pp. 157–58.

64. *Auburn Journal and Advertiser,* June 3, 1846.

65. "Trial of William Freeman," 368–69.

66. Seward to Weed, May 29, 1846, Weed Papers.

67. Ibid.

68. Ibid., June 10, 1846.

69. Ibid., July 13, 1846.

70. Ibid., July 8, 1846.

71. Ibid., August 29, 1846.

72. The solicitation of Van Buren's services is discussed in the *Albany Evening Atlas,* June 8, 1846, and *Auburn Journal and Advertiser,* June 24, 1846. Van Buren ventured to Auburn amid speculation in the press that Cayuga County required his services because District Attorney Luman Sherwood was incompetent. Van Buren's services did not come cheap; the expense that counties incurred for his assistance was reported to be in the neighborhood of seventy-five dollars per day. The *Auburn Journal and Advertiser* estimated that Van Buren's services would nearly double the daily expense of the Wyatt proceedings.

73. Seward to Weed, July 8, 1846, Weed Papers.

74. Douglas L. Wilson, *Honor's Voice: The Transformation of Abraham Lincoln* (New York: Alfred A. Knopf, 1998), 295–97. Michael Fellman devotes considerable attention to nineteenth-century notions of honor in *Citizen Sherman: A Life of William Tecumseh Sherman* (New York: Random House, 1995). See, in particular, chapter 4, which is entitled "Failure as a Banker and Debts of Honor."

75. Van Deusen, *William Henry Seward,* 97.

76. Holt, 118.

77. Daniel Walker Howe, *The Political Culture of the American Whigs* (Chicago: Univ. of Chicago Press, 1979), 30, 35.

78. John Ashworth, *Agrarians and Aristocrats: Party Ideology in the United States, 1837–1846* (Cambridge: Cambridge Univ. Press, 1987), 54–61.

79. Rush Welter, *The Mind of America, 1820–1860* (New York: Columbia Univ. Press, 1975), 205–11.

80. Merrick, 217.

81. Van Deusen, *William Henry Seward,* 94.

82. Seward to Weed, June 10, 1846, Weed Papers.

83. Ibid., August 29, 1846.

84. Ibid., August 1, 1846.

85. Seward to James Bowen, September 15, 1846, Seward Papers.

86. *Auburn Journal and Advertiser,* June 3, 1846.

87. Ibid.

88. Ibid.

4. Controversial Verdict, Controversial Defense

1. *New York Daily Tribune,* June 8, 1846.

2. Ibid.; *Cayuga Patriot,* June 3, 1846.

3. *Auburn Journal and Advertiser,* July 1, 1846.

4. *Albany Argus,* June 11, 1846.

5. *Rochester Daily Advertiser,* June 20, 1846.

6. *New York Herald,* June 6, 1846.

7. Ibid.; *Auburn Journal and Advertiser,* July 1, 1846.

8. *Auburn Journal and Advertiser,* June 3 and July 1, 1846.

9. Ibid., July 1, 1846.

10. *Rochester Daily Advertiser,* June 20, 1846; *Albany Argus,* June 11, 1846.

11. *Albany Argus,* June 11, 1846.

12. *Albany Evening Atlas,* June 24, 1846.

13. *Albany Evening Journal,* June 27, 1846. After Wyatt's conviction, the *Cayuga Patriot* expressed considerable relief. The *Patriot* did not fail to notice, however, that there was "something startling too in the nature of the defence, which was such as might be used to screen all murderers from punishment, and thus render life insecure, and sunder the bonds that hold society together." See *Cayuga Patriot,* July 8, 1846. An exchange between the *Daily Cayuga Tocsin* and the *New York Morning News* illustrates the ongoing debate between an angry community and the antigallows reformers. In 1846, Democrat and antigallows reformer John L. O'Sullivan was using the *Morning News* as a mouthpiece for his opposition to capital punishment. The *Tocsin* printed an article by a contributor that the *Morning News* tagged "an ultra capital punishment man." The writer, obviously upset that Wyatt was being allowed a second, prolonged trial, advocated a new scheme of justice for convicts accused of committing murder while in prison. He argued that such accused convicts should be tried before the prison authorities, in much the same way that accused soldiers were tried before courts-martial. The *Morning News* retorted in language that clearly reflected the influence of liberal theology and the New Testament. "In this writer's estimation, human life must be next to worthless," the editorial began. O'Sullivan then attacked the *Tocsin* writer for holding "opinions that foster crime, and result in much evil to society, regarding the convict as a wretch who, by one false step, has forfeited all claim to tolerance or incentive to reform." O'Sullivan was disturbed by the *Tocsin* writer's focus on human depravity and dubbed the doctrine revealed in the *Tocsin,* "He sinned once—he must sin ever." See *New York Morning News,* June 22, 1846.

14. Seward to Weed, June 10, 1846, Weed Papers.

15. *Albany Argus,* June 29, 1846; "Trial of William Freeman," 328–29.

16. "Trial of William Freeman," 329–30, 352–61.

17. *Auburn Journal and Advertiser,* July 8, 1846.

18. "Trial of William Freeman," 329–30.

19. Ibid., 330.

20. *Auburn Journal and Advertiser,* July 8, 1846.

21. Ibid.

22. "Trial of William Freeman," 330.

23. Benjamin Hall, 143.

24. "Trial of William Freeman," 331; Benjamin Hall, 143–44.

25. Benjamin Hall, 144.

26. "Defence of William Freeman," 414.

27. *Albany Evening Atlas,* July 7, 1846.

28. *Cayuga Patriot,* July 22, 1846.

29. Benjamin Hall, 145.

30. This dialogue is reconstructed from Benjamin Hall, 145, and *New York Daily Tribune,* November 27, 1846.

31. *New York Daily Tribune,* November 27, 1846.

32. Benjamin Hall, 145; "Defence of William Freeman," 418.

33. *Auburn Journal and Advertiser,* July 8, 1846.

34. "Trial of William Freeman," 332. For a discussion of the role of Quakers in opposing the death penalty, see Mackey, 214, 217.

35. *Auburn Journal and Advertiser,* July 8, 1846.

36. *Albany Argus,* July 13, 1846; "Trial of William Freeman," 332. Joining Whiting at the bench were associates Joseph L. Richardson, Isaac Sisson, Abner Hollister, and Walter G. Bradley. See Benjamin Hall, 169.

37. "Trial of William Freeman," 513.

38. Ibid., 357–58; "Defence of William Freeman," 456–58.

39. "Trial of William Freeman," 336, 469–70. As noted in the previous chapter, the ability to distinguish between right and wrong was the central element of the McNaughtan rules.

40. "Defence of William Freeman," 419–20. Testimony taken at Kleim's trial revealed that he set fire to the residence of his neighbors, Catharine Hanlin and her family, on the morning of December 23, 1844. When Hanlin attempted to flee the building through the only existing door, Kleim blocked her path and thrust her back into the blaze. He pursued her into the residence and stabbed her in the thigh with an iron spike that was mounted at the end of a stick. A postmortem examination revealed that Hanlin died from asphyxiation caused by severe burns to the throat, larynx, trachea, and lungs. She had also suffered three broken ribs. Nothing in the testimony indicated that Kleim had any rational motive to harm the Hanlins. Defense witnesses testified that before the crime, Kleim had expressed concern about threats made upon his life. Dr. Pliny Earle, superintendent of the Bloomingdale Lunatic Asylum in New York City, testified that Kleim's social feelings were "evidently destroyed or perverted." Earle concluded that Kleim manifested "no consciousness of the relation in which he is now placed with reference to the law." Prosecution witnesses, including physicians and laymen, testified that Kleim understood the wrongful nature of his actions and exhibited no evidence of insanity. See "Homicidal Insanity," 245–61.

41. "Defence of William Freeman," 421.

42. Ibid., 420, 423.

43. "Trial of William Freeman," 358.

44. "Defence of William Freeman," 423.

45. Ibid., 422.

46. "Trial of William Freeman," 355–56, 358; "Defence of William Freeman," 422.

47. "Defence of William Freeman," 420.

48. "Trial of William Freeman," 340–41.

49. Ibid., 360–61.

50. Dain, 72–73.

51. Seward's praise for the medical witnesses that testified on Freeman's behalf appears in "Defence of William Freeman," 466–67. The relationship between Briggs and Freeman, and between Van Epps and Freeman, was revealed in the doctors' testimony. See "Trial of William Freeman," 375, 380; and David Dimon, *The Freeman Trial: Presenting the Testimony Given in This Remarkable Case, with Comments* (Auburn: Dennis Bro's and Thorne, 1871), 25.

52. "Defence of William Freeman," 462–63.

53. "Trial of William Freeman," 375–76.

54. Ibid., 380–81.

55. Ibid., 369–70.

56. Dimon, 28.

57. "Trial of William Freeman," 388. Van Buren indicated in his closing argument that other prisoners thought that they were entitled to pay for time lost in prison. See "Trial of William Freeman," 501.

58. Dimon, 25, 27.

59. "Trial of William Freeman," 387; Benjamin Hall, 309.

60. Dimon, 27.

61. "Trial of William Freeman," 386–87.

62. Ibid., 386–87.

63. Benjamin Hall, 307–8.

64. "Homicidal Insanity," 265. For Shaw's influential discussion of irresistible impulse, see "Medical Jurisprudence of Insanity," 269.

65. Benjamin Hall, 298–99; Dimon, 46.

66. Dimon, 42.

67. "Trial of William Freeman," 382–83.

68. Dimon, 43–47.

69. Ibid., 18, 40.

70. Ibid., 45, 47.

71. Brigham is quoted in this manner in both "Trial of William Freeman," 384, and Dimon, 45.

72. Dimon, 45; Brigham also offered an assessment of Kleim's condition in "Homicidal Insanity," 266.

73. "Defence of William Freeman," 445.

74. Ibid., 446–47; Austin's testimony appears in "Trial of William Freeman," 368, and Benjamin Hall, 250. Hotchkiss's testimony appears in "Trial of William Freeman," 378.

75. "Trial of William Freeman," 359, 361.

76. Ibid., 360.

77. Benjamin Hall, 251–53.

78. "Defence of William Freeman," 470–71.

79. Ibid., 439–40. Ironically, the creation of a special public school district for the bene-

fit of black children, as discussed in chapter 1, took place just weeks after Freeman was convicted of the murder of John G. Van Nest. Before that date, the only educational opportunities available to black children apart from private instruction inside the home (which was
rarely feasible) were in Sunday schools established in both white and black churches. See
Henry Hall, 150, 280–82; also see Allen, 39.

80. "Defence of William Freeman," 440.

81. Kristin Hoganson, "Garrisonian Abolitionists and the Rhetoric of Gender,
1850–1860," *American Quarterly* 45 (1993): 586–87.

82. Frederick Douglass's vision of masculinity was personified in the character of Madi-
son Washington, the protagonist in Douglass's fictionalized account of a successful slave
mutiny, "Heroic Slave" (1853). Washington, the leader of the revolt, "rejects the Andrew
Jackson model of masculine aggression and acquisition in favor of a different masculine model
that incorporates moral restraint and respect for other peoples." Washington prevents the "re-
vengeful killing" of the slaver's white crew because it is "unnecessary for the slaves' victory."
He displays bravery and physical strength in rising up against an unjust oppressor, but his character is tempered by "a moral restraint that recognizes the natural rights of his opponents, regardless of their race." In his insistence "that moral and ethical considerations must transcend
racial distinctions," Washington gives voice to Douglass's vision of an "heroic manhood."
Douglass rejected notions of a "gendered racial hierarchy" that were used by whites to support
"unrestrained aggressiveness" toward blacks. Black men, Douglass asserted, were equal to
white men in physical prowess and courage. Ideally, however, Douglass's black revolutionary
operated at a higher moral level than his white counterpart. See Maggie Sale, "Critiques from
Within: Antebellum Projects of Resistance," *American Literature* 64 (1992): 702–3. Charles
Sellers observes, additionally, that the popular mid-nineteenth-century image of manhood
placed tremendous pressure on American men to succeed in the competitive world of the
market. "With the traditional patriarchy of household production shattered," Sellers notes,
"sons had to compete for elusive manhood in the market rather than grow into secure manhood by replicating fathers." In a culture where many could never attain the "self-made manhood of success," he adds, "middle-class masculinity pushed egotism to extremes of
aggression, calculation, self-control, and unremitting effort." With encouragement from
politicians of both parties, Sellers concludes, working-class white men found an outlet for
their insecurities in "dehumanizing 'niggers'—as stupid, lazy, obsequious, larcenous, and immoral." Fear of failure, which was viewed as unmanly, "both energized effort and turned the
shame of proletarianized whites against even more vulnerable blacks." If blacks were not allowed to rise to an equal socioeconomic level with whites, precarious white masculinity
would remain sheltered from at least one potential threat. Given the scope of his involvement
in public service, it is likely that Seward was aware that such feelings at least partially ac-
counted for white prejudice. Along with northern social reformers, he participated in an ongoing effort to shift antebellum notions of masculinity away from competition, insecurity,
and aggression. The reformers' concept of Christian manhood clearly rejected the neglect

and dehumanization of blacks. See *The Market Revolution: Jacksonian America, 1815–1846* (New York: Oxford Univ. Press, 1991), 245–46, 386–87.

5. The Tried Experience and Security of Law

1. "Trial of William Freeman," 336. Daniel N. Robinson discusses, in detail, many of the treatises and decisions that Sherwood cited. Among them were the trials in England of Edward Arnold in 1724, and of Lawrence, the Earl Ferrers, in 1760. The standard used to define insanity in these cases was that the accused must be indistinguishable from "infant, brute or wild beast." See Robinson, 134, 138.

2. "Trial of William Freeman," 336–37.

3. Ibid., 469; Sir Matthew Hale, in his 1680 treatise entitled *The History of the Pleas of the Crown*, maintained that only total insanity or a total want of reason excused capital crimes. See Robinson, 118–19.

4. "Trial of William Freeman," 469–71.

5. Ibid., 511–12. Wyatt's conviction, in which the attorney general was involved, certainly bolstered Van Buren's confidence that jurors in New York could be persuaded to view moral insanity with suspicion. Van Buren's reasoning resembled that of Justice Robert Tracy, who in Edward Arnold's trial weighed the importance of general deterrence when defining insanity. Tracy postulated that the "jury must consider the plea in the context of the offense itself, weighing the cost to justice of excusing so grave an offense on less than the most compelling grounds." See Robinson, 134–35.

6. Levy, 214–16.

7. "Trial of William Freeman," 336–38.

8. Ibid., 369, 387, 474, 479.

9. Ibid., 475.

10. Shaw's rulings with regard to implied malice are discussed in Levy, 220–27.

11. "Trial of William Freeman," 340.

12. Dimon, 7–8.

13. "Trial of William Freeman," 350.

14. Ibid., 472.

15. Ibid., 346; Benjamin Hall, 195–96.

16. "Trial of William Freeman," 351.

17. Benjamin Hall, 332; "Trial of William Freeman," 394.

18. "Trial of William Freeman," 364.

19. Ibid., 370.

20. Dimon, 40.

21. "Trial of William Freeman," 342.

22. Dimon, 4–5.

23. "Trial of William Freeman," 352.

24. Dimon, 49.

25. Van Buren realized that despite his distaste for it, he had to acquire an understanding of the theory of moral insanity in order to argue that Freeman did not fit the general description. Van Buren astutely quoted from the major antebellum authorities on the theory, including Esquirol, Prichard, and of course, the authority that had most greatly influenced Chief Justice Shaw, Isaac Ray. According to Ray, the homicidal monomaniac (a term commonly used to refer to morally insane killers) "falls upon the object of his fury, oftentimes, without the most proper means for accomplishing his purpose, and perhaps in the presence of a multitude, as if expressly to court observation; and then voluntarily surrenders himself to the constituted authorities." Ray also observed that criminal behavior among the morally insane resulted from "a strong, and perhaps sudden impulse, opposed to [their] natural habits." Esquirol noted a lack of "regret, remorse or fear" among homicidal monomaniacs, as well as their tendency to remain at the crime scene or hastily reveal their acts to the authorities. Their acts were usually not the result of any immediate, external provocation that was proportional to the resulting violence. Van Buren argued that Freeman most closely resembled the descriptions of the malicious murderer, presented by Ray and Esquirol for the purpose of differentiating depravity from insanity. See "Trial of William Freeman," 498–500.

26. Ibid., 498.

27. Dimon, 11.

28. "Trial of William Freeman," 350.

29. Ibid., 382.

30. Dimon, 40.

31. "Trial of William Freeman," 377.

32. Dimon, 37.

33. James H. Cassedy, *Medicine in America: A Short History* (Baltimore: Johns Hopkins Univ. Press, 1991), 33–34.

34. Mohr, 87–88.

35. Joseph F. Kett, *The Formation of the American Medical Profession: The Role of Institutions, 1780–1860* (New Haven: Yale Univ. Press, 1968), 31.

36. Cassedy, 34.

37. Mohr, 88.

38. Cassedy, 34.

39. Richard Hofstadter, *Anti-Intellectualism in American Life* (New York: Alfred A. Knopf, 1966), 154–56, 170.

40. Mohr, 88.

41. Perry Miller, *The Life of the Mind in America from the Revolution to the Civil War* (New York: Harcourt, Brace and World, Inc., 1965), 102–3.

42. Hofstadter, 151, 161, 164.

43. Paul Starr, *The Social Transformation of American Medicine* (New York: Basic Books, 1982), 56–59.

44. Ibid., 57–59. Clergy and laymen of the Calvinist denominations viewed the defense of moral insanity with suspicion, as well. Religious commentators concluded that it was merely a new word for sin, presented to protect "desperate culprits" whose only indications of insanity were the "enormity of their crimes." The security of society would be better preserved if the intelligent public, rather than physicians, were trusted with determining "when insanity reached the level at which moral accountability no longer existed." Calvinists did not regard physicians as "especially competent in philosophy or ethics." Laymen were better able to judge with "intuitive certainty" on such matters. The "unperverted common sense of mankind" was the better source of judgement regarding the point at which legal responsibility ended. See Dain, 192–93.

45. Mohr, 96, 104–7. The author notes that "juries of experts" were contemplated by antebellum doctors and lawyers as a possible solution to the problems that arose in trials involving medical issues. Under the adversarial system, the opposing sides presented medical witnesses of varying levels of expertise. Juries were confused and justice compromised by the testimony of these so-called experts, some of whom knew painfully little about the subject at hand. Juries of truly qualified physicians, it was suggested, could convene in the manner of a grand jury for the purpose of settling cases involving poisoning, insanity, or other vexing medical issues.

46. "Trial of William Freeman," 341.

47. "Medical Jurisprudence of Insanity," 270–71.

48. "Trial of William Freeman," 466–67.

49. Ibid., 467–68, 489.

50. Ibid., 340–41.

51. Dimon, 28.

52. Ibid., 29–30.

53. Ibid., 30–31; "Trial of William Freeman," 394.

54. Dimon, 35.

55. "Trial of William Freeman," 376–77, 395.

56. Dimon, 39.

57. "Trial of William Freeman," 396.

58. Dimon, 51.

59. Ibid., 57–58; "Trial of William Freeman," 402–3. Earl Conrad asserts, with good reason, that Seward believed Dr. Spencer was nothing more than a quack who tarnished the reputation of legitimate science. "The doctor overwhelms us with learning, universal and incomprehensible," Seward complained during the trial. Freeman's counsel believed that if anyone exemplified the deliberate attempt to render the science of the human mind beyond the ordinary man's comprehension, Spencer certainly did. Seward was amazed that, given the venom with which the counsel for the people denounced men of science, such a witness was called to testify. See Conrad, 218–19, 245; see also "Defence of William Freeman," 463–64.

60. "Trial of William Freeman," 335–36, 342. Robert F. Berkhofer Jr. traces "savage" im-

ages of Native Americans back to the need of whites to justify forcing cultural change upon native peoples. The image of the "bad Indian" was used as a justification for the forced transformation of Native Americans from "savage" ways to civilized ways through European exploitation and religious conversion. See *The White Man's Indian: Images of the American Indian from Columbus to the Present* (New York: Alfred A. Knopf, 1978) 93, 119.

61. "Trial of William Freeman," 342–43.

62. Dain, 199.

63. Dimon, 16–17; George M. Fredrickson concludes that after the 1830s, "widespread, almost universal agreement existed on the following points: blacks are physically, intellectually, temperamentally different from whites; blacks are also inferior to whites in at least some of the fundamental qualities wherein the races differ, especially in intelligence and in the temperamental basis of enterprise or initiative." See *The Black Image in the White Mind: The Debate on Afro-American Character and Destiny, 1817–1914* (Hanover: Wesleyan Univ. Press, 1987), 321.

64. "Trial of William Freeman," 394.

65. Dimon, 30–31.

66. Ibid., 33.

67. "Trial of William Freeman," 397.

68. Dimon, 61–63.

69. Ibid., 9, 30.

70. Ibid., 33.

71. "Trial of William Freeman," 365–66.

72. Ibid., 483. The second white witness to contradict De Puy was Thomas F. Monroe. For his testimony, see "Trial of William Freeman," 304; and Dimon, 31.

73. Dimon, 34; "Trial of William Freeman," 396.

74. Dimon, 24; "Trial of William Freeman," 380.

75. "Trial of William Freeman," 477.

76. Dimon, 36.

77. "Trial of William Freeman," 480.

78. Dimon, 25.

79. Dimon, 53; "Defence of William Freeman," 439.

80. "Trial of William Freeman," 393, 480.

81. Ibid., 378–79, 477, 480, 494.

82. Ibid., 364.

83. Ibid., 482.

84. "Defence of William Freeman," 470.

85. Dimon, 23.

86. "Defence of William Freeman," 470; "Trial of William Freeman," 379–80.

87. "Trial of William Freeman," 477.

88. Ibid., 494. The white witness to which Van Buren referred was Levi Hermance, an

assistant keeper at Auburn State Prison who claimed to have practiced medicine. Van Buren in turn attacked Hermance's credibility on the grounds of limited medical experience and limited exposure to Freeman.

89. *Cayuga Patriot,* July 29, 1846.

90. "Trial of William Freeman," 463, 493. The attorney general was well aware, however, that certain members of the community did not share the prosecution's views regarding the character of nonwhite peoples. He challenged the acceptance of three men that were eventually sworn as jurors, for belonging "to a class termed abolitionists." Van Buren "desired to know whether they entertained any peculiar views in regard to the general neglect of the colored race, which would induce them to hold society, and not the individual, responsible for the crimes which this race commits." The attorney general withdrew the challenges after he became satisfied that these men "were disposed to try this case precisely like that of a white man." Van Buren's concerns were not unwarranted; certain commentators, as demonstrated, did hold society in some measure responsible for the killer's actions. See "Trial of William Freeman," 510–11.

91. "Defence of William Freeman," 417, 463. Leon Litwack concludes that whites created the condition of blacks and then used that condition as evidence of blacks' inferiority and inability to become educated or rise economically. See Litwack, 279.

92. "Defence of William Freeman," 417–18.

93. Ibid., 418–19; Norman Dain notes that though loss of reason and inability to tell right from wrong at the time of the crime were the criteria most commonly used to determine legal insanity, these standards were "not applied in cases of the defendant's obvious idiocy or imbecility." Evidence of "great intellectual deficiency seemed to be enough proof of irresponsibility and thus insanity," he adds. Seward was aware of this, and he claimed that Freeman's case was treated differently because the accused was not white. Dain's research into antebellum insanity trials supports Seward's conclusion. See Dain, 45, 199.

94. "Defence of William Freeman," 471. At this time, every state except Massachusetts barred blacks from testifying against whites in court. *America's History,* vol. 1, ed. James A. Henretta et al. (New York: Worth Publishers, 1997), 392.

95. "Defence of William Freeman," 470–71.

96. Ibid., 471. Vivienne L. Kruger observes that in order to secure passage of the 1799 emancipation bill, the New York State legislature made a number of concessions to "Dutch and other slaveholding interests." Slavery was to be "phased out in a way that would preserve the rights of property owners; current slaves would remain enslaved for life so that no slaveholder would lose his investment." The 1799 act stipulated that all children born of slave women after July 4, 1799, were legally born free but owed a period of service to their mothers' masters. The period of service was twenty-five years for females and twenty-eight years for males. Until an amendment was passed in 1804, owners of newborns could "legally abandon them at age one to local overseers of the poor if they felt that the cost of rearing them would not be compensated by the limited twenty-five or twenty-eight years of service."

Abandoned newborns were bound out to service by authorities "as early as practicable," the authorities having the option to grant the children freedom at either age eighteen or twenty-one. Several provisions that had been "inserted into the program to mollify slaveholders," including the provision allowing abandonment, were slowly removed. In 1817, a "major revision" of the original 1799 gradual emancipation act was passed. Children born to slave women between July 4, 1799, and March 31, 1817, "were still to be retained as servants until age twenty-five or twenty-eight" as per the original act. Children of either sex born between April 1, 1817, and July 4, 1827, owed service for a period of twenty-one years prior to receiving their freedom. The 1817 act gave slave owners "notice that their permanent slaves were to be taken away in ten years' time." All slaves born before July 4, 1799, were to be freed on July 4, 1827. Kruger draws attention to the frequently overlooked fact that the very last children born to slave mothers in New York did not complete their service obligations until July 4, 1848. See *Born to Run: The Slave Family in Early New York, 1626–1827* (Ph.D. diss., Columbia Univ., 1985; Ann Arbor: University Microfilms International, 1988), 818–24, 839, 862–63. Edgar J. McManus adds that as slavery passed away in the North, racial restrictions enacted by states increased. Slaves were freed in New York when their labor was no longer needed but were then excluded from opportunities to support themselves in decent fashion. See *A History of Negro Slavery in New York* (Syracuse: Syracuse Univ. Press, 1966), 184–85, 193–95.

97. Maxwell Bloomfield, *American Lawyers in a Changing Society, 1776–1876* (Cambridge: Harvard Univ. Press, 1976), 106.

98. Ibid., 108; Lawrence M. Friedman, *A History of American Law,* 2nd ed. (New York: Simon and Schuster, 1985), 204.

99. Bloomfield, 106–7.

100. Michael Grossberg, *Governing the Hearth: Law and the American Family in Nineteenth-Century America* (Chapel Hill: Univ. of North Carolina Press, 1985), 70–71; Friedman also observes that common-law marriage had a "solid basis in the social context" of early America. Rejection of oppression by an official church was part of the intellectual climate dating back to the colonial period. Informal unions were a traditional means of defending private decision making from church interference. All colonies except Maryland offered couples the right to choose between civil and religious marriage rites, but as Grossberg observes, dissenters from both forms of public regulation pursued informal unions. Religious dissenters, and others who resented contractualism in marriage law and the bureaucratic controls instituted by provincial statutes, wed clandestinely despite the threat of legal sanctions. Friedman adds that in the early days of colonization, and later in rural areas, the lack of "a reliable corps of religious and lay officials" forced some couples to wed informally. The rising cost of marriage fees, "sometimes as high as a month's wages," encouraged others to "bypass formal ceremonies." By the beginning of the nineteenth century, the interference of official churches in private decision making was becoming a memory. Nevertheless, a tradition of informal marriage was firmly implanted in American culture. See Friedman, *A History of American Law,*

203. Grossberg notes that the formation of the American republic had positive effects for those that wanted or needed informal marriage. In the first half of the nineteenth century, "American marriage law reflected, and in turn fostered, a republican ethos that weakened the public regulation of matrimony, whether by parents, the local community, or the state." The judicial recognition of common-law marriage reflected a "faith in competitive individualism and voluntary choice," asserting that the "commonwealth was better served by judicially supervised self-regulation than by public scrutiny." The evils of state intervention in the "private sphere of life" were assumed to far outweigh the "inevitable problems arising from flawed human nature." By legitimizing private practice, Grossberg states, "marriage law strengthened the proposition that social order came through the validation of voluntary decisions rather than through regulated conduct." By mid-century, judicially inspired "liberal rules" governed marital rites in almost every state. Based in part on practicality and in part on republican notions of social order, judicial recognition of informal marriage legitimized traditional behavior. See *Governing the Hearth,* 70, 82–83.

101. "Defence of William Freeman," 471–72.

102. "Trial of William Freeman," 516.

103. *Albany Evening Atlas,* July 24, 1846.

104. "Trial of William Freeman," 513.

105. Ibid., 513–14.

106. For Edmonds's charge in the trial of Andrew Kleim, see "Homicidal Insanity," 265.

107. "Trial of William Freeman," 513–14.

108. "Medical Jurisprudence of Insanity," 272; Hornblower's ruling was laid down in *State v. Spencer,* quoted in "The People v. McCann," *Reports of Cases Argued and Determined in the Court of Appeals in the State of New York,* vol. 2, ed. E. Peshine Smith (New York: Banks and Brothers, 1858), 62.

109. "Trial of William Freeman," 513–14; the clear and convincing standard is defined in Edward W. Cleary et al., eds., *McCormick on Evidence,* 3d ed. Hornbook Series, Lawyer's Edition (St. Paul: West Publishing Co., 1984), 959–60.

110. Shaw attempted in *Commonwealth v. Rogers* to establish the relevance of expert medical opinion when a defendant's guilt or innocence depended upon his state of mind. He included mental illness among the subjects that produced questions "beyond the scope of the observation and experience of men in general." Such questions were, however, "quite within the observation and experience of those whose peculiar pursuits and profession, have brought that class of facts frequently and habitually under their consideration." Judge Edmonds, as noted, agreed as to the utility of expert witnesses in insanity trials. See "Medical Jurisprudence of Insanity," 270; "Homicidal Insanity," 263.

111. "Trial of William Freeman," 515–16.

112. Ibid., 516.

113. Ibid.

114. *Albany Evening Journal,* July 29, 1846.

6. Aftermath: Vindication Denied

1. *New York Herald,* July 28, 1846.

2. Sentencing of Freeman from *Daily Cayuga Tocsin,* as quoted in *Albany Evening Atlas,* July 28, 1846, and from *Auburn Daily Advertiser,* as quoted in *Albany Evening Journal,* July 29, 1846.

3. Ibid., "Trial of William Freeman," 517.

4. "Trial of William Freeman," 518.

5. *Daily Cayuga Tocsin* quoted in the *Albany Argus,* July 27, 1846.

6. "Trial of William Freeman," 516.

7. *Cayuga Patriot,* July 29, 1846.

8. "Plea of Insanity in Criminal Cases," *Law Reporter* 10 (May 1847): 1–4.

9. Ibid., 6.

10. Ibid., 4, 7–12.

11. "Plea of Insanity in Criminal Cases," *Law Reporter* 10 (July 1847): 103.

12. "Medical Jurisprudence," *New York Journal of Medicine and the Collateral Sciences* 7 (1846): 262–63.

13. Ibid., 260–63.

14. John McCall to Seward, July 4, 1846, Seward Papers.

15. Gerrit Smith to Seward, February 18, 1847, Seward Papers.

16. Seward to Weed, September 8, 1846, Weed Papers.

17. *New York Courier and Morning Enquirer* quoted in *Albany Evening Journal,* September 12, 1846.

18. *Daily Cayuga Tocsin* quoted in *Albany Evening Journal,* September 5, 1846.

19. *New York Daily Tribune,* November 27, 1846.

20. *Albany Evening Atlas,* August 21, 1846.

21. *Daily Cayuga Tocsin*'s account of the execution of Wyatt quoted in *Albany Evening Atlas,* August 19, 1846.

22. *Albany Evening Journal,* September 12, 1846.

23. *American Journal of Insanity* 4 (1847): 183.

24. *Albany Argus,* July 27, 1846.

25. *Albany Evening Journal,* September 12, 1846.

26. *New York Daily Tribune,* September 15, 1846.

27. "Freeman v. the People," in *Reports of Cases Argued and Determined in the Supreme Court and in the Court for the Correction of Errors of the State of New York,* vol. 4, ed. Hiram Denio (New York: Banks and Brothers, 1859), 18–19.

28. *Albany Evening Journal,* September 14, 1846.

29. Conrad, 294.

30. "Trial of William Freeman," 518; "Freeman v. the People," 18.

31. "Freeman v. the People," 9–10; *Auburn Journal and Advertiser,* February 10, 1847.

32. "Freeman v. the People," 24–25, 27–28.

33. Ibid., 28.

34. "Trial of William Freeman," 330, 376.

35. "Freeman v. the People," 30.

36. "Trial of William Freeman," 344, 465.

37. Ibid., 388–89.

38. Ibid., 389.

39. "Defence of William Freeman," 468. Since the preliminary verdict was rendered on July 5, no evidence obtained on or after July 6 was deemed admissible.

40. "Freeman v. the People," 39–40.

41. Ibid., 40–41.

42. "Trial of William Freeman," 356.

43. "Case of William Freeman, Indicted for Murder," *New York Journal of Medicine and the Collateral Sciences* 9 (1847): 251.

44. Ibid., 251–53. For the relevant text of Beardsley's opinion, see also "Freeman v. the People," 28–29.

45. "Plea of Insanity in Criminal Cases," *Law Reporter* 10 (July 1847), 105–7.

46. Seward to Weed, February 2, 1847, Weed Papers.

47. *Albany Evening Journal,* August 26, 1846.

48. *Albany Evening Journal* quoted in *Cayuga Patriot,* March 3, 1847.

49. *Albany Evening Atlas* quoted in *Cayuga Patriot,* March 3, 1847; "Trial of William Freeman," 332, indicates that sixty-five jurors were examined in the process of selecting the jury in the trial on the indictment.

50. *Auburn Daily Advertiser* quoted and commented on in *Cayuga Patriot,* February 17, 1847.

51. Cornwell is quoted and commented on in *Cayuga Patriot,* February 17, 1847. Michael Holt discusses Cornwell's background in *The Rise and Fall of the American Whig Party,* 587.

52. *Cayuga Patriot,* February 24, 1847.

53. *New York Daily Tribune,* February 19, 1847.

54. Gerrit Smith to Seward, February 18, 1847, Seward Papers.

55. Smith's letter to Seward was published in *Frederick Douglass' Paper,* March 23, 1855. James McCune Smith, in an 1855 letter to Gerrit Smith, also acknowledged that the Freeman trial remained a source of Gerrit Smith's respect for Seward. See James McCune Smith to Gerrit Smith, March 31, 1855, in *The Black Abolitionist Papers,* vol. 4, The United States, 1847–1858, ed. C. Peter Ripley (Chapel Hill: Univ. of North Carolina Press, 1991), 275.

56. Phillips is quoted from a speech entitled "Progress," delivered before the Twenty-eighth Congregational Society in Music Hall, Boston, February 17, 1861. See Wendell Phillips, *Speeches, Lectures, and Letters* (Boston: Lothrop, Lee, and Shepard Co., 1891), 382.

57. James McCune Smith to Gerrit Smith, March 31, 1855, *Black Abolitionist Papers,* 4: 275.

58. "Defence of Freeman," 474.

59. Seward, as noted, referred to both William and Sally Freeman as "degraded." See "Defence of Freeman," 419, 439.

60. *Black Abolitionist Papers,* 4: 274–76.

61. Lawrence J. Friedman, *Gregarious Saints,* 166, 170, 193–94; Van Deusen supports this assessment of Seward, noting that Seward "did not believe that the black man in America was the equal of the white, or that he was capable of assimilation as were the Irish and German immigrants." See *William Henry Seward,* 94.

62. Case and Action Registers, 1813–1831, 1841–1883, Attorney General's Office, Record Series B0606–82, New York State Archives, Albany, N.Y.

63. "Review of Benjamin F. Hall, *The Trial of William Freeman, for the murder of John G. Van Nest, including the Evidence and the Arguments of Counsel, with the Decision of the Supreme Court granting a new trial—And of the post-mortem examination of the body by Amariah Brigham, M.D., and others* (Auburn: Derby, Miller, and Co., 1848)," *American Journal of Insanity* 5 (1848): 59.

64. *Cayuga Patriot,* March 3, 1847. Recognizance referred to "an obligation undertaken by a person, generally a defendant in a criminal case, to appear in court on a particular day or to keep the peace." See Joseph R. Nolan, et al., *Black's Law Dictionary,* 6th ed. (St. Paul: West Publishing Co., 1990).

65. The bulk of this account is taken from "Review of Hall," 47–48; David Dimon makes reference to Freeman's difficulty breathing in *Freeman Trial,* 76.

66. "Review of Hall," 49–51.

67. This summary of the autopsy report appears in Dimon, 76; for additional details, see "Review of Hall," 55.

68. Dimon, 76–77.

Conclusion

1. Influenced by Ray, Doe formulated what became known as the New Hampshire rule. Under this rule, criminal responsibility hinged not upon delusion or knowledge of right and wrong but upon whether or not the alleged criminal act "was the offspring of mental disease in the defendant." See Maeder, 43–46.

Bibliography

Primary Sources

Manuscript Collections

George J. Mastin Collection, New York State Historical Association, Cooperstown, N.Y.
William Henry Seward Papers, University of Rochester, Rochester, N.Y.
Thurlow Weed Papers, University of Rochester, Rochester, N.Y.

Government Records

Case and Action Registers, 1813–1831, 1841–1883, Attorney General's Office, Record Series B0606–82, New York State Archives, Albany, N.Y.
Daily Punishment Reports, 1836–1846, Auburn Prison, Record Series A0780–80, New York State Archives, Albany, N.Y.
Registers of Male Inmates Discharged, 1817–1949, Auburn Prison, Record Series B0068–77, New York State Archives, Albany, N.Y.

Published Trial Reports

"Defence of William Freeman." In *The Works of William H. Seward*, vol. 1, ed. George E. Baker, 409–75. New York: Redfield, 1853.
Dimon, David. *The Freeman Trial: Presenting the Testimony Given in This Remarkable Case, with Comments.* Auburn: Dennis Bro's and Thorne, 1871.
"Freeman v. the People." In *Reports of Cases Argued and Determined in the Supreme*

Court and in the Court for the Correction of Errors of the State of New York, vol. 4, ed. Hiram Denio, 9–41. New York: Banks and Brothers, 1859.

Hall, Benjamin F. *The Trial of William Freeman, for the Murder of John G. Van Nest, Including the Evidence and the Arguments of Counsel, with the Decision of the Supreme Court Granting a New Trial, and an Account of the Death of the Prisoner, and of the Post-Mortem Examination of His Body by Amariah Brigham, M.D., and Others.* Auburn: Derby, Miller, and Co., 1848.

"The People v. McCann." In *Reports of Cases Argued and Determined in the Court of Appeals of the State of New York*, vol. 2, ed. E. Peshine Smith, 58–65. New York: Banks and Brothers, 1858.

Report of the Trial of Henry Wyatt, a Convict in the State Prison at Auburn, Indicted for the Murder of James Gordon, Another Convict Within the Prison. Auburn: J. C. Derby, 1846.

"The Trial of William Freeman for the Murder of John G. Van Nest, Auburn, New York, 1846." In *American State Trials*, vol. 16, ed. John D. Lawson, 323–519. St. Louis: Thomas Law Book Co., 1928.

Periodicals

Albany Argus

Albany Evening Atlas

Albany Evening Journal

American Journal of Insanity

Auburn Journal and Advertiser

Cayuga Patriot

Frederick Douglass' Paper

Liberator

Morning Courier and New York Enquirer

National Anti-Slavery Standard

New York Daily Tribune

New York Herald

New York Morning Express

New York Morning News

The Prisoner's Friend

Rochester Daily Advertiser

Articles on Cases Involving Insanity

"Case of William Freeman, Indicted for Murder." *New York Journal of Medicine and the Collateral Sciences* 9 (1847): 251–53.

"Homicidal Insanity. Court of Oyer and Terminer, City of New York. Before Judge Edmonds and Aldermen Henry and Seaman.—M. C. Paterson, Esq., District Attorney. May 21, 1845.—Case of Murder. (Trial of Andrew Kleim for Murder of Catharine Hanlin, December 23, 1844)." *American Journal of Insanity* 2 (1846): 245–66.

"Medical Jurisprudence." *New York Journal of Medicine and the Collateral Sciences* 7 (1846): 260–64.

"Medical Jurisprudence of Insanity: Review of George Tyler Bigelow, and George Bemis, *Report of the Trial of Abner Rogers, Jr., indicted for the murder of Charles Lincoln, Jr., late Warden of the Massachusetts State Prison; before the Supreme Judicial Court of Massachusetts; holden at Boston, on Tuesday, January 30, 1844* (Boston: Charles C. Little and James Brown, 1844)." *American Journal of Insanity* 1 (1845): 258–74.

"Plea of Insanity in Criminal Cases." *Law Reporter* 10 (May 1847): 1–12.

"Plea of Insanity in Criminal Cases." *Law Reporter* 10 (July 1847): 97–112.

"Review of Benjamin F. Hall, *The Trial of William Freeman, for the murder of John G. Van Nest, including the Evidence and the Arguments of Counsel, with the Decision of the Supreme Court granting a new trial—And of the post-mortem examination of the body by Amariah Brigham, M.D., and others* (Auburn: Derby, Miller, and Co., 1848)." *American Journal of Insanity* 5 (1848): 34–60.

Published Papers and Correspondence

Phillips, Wendell. *Speeches, Lectures, and Letters.* Boston: Lothrop, Lee, and Shepard Co., 1891.

Ripley, C. Peter., ed. *The Black Abolitionist Papers,* vol. 4, The United States, 1847–1858. Chapel Hill: Univ. of North Carolina Press, 1991.

Secondary Sources

Books, Articles, and Published Dissertations

Allen, Henry Mott. *A Chronicle of Auburn from 1793 to 1955, Being a Chronicle of Early Auburn, and Chronicle of Auburn Consolidated.* Auburn: Henry M. Allen, 1955.

Ashworth, John. *Agrarians and Aristocrats: Party Ideology in the United States, 1837–1846.* Cambridge: Cambridge Univ. Press, 1987.

Baur, John I. H. *American Painting in the Nineteenth Century: Main Trends and Movements.* New York: Frederick A. Praeger, 1953.

Benson, Lee. *The Concept of Jacksonian Democracy: New York as a Test Case.* Princeton: Princeton Univ. Press, 1961.

Berkhofer, Robert F., Jr. *The White Man's Indian: Images of the American Indian from Columbus to the Present.* New York: Alfred A. Knopf, 1978.

Bloomfield, Maxwell. *American Lawyers in a Changing Society, 1776–1876.* Cambridge: Harvard Univ. Press, 1976.

Brundage, W. Fitzhugh. *Lynching in the New South: Georgia and Virginia, 1880–1930.* Urbana: Univ. of Illinois Press, 1993.

Cassedy, James H. *Medicine in America: A Short History.* Baltimore: Johns Hopkins Univ. Press, 1991.

Christianson, Scott. *With Liberty for Some: 500 Years of Imprisonment in America.* Boston: Northeastern Univ. Press, 1998.

Cleary, Edward W., et al., eds. *McCormick on Evidence,* 3d ed. Hornbook Series, Lawyer's Edition. St. Paul: West Publishing Co., 1984.

Conrad, Earl. *Mr. Seward for the Defense.* New York: Rinehart and Co., Inc., 1956.

Dain, Norman. *Concepts of Insanity in the United States, 1789–1865.* New Brunswick: Rutgers Univ. Press, 1964.

Davies, John D. *Phrenology, Fad and Science: A Nineteenth Century American Crusade.* New Haven: Yale Univ. Press, 1955.

Davis, David Brion. *Homicide in American Fiction, 1798–1860: A Study in Social Values.* Ithaca: Cornell Univ. Press, 1957.

Dunn, James Taylor, and Louis C. Jones. "Crazy Bill Had a Down Look: Quaint Pictures and a Grim Story Tell of Prejudice and Mob Passion in Upstate New York of the 1840's." In *Stories of Great Crimes and Trials from American Heritage Magazine,* 26–30. New York: American Heritage Publishing Co., Inc., 1973.

Fellman, Michael. *Citizen Sherman: A Life of William Tecumseh Sherman.* New York: Random House, 1995.

Field, Phyllis F. *The Politics of Race in New York: The Struggle for Black Suffrage in the Civil War Era.* Ithaca: Cornell Univ. Press, 1982.

Fredrickson, George M. *The Black Image in the White Mind: The Debate on Afro-American Character and Destiny, 1817–1914.* Hanover: Wesleyan Univ. Press, 1987.

Friedman, Lawrence J. *Gregarious Saints: Self and Community in American Abolitionism, 1830–1870.* Cambridge: Cambridge Univ. Press, 1982.

Friedman, Lawrence M. *A History of American Law,* 2d ed. New York: Simon and Schuster, 1985.

Grob, Gerald. "Origins of DSM-I: A Study in Appearance and Reality." *American Journal of Psychiatry* 148 (1991): 421–31.

Grossberg, Michael. *Governing the Hearth: Law and the American Family in Nineteenth-Century America.* Chapel Hill: Univ. of North Carolina Press, 1985.

———. *A Judgement for Solomon: The D'Hauteville Case and Legal Experience in Antebellum America.* New York: Cambridge Univ. Press, 1996.

Hall, Henry. *History of Auburn.* Auburn: Dennis Bro's, 1869.

Hofstadter, Richard. *Anti-Intellectualism in American Life.* New York: Alfred A. Knopf, 1966.

Hoganson, Kristin. "Garrisonian Abolitionists and the Rhetoric of Gender, 1850–1860." *American Quarterly* 45 (1993): 558–95.

Holt, Michael F. *The Rise and Fall of the American Whig Party: Jacksonian Politics and the Onset of the Civil War.* New York: Oxford Univ. Press, 1999.

Howe, Daniel Walker. *The Political Culture of the American Whigs.* Chicago: Univ. of Chicago Press, 1979.

Jordan, Winthrop D. *White over Black: American Attitudes Toward the Negro, 1550–1812.* Chapel Hill: Univ. of North Carolina Press, 1968.

Kett, Joseph F. *The Formation of the American Medical Profession: The Role of Institutions, 1780–1860.* New Haven: Yale Univ. Press, 1968.

Kruger, Vivienne L. *Born to Run: The Slave Family in Early New York, 1626–1827.* Ph.D. diss., Columbia Univ., 1985. Ann Arbor: Univ. Microfilms International, 1988.

Levy, Leonard W. *The Law of the Commonwealth and Chief Justice Shaw.* Cambridge: Harvard Univ. Press, 1957.

Lewis, W. David. *From Newgate to Dannemora: The Rise of the Penitentiary in New York, 1796–1848.* Ithaca: Cornell Univ. Press, 1965.

Litwack, Leon F. *North of Slavery: The Negro in the Free States, 1790–1860.* Chicago: Univ. of Chicago Press, 1961.

Llewellyn, K. N., and E. Adamson Hoebel. *The Cheyenne Way: Conflict and Case Law in Primitive Jurisprudence.* Norman: Univ. of Oklahoma Press, 1941.

Mackey, Philip English. *Hanging in the Balance: The Anti-Capital Punishment Movement in New York State, 1776–1861.* New York: Garland Publishing, 1982.

Maeder, Thomas. *Crime and Madness: The Origins and Evolution of the Insanity Defense.* New York: Harper and Row, 1985.

Masur, Louis P. *Rites of Execution: Capital Punishment and the Transformation of American Culture, 1776–1865.* New York: Oxford Univ. Press, 1989.

McManus, Edgar J. *A History of Negro Slavery in New York.* Syracuse: Syracuse Univ. Press, 1966.

Merrick, Wayne Reynolds. *A Study of William Henry Seward, Reformer.* Ph.D. diss., Syracuse Univ., 1957. Ann Arbor: Univ. Microfilms, Inc., 1963.

Miller, Perry. *The Life of the Mind in America from the Revolution to the Civil War.* New York: Harcourt, Brace and World, Inc., 1965.

Mohr, James C. *Doctors and the Law: Medical Jurisprudence in Nineteenth-Century America.* Baltimore: Johns Hopkins Univ. Press, 1993.

Moran, Richard. *Knowing Right from Wrong: The Insanity Defense of Daniel McNaughtan.* New York: Free Press, 1981.

Perlin, Michael. *The Jurisprudence of the Insanity Defense.* Durham: Carolina Academic Press, 1994.

Robinson, Daniel N. *Wild Beasts and Idle Humours: The Insanity Defense from Antiquity to the Present.* Cambridge: Harvard Univ. Press, 1996.

Rothman, David J. *The Discovery of the Asylum: Social Order and Disorder in the New Republic.* Boston: Addison Wesley Educational Publishers, 1971.

Rotundo, E. Anthony. *American Manhood: Transformations in Masculinity from the Revolution to the Modern Era.* New York: Basic Books, 1993.

Sale, Maggie. "Critiques from Within: Antebellum Projects of Resistance." *American Literature* 64 (1992): 695–718.

Schuckers, J. W. *The Life and Public Services of Salmon Portland Chase.* New York: D. Appleton and Co., 1874.

Sellers, Charles. *The Market Revolution: Jacksonian America, 1815–1846.* New York: Oxford Univ. Press, 1991.

Stanley, John L. "Majority Tyranny in Tocqueville's America: The Failure of Negro Suffrage in 1846." *Political Science Quarterly* 84 (1969): 412–35.

Starr, Paul. *The Social Transformation of American Medicine.* New York: Basic Books, 1982.

Stern, Madeleine B. *Heads and Headlines: The Phrenological Fowlers.* Norman: Univ. of Oklahoma Press, 1971.

Storke, Elliot G. *History of Cayuga County, New York, with Illustrations and Biographical Sketches of Some of Its Prominent Men and Pioneers.* Syracuse: D. Mason, 1879.

Taylor, John M. *William Henry Seward: Lincoln's Right Hand*. New York: Harper Collins, 1991.

Tolnay, Stewart E., and E. M. Beck. *A Festival of Violence: An Analysis of Southern Lynchings, 1882–1930*. Chicago: Univ. of Illinois Press, 1995.

Tucher, Andie. *Froth and Scum: Truth, Beauty, Goodness, and the Ax Murder in America's First Mass Medium*. Chapel Hill: Univ. of North Carolina Press, 1994.

Tucker, Sheila Saft. *The Township of Fleming, Cayuga County, New York, 1823–1973*. Auburn: Brunner the Printer, 1973.

Van Deusen, Glyndon G. *Horace Greeley: Nineteenth-Century Crusader*. New York: Hill and Wang, 1964.

———. *Thurlow Weed: Wizard of the Lobby*. Boston: Little, Brown, 1947.

———. *William Henry Seward*. New York: Oxford Univ. Press, 1967.

Welter, Rush. *The Mind of America, 1820–1860*. New York: Columbia Univ. Press, 1975.

Wilmerding, John., ed. *The Genius of American Painting*. New York: William Morrow, 1973.

Wilson, Douglas L. *Honor's Voice: The Transformation of Abraham Lincoln*. New York: Alfred A. Knopf, 1998.

Wolff, Cynthia Griffin. " 'Masculinity' " in *Uncle Tom's Cabin*." *American Quarterly* 47 (1995): 595–618.

Index